ALFRED M. FLETT

BREAKING CHAINS
From the Projects to the Pulpit

BREAKING CHAINS
Copyright © 2024 by Alfred M. Flett

All rights reserved. Neither this publication nor any part of this publication may be reproduced or transmitted in any form or by any means, electronic or mechanical, including photocopying, recording or any information storage and retrieval system, without permission in writing from the author.

Unless otherwise indicated, all scripture quotations are taken from the New King James Version®. Copyright © 1982 by Thomas Nelson. Used by permission. All rights reserved. • Scripture quotations marked (TPT) are taken from The Passion Translation®. Copyright © 2017, 2018, 2020 by Passion & Fire Ministries, Inc. Used by permission. All rights reserved. ThePassionTranslation.com.n • Scripture quotations marked (GW) are taken from GOD'S WORD®. © 1995, 2003, 2013, 2014, 2019, 2020 by God's Word to the Nations Mission Society. Used by permission. • Scripture quotations marked (KJV) are taken from the Holy Bible, King James Version, which is in the public domain.

The content of this publication is based on actual events. Names may have been changed to protect individual privacy.

ISBN: 978-1-4866-2622-9
eBook ISBN: 978-1-4866-2623-6

Word Alive Press
119 De Baets Street Winnipeg, MB R2J 3R9
www.wordalivepress.ca

Cataloguing in Publication information can be obtained from Library and Archives Canada.

Like all too many Indigenous youth in Canada, Alfred M. Flett's formative years were scarred by discrimination, dysfunction, poverty, and alcoholism. Like all too few Canadian young adults, Alfred and Lynda Flett surrendered their lives and chains to the Lord Jesus and were launched on an amazing ministry journey to (but not limited to) Indigenous peoples across Canada and in many countries all around the world. One cannot spend time with the Fletts without being impressed by their compassion, integrity, and vision and be challenged to the core by their spiritual vitality and demanding ministry schedule.

Breaking Chains is more than an inspiring true story—it's a powerful, biblically-grounded call to faith.

—Fred Fulford, B.Sc. MA, Professor Emeritus, Summit Pacific College

Breaking Chains is a transparent story of how life can be transformed from despair to hope, from darkness to light, and from bondage to freedom. Alfred M. Flett has chosen to pour out the emotional dregs of the past to remind us all that in King Jesus, even the worst of situations can be rescued, and in the worst of heartache, Jesus can bring release and relief!

You must pick up this book and read it today. It will not only inspire you, but it will show you how to go from victim to victor and from wounded to warrior through the transformative power of God's Son, Jesus of Nazareth.

Real life. Real pain. Real gloom. They met the one who gives Life Eternal, who showers us with wholeness of the Soul, who is Light itself! Global missionary Alfred M. Flett has given us a path out of our prison and into God's palace in his new book, *Breaking Chains*! Isn't it time you allowed God to break your chains? Buy a copy for yourself and one for a friend and be released!

—Dr. Matthew Lee Smith, Executive Director, Eagles in Leadership

This is a must-read book of testimonies of Alfred M. Flett—I was reminded of the apostle Paul's conversion and the mandate Christ had set up for him recorded in Acts 9:15–16 (KJV), *"But the Lord said unto him, Go thy way: for he is a chosen vessel unto me, to bear my name before the Gentiles, and kings, and the children of Israel: For I will shew him how great things he must suffer for my name's sake."*

For Alfred, it wasn't a religious persecution but a story of God's grace pulling an impoverished Indigenous person living in Winnipeg, Canada, out of bondage to sin, alcohol, and others forms of abuse and raising him up to reach the nations of the world for such a time as this.

He is indeed a chosen, yielded vessel of God destined to walked in places of extremely harsh conditions to share the gospel of the Kingdom to the lost and dying. This is a message of hope to those with a desire to be used of God no matter what situation they're in. I admire both him and his wife, Lynda, for answering the call of God in their lives to reach the nations of the world and to witnessed revivals globally. Well done, and to God be the glory!

—Raymond McLean, Lead Pastor of The Launching Place, Winnipeg, Manitoba

Praise God for delivering us from the grave and being hope when it seemed there was no hope. I myself have been in dark despair until my beautiful Saviour opened the prison doors for me and set me free, truly free indeed. This is why this book will greatly encourage you to know that there is no one or no situation beyond the reach of the Saviour, Jesus Christ, No one.

"God has rescued us from the power of darkness and has brought us into the kingdom of his Son, whom he loves" (Colossians 1:13, GW).

—Charlene Thomas, B. Arts, LLB, Calvary Temple, Winnipeg, Board Member

Dedication

THIS BOOK IS written in memory of my parents, who instilled in me to drive to never give up on my dreams. They both played a part in my life and demonstrated a loyalty to this country called Canada. My dad fought in the Second World War, and my mom's first husband never returned home from the battlefield of Europe. A big shout out to all veterans who served our country with honour and bravery.

Contents

Dedication	v
Acknowledgements	ix
Foreword	xi
Preface	xiii
Introduction	xv
Prologue	xvii

Chapter One
The Early Years — 1

Chapter Two
The 1960s — 19

Chapter Three
The 1970s — 41

Chapter Four
The Restoration of the 1980s — 61

Chapter Five
The 1990s — 111

Chapter Six
International Evangelism — 117

Afterword	199
Photo Gallery	201
About the Author	203

Acknowledgements

I WANT TO thank my wife, Lynda, for her meticulous reading and re-reading of this manuscript and her ongoing support to see the book complete.

I want to thank my home church, Calvary Temple here in Winnipeg, for their prayers and support over the many years. Special thanks to Calvary Temple Board members who served over the years, showing their love for lost souls and their support of mission work around the globe.

A special thanks to the bus driver and bus captain who knocked on our door to pick us up for Sunday school. That knocked changed the course my life and the lives of thousands of people around the globe.

H.H. Barber was a special friend who believed in me and gave me an opportunity serve alongside of him in ministry.

I wish to acknowledge the Truth and Reconciliation committees who worked tirelessly to bring forth the tragic stain of the mistreatment our people in residential schools.

Thank you to Dr. M. Mollering, who came alongside us during the infancy stage of our Indigenous church plant. She was a trained psychologist who helped the people with her knowledge and heart of compassion.

So many people have helped, and if you're reading this and you are one of them, thank you so much.

Foreword

IT HAS BEEN my privilege to know international evangelists Alfred and Lynda Flett since Alfred served under his lead pastor, H. H. Barber, as a deacon at Calvary Temple in Winnipeg, Manitoba. Eventually, they served as Indigenous pastors of Calvary Temple Native Fellowship Church with the Pentecostal Assemblies of Canada, and he was later ordained.

I was unaware of his conversion experience as described in his book, since he felt it was more important just to preach the gospel of Christ who died, was buried, and rose again to cleanse sinners and set them free from their sins. He addresses the sinner again and again and encourages him not to give up on believing God for a breakthrough that will set him free from his sin. It would be wise for the sinner to take heed of Alfred's admonitions and follow his scriptural teachings, which are able to break the chains that keep him in bondage.

It's clear Alfred has a burden and vision to win the lost. This is what has compelled him to take the gospel message to the "uttermost parts of the world" as he travelled several times around the world. What a testimony to our Native people! God is able to take a Native person, save him from his sin, cleanse him with Jesus' blood, fill him with the Holy Ghost, and set him on fire with a powerful anointing to preach the Word to the nations. God called him to evangelize people living under third-world conditions, and he was able to adapt to those conditions because he came out that particular lifestyle.

He was open to God clarifying his calling into the ministry, because he felt it necessary to be equipped in his faith so he could persevere in his service. His calling led him into leadership training, so he did this around the world. He felt he was old fashioned, but he insisted on also being biblical and adhering to his Pentecostal roots. This is evident in his writing as he shares the experiences in his ministry of the Holy Spirit manifested himself in signs and wonders during his crusades.

He doesn't apologize for behaviour that is questionable in church services today, as long as the behaviour is soundly rooted in the Word of God. His crusades are filled with experiences that can be described with words such as "the Holy Ghost fell," "a powerful anointing filled the house," "signs and wonders followed," "filled with the Holy Ghost with the evidence of speaking in tongues," "gifts of the Spirit," "your breakthrough is going to come," "dancing in the Spirit," and most importantly, "the salvation and deliverance of sinners."

Thousands attended his crusades, and thousands were converted. The reader can learn about topics such as: spiritual warfare, spiritual oppression and demon possession, baptism in the Holy Spirit, speaking in tongues, gifts of the Spirit, casting out demons, divine healing, leadership development, discipleship, the call of God, witnessing, preaching and praying, and evangelizing. The value of these topics is their scriptural references.

This could be Alfred's testimony, *"My love for you has my heart on fire! My passion for your house consumes me! Nothing will turn me away, even though I endure all the insults of those who insult you"* (Psalm 69:9, TPT). Alfred has endured, and he continues to persevere in his ministry to hear chains fall off captives. I wholeheartedly endorse his book.

—Rev. James Kallappa, Retired

Preface

THIS BOOK IS a real-life story of a person who was born ten years after the Second World War but had to endure the grief and trauma of a previous generation. The cycle of grief lasted for decades and was passed down to the next the generation. The memories left scars on many hearts, including my own. Today I am healed from those scars, but the memories remain. As I have gained more understanding over the years, I appreciate even more the great sacrifice my parents paid for the freedom we enjoy today. But I hold greater gratitude for my God, who has taken a broken heart and given me a new one.

Introduction

OVER THE YEARS, I've shared stories of my mission trips around the world with people who would listen. I must have told my grandchildren the same stories many times over the years at our family gatherings. People often encouraged me to write a book. Well, over the years I thought about it, and I finally put some action behind their words of encouragement and sat down to write my personal story. I didn't think my story was all that unique, but the more I thought about it, the more it became a reality.

I also want to help others who might be struggling with addictions and thoughts of suicide. I know my people throughout Canada and USA have had to deal with this subject for far too long, and we have lost many of our youth to that horrible mental health issue.

I have worked as a social worker, youth leader, case worker, and a pastor in the inner city of Winnipeg. I've travelled to over eighty-five First Nations communities in North and South America. The years of trauma have left many Indigenous communities struggling for answers to help these youth who have died far too early in life. I hope and pray that this book will be an encouragement to as many people possible. You might know someone who is struggling with this condition, or you might be the person dealing with it now. There is hope and help for you, so please don't give up. Please take the first step and tell someone what you're struggling with. Let your parents, teacher, elder, or pastor know.

I gave my life to Christ when I was twenty-four years old. I never imagined that God would take my broken life and turned into a miracle of His amazing grace.

Jeremiah 29:11 says, *"For I know the thoughts that I think toward you, says the Lord, thoughts of peace and not of evil, to give you a future and a hope."* God thinks much differently than anyone else in this world. He loves us with a love that passes knowledge and understanding. Now if I was God (and I am not), I might have just passed me by and found someone more qualified to serve His purposes. There I was sitting on a bench outside the steel mill I was working at, wearing my dirty and greasy coveralls. It was lunch break, and I was looking up into the sky and saw an airplane flying above. The Spirit of the Lord came upon me, and I said to myself as I pointed toward the plane, "One day I'm going to get on a plane and preach around the world for Jesus."

My circumstance looked bleak and my surrounding didn't look favourable, but God spoke into my spirit. Sometimes in your walk of faith, all you may receive from the Lord is a directive, and the destination won't come until later. That is so true in my life; the places and people God would take me to were just amazing. When God opens the door, no man can close it!

Don't give up! You have been called for such a time as this! He will take you to places unimaginable; you are someone's breakthrough. An eight-year-old boy in Barrow, Alaska handed me a note and two dollars to win souls for Jesus. You could be the change agent for someone who struggles with the complexities of a crisis. My responsibility as well as yours is now to become a catalyst of change in someone else's life.

Prologue

OUR FAMILY ARRIVED in the city of Winnipeg near the end of the 1950s. My parents had moved from the Patricia Beach area as part of a migration of Indigenous people moving to the city for a better life. In my parents' case, it was for employment. A number of my mother's siblings moved to Winnipeg as well. For them, it was a new and exciting place to live. Unfortunately, it didn't turn out that well for most of them.

My parents were both addicted to alcohol, and for them it was a means to numb their feelings from their trauma. My mother lost her first and only husband, Mr. Flett. He never returned to Canada was buried overseas. They must have been around twenty years old when they got married. My mother was buried with her husband's Silver Star next to her in her coffin. She'd fought a long, hard battle, and near the end of her life, she gave her heart to another person—Jesus Christ.

My dad was a broken young man when he came back from being wounded and a prisoner of war. Life in the city didn't bring a bright tomorrow for them. It only brought years of alcoholism and abuse. We moved to a different location in Winnipeg, mostly rentals that were dire need of upkeep. My mother found us a place in the northwest of the city, known as Jig Town. It was the first brand-new place we lived in, but it was still a rental.

This story stems from years of alcohol abuse and violence that left me broken and wounded, just like my parents. They passed down their brokenness and grief. I was carrying on the family tradition, and it left me a broken young man, until I met the man called Jesus.

Chapter One
The Early Years

THE YEAR WAS 1959–1960. The evening turned out to be a very long, hot, summer night. It seemed that everything was so dark around me. As a matter of fact, most of my early childhood memories are dark and confusing. What I understand of those early days was the foundation that would determine my outlook on life in general.

The only light shining through the window was a light from the street lamp outside our bedroom window. I remember being left alone with my younger brother and sister. I was only four or five years old at the time. It seemed like I cried for hours looking out the window and asking myself when would my sisters return home. Those deep emotions of feeling left alone came from insecurity and abandonment by my family. In the moments of despair, a child doesn't have an understanding of the concept of time; all they feel and know is that no one is providing security and comfort. The crying went on for what seemed like an eternity. My older sister went searching the neighbourhood, looking for my other sister. My mother left them to watch us younger children while she was out on the town drinking and partying. Children watching children, and my sisters weren't much older than me.

This story is being re-created again and again in the lives of many people living in the inner-city and for those growing up in alcoholic homes. Back in those days, the child welfare system could have easily scooped us up and taken us away and placed us in some foster home, because none of us were of the age to look after each other. That would have been devastating for all of us. We would have been part of the 1960s Scoop that ran rampant in that decade, especially among our Indigenous people. My understanding is that the Sixties Scoop children were sent to different places in Canada, the USA, and even as far away as Europe.

That particular neighbourhood was always kind of spooky. There was this vehicle parked outside our house, and this person would sit in it for very long periods of time. That seemed to have gone on for weeks. We could only guess he was up to no good. We were living at that time on Robinson and Dufferin. The building was quite old; it must have been built in the early 1900s. We lived in the upper part of the house; looking back, it was more or less a rooming house with units upstairs and down. I believe these homes were built to accommodate the railroad workers and their families. It was old and rundown—not a place to raise a family. It was full of alcohol and violence and was unsafe. But it was our playground and it was close to the main street, and that has a lot of memories as well.

One neighbour would gather all the children and buy everyone ice cream cones. It was actually an ice cream truck on wheels that played music to let everyone know he was in the hood. This man and his family would also eventually move to Jig Town or Gilbert Park, as it's known. As a matter of fact, on one of my adventures back to the old neighbourhood from Jig Town, I got lost trying to find my way back home. I took a bus and came home late and was confused on where I lived. The townhouses all looked the same to me, and I forgot where I lived. I was only seven or eight years old. I ended up at the man's home who bought everyone ice cream cones. I got the directions to my home and made it home late in the evening. When he and his family moved to the same area, their tradition continued, but there were a whole lot more children to buy ice cream for. When the music that played on the ice cream truck could be heard, a stampede of young people would come running.

We moved to a variety of places back then, mostly older rented homes that accommodated people living with little or no income. The neighbourhood was filled with older homes, all of them rundown looking. Anyone living in the area knew that the row of red buildings on Jarvis was where the poorest people lived.

At the back of the building were what seemed like storage sheds at least six feet apart. That was our playground as we jumped from one building to another. It was quite a leap to take a run-and-jump approach for us little people. It seemed we were jumping over the Grand Canyon. It was fun, but it was also dangerous. We moved to a variety of homes, mostly in the inner-city and in the north end.

One particular home on Pioneer Street was across from what is now called the Canadian Human Rights Museum. This is where the Red River and the Assiniboine River meet; it's an historical place. It was a trading place for the Indigenous people and the new settlers that came to Canada. The rivers acted like a highway that transported goods into the province and down to the Mississippi River. I'm not quite sure how long we lived in this area, but I remember some tragic incidents back then. Our family friends experienced a serious incident. The young boys were playing with a loaded rifle, and the one boy pointed at his brother and shot him. It was just devastating news for these people, whom my parents knew.

My cousins lived next door. We were around the same age and attended an elementary school somewhere in the downtown area. It seemed like we moved quite a few times back then. I'm not sure why we moved so much. I guess the landlord would raise the rent or we got evicted because of the parties, or just falling behind in the rent payments.

The Nutty Club was down the street, and when we were hungry one of us would reach into the truck and help ourselves to nuts or candies. "Grab and run, boys" was our motto! The driver would spot us and the chase would be on, and at the same time we'd try to empty our pockets of the evidence.

At times we were mischievous. One day, we decided not to go to school. My cousin's mother found out from the school that we weren't in attendance. I guess her boys were disciplined and had their butts hit with a belt. My auntie then came over to our house and informed my mother of what had happened that day. So her boys got disciplined, and then it was my turn. I don't remember missing school after that, or at least we didn't get caught.

During one of these mischievous moments, we were playing under the bridge by the rail station. Ice was building up, and we decided that it would make a nice climb. We climbed a slope toward the top. I slipped and grabbed on to whatever I could find. There just happened to be a wire of sorts hanging, so I grabbed it and felt a bolt of electricity go through my body. It scared me big time! Not sure how much live electricity flowed through me, but enough that I would never become an electrician.

The parties seemed endless no matter where we lived, whether in the inner-city or the north end. I do remember changing schools quite often. We would make friends with local families and then be gone again. I remember one particular house on Manitoba Avenue, where we had a coal furnace to heat the building. The truck would deliver the coal next to the building and into the furnace room.

I have many other memories. I'd often go down to the local bakery to buy bread; the lady wrapped the day-old bread in a newspaper. Can you believe the bread only cost five cents a loaf? There was a store on Selkirk and McGregor where the butchers would throw away bones that had a little bit of meat left on them. I'd come by and take home the bones from the barrel that sat outside the store. My mother would make neck bone soup, or as it was called, hangover soup. Believe me, she and her relatives had plenty of soup always cooking. They really believed it would bring relief to their hangover from drinking too much booze.

Back to Robinson. One day a tragic event occurred. Our next-door neighbour down the hall was found dead inside her unit. I overheard that it was a suicide. I remember standing in the hallway while the ambulance personnel took her body away. She was lying on the floor, but I could see that her legs had turned blue and she was motionless.

I believe that at this point, a spirit of suicide came upon me as a young boy. I want to deal with the subject somewhat in length because it has affected so many young people, especially among Indigenous people who lived in the city or back on the reservations. Over the years they have renamed the reservations "First Nations communities," and they have added their original-language names to the communities. But back in the day, they were basically called reservations.

My dad grew up in the Métis community called Stony Point, or Patricia Beach. My grandfather refused to move with the Peguis people from Petersfield to the Interlake, which is known today as Peguis First Nation; the people were the descendants of Chief Peguis. The Ojibway people!

My parents were the first Indigenous people to live in the urban setting. So I am a second-generation Indigenous person who grew up, for most of my life, in the city of Winnipeg. My parents moved to the city for employment reasons. My dad was a commercial fisherman, and at that time, my mother had a variety of jobs, mostly cooking.

My parents were always hard workers, but unfortunately, they didn't spend their resources wisely. It seemed that money wasn't a priority for them, nor was thinking about the future. The funds came into the family and left very quickly. The amount of money spent on alcohol consumed over 50 per cent of their income, if not more. Our relatives were in the same situation. It seemed normal at times because everyone was doing it. It became a lifestyle, and abuse of alcohol created nothing but havoc in our homes. The parties would start off with a great deal of laughter, dancing, and poking fun at one another. It was guaranteed that by the end of the evening, there would be a fight among themselves. Can you imagine the effect it had on young people? I think most of us just hid in our back bedrooms hoping the party would end. There was no peace in our home, mostly strife and unforgiveness. People back then simply held grudges against one another, probably due to the fights among themselves.

Alcohol had become a curse in our family, from generation to generation and passed down the family line. The bondage of alcoholism affected so many of that generation. When my dad returned from the Second World War, he was a broken young man, having been captured during the war. He was wounded on the battlefields of Europe and spent many months as a prisoner of war. Unfortunately, in his grief and pain, he could only find comfort in consuming alcohol. Like so many veterans, he came back to Canada suffering what we would call PTSD today.

When he'd enlisted for war, he'd been assigned to the regiment of the Winnipeg Rifles, also known as the Little Black Devils. His younger brother, my uncle, tried to join the military but was underage. These Indigenous veterans came back from the war to the reservation and had no right to vote for elected leaders in Canada. In some cases, some of these veterans needed permission to leave the reservation. It's beyond my thinking why these men would volunteer and defend our freedom that we enjoy today when they had no freedom to live as free citizens of this nation called Canada.

I'm not quite sure his reasonings, but my guess is that they were aware that the Indigenous children were being sent to residential schools to be educated. My late uncle must've dropped out of school, because he didn't know how to read or write. When he came to the city of Winnipeg, he needed to come with someone who knew how to read the street signs. Although my uncle didn't make it to the Second World War, like so many in the community, he also turned to alcohol, which had devastating results for his family. Alcohol is a curse that has been passed down from generation to generation.

When I was seeking the Lord for answers about this generational curse, God gave me a vision of a forest that was set on fire, and the fire was moving from tree to tree until there was nothing left but ashes. This described the effects and consequences of a lifestyle of drunkenness and alcoholism that has ruined so many lives in my family and the lives of so many of my relatives. It's a terrible curse among Indigenous people; it has ruined so many lives. It left nothing but poverty and brokenness in its path. Our families lived from paycheque to paycheque and never prospered or left any inheritance to the next generation.

My parents and those in their generation lived through the Great Depression as children in the 1930s. They lived without electricity or running water. I imagine they never celebrated birthdays or had any Christmas gifts to give. Everything was a struggle for them, but they survived as family units because my grandparents knew how to live off the land. They were trappers and fishermen who worked hard to supply for their families the basic necessities of life. When my grandfather died, my mom had to pawn our television set to help pay the funeral bill. There was just no money or any type of savings available. I think the TV we owned was pawned more than once or twice. I never knew my grandfather, my mother's dad, but she was broken up and cried when she was drinking. So the grief cycle continued.

There was a downtown church in Winnipeg. One day I walked inside and saw all these candles burning. So I prayed, "God, why did you take my grandfather away? Could you please bring him back?" I was only a child. There were confession booths set up inside the building, but it was kind of spooky, so I didn't bother going inside. One after another my uncles passed away, leaving nothing for their families. Of course, the grief led to more alcohol consumption.

Solomon, the wisest man who ever lived, wrote Proverbs, and this is what he says in Proverbs 23:29–35:

Who has woe?
Who has sorrow?
Who has contentions?
Who has complaints?
Who has wounds without cause?
Who has redness of the eyes?
Those who linger long at the wine,
Those who go in search of mixed wine.
Do not look on the wine when it is red,
When the sparkles in the cup,
When it swirls around smoothly,
At the last it bites like a serpent,
and stings like a viper.
Your eyes will see strange things,
And your heart will utter perverse things.
Yes, you will be like one who
lies down in the midst of the sea,
Or like the one who lives at the top of a mast, saying:
"They have struck me,
but I was not hurt;
They have beaten me,
but I did not feel it.
When shall I awake,
that I may seek another drink?"

The 1960s was a *decade* of rebellion and self-centredness.

After living in a variety of rundown places, our family finally got a break. My mother received a notice that a government housing project was being built in the northwest of Winnipeg. At that time, it seemed like it was at the edge of the city. As a matter of fact, it was at the edge of the city; there were family farms across the field. This area would eventually become more developed with more family housing.

Most of the people who lived in the complex came from similar backgrounds. Some were single-parent homes, others had both parents. Some of the families had working parents, and others had single-parent families with no one working, and that included our family. My mother was able to raise five of us children on her own efforts.

Mom was a hard-working woman and very independent. At the time we moved into the complex, she was working, mostly as a community outreach worker. Apparently, a friend of hers who was a social worker was a very helpful and kind person. He helped my mom with her skill level and saw the potential in her to become a community worker. She worked at this job for many years, helping the Indigenous people who were continually arriving in Winnipeg. She had to deal with the bureaucracy and unjust landlords, and help her clients navigate for employment, self-improvement, and better housing. My mother was very outspoken and always helpful to people who were down and out. She became quite an advocate for many over the years, in spite of her own grief over the death of her husband in the Second World War. During her times of grief, which came out usually when alcohol was being served, there would be endless tears.

She would have been married in the 1940s before her husband, Mr. Flett, went off to war. Over the years she refused to remarry or change back to her maiden name, so she was Mrs. Flett. My mother's maiden name was Thomas. She grew up in the Victoria Beach area and came from a very large family. I don't know much of her history or the problems she had to face. But I guess the generational curse of alcoholism was passed down to her and her siblings. I know this because of the comments that were made over the years. Mom was a very hard worker from a young age. She drove a truck and could handle any task a man could do. She worked on the fishing boats as a cook, and she worked cleaning other people's homes.

For some reason, I was the only family member that I'm aware of who had to go with her on those long bus rides from Jig Town to Tuxedo. She worked for Mrs. Henry, who was employed as a journalist for the *Winnipeg Tribune* newspaper. Today, we would look at her as being a feminist and an advocate for the poor and for women of her generation. Mrs. Henry was my mother's mentor, and she learned much from her. She considered Mrs. Henry not only her employer but a friend.

My memories of those early days are of those long bus rides to the other side of the city, but it paid off at the end. Mrs. Henry would feed us lunch, and I would have my own bottle of Coca-Cola beside the refrigerator. I hit the jackpot. Mrs. Henry's sons would go on to become famous actors on their own TV programs. My mother would often say I helped those boys when they were younger; I cleaned their rooms and fed them. I always wondered why they had so many swords in their bedrooms. My guess is that it was part of the drama class in high school or university years.

At Mrs. Henry's funeral, her sons gave eulogies about their mother and their upbringing. One of her sons included how much of a positive attitude she had. He said they grew up dirt poor, but they never knew it. Mrs. Henry would tell her boys that they came from royalty and that their family history was tied to the King of Scotland. In their minds, they believed that they were important and had value in society because they came from royalty. He repeated that, in reality, they were a poor family. But their mother never allowed them to think that way, because they came from royalty, and they believed it.

My mother, my brother, and I attended the service. My mother embraced the boys, now men, as her own sons. The family members greeted everyone as we said our final goodbyes. One of the members standing with them was a young Indigenous lady. It spoke volumes to me that these people had a burden and felt a responsibility to reach out to Indigenous people, just like Mrs. Henry reached out to my mother and became her mentor and helped her navigate through life as a single parent. She became an anchor for my mother during the many trials of her life. In the good times and the bad, she was always there. She was a source of strength, a person of integrity, a person filled with compassion, and she knew the struggles of life and just wanted to help someone else in need.

Mrs. Henry no longer lived in poverty but obtained a better lifestyle for herself and family. In my young mind, she was one of the richest people I'd ever met, because she lived in an area of the city where the rich people lived. It's amazing what an act of kindness does. It left an impression in my mind and heart even to today. That happened almost sixty years ago! That could also be said about being unkind and cruel. That can remain with someone for years. The act of kindness can remain with many people for many years.

It was that act of kindness that I held on to over many years in my own struggles of life. I knew from young age that there was a better life to live, at least materially. Throughout my younger years, God put several individuals in my life who spoke volumes of kindness and believed in me when I didn't believe in myself. My elementary school teacher was a kind and generous man. He was also a man who believed in you and would discipline you when he needed to. Later on in my Christian life, I would meet that teacher again when he worked as a marriage counsellor.

I called him at his office one day and said, "Mr. Koop, I don't know if you remember me, but you were my teacher in elementary school, and I'm calling you to thank you for believing in me and being such an encouragement." I met him at his office and we shared memories and cried over the reunion. He told me that he'd left to teach in South America, as it was getting impossible to teach in the Canadian system. They were no longer allowed to discipline the children like the days when I grew up in his classroom. He was old school and he meant not to be mean but to demonstrate that he really cared. Once you got out of line or were fighting, out came that twelve-inch, black, thick leather belt. It would sting for a very long time. If you moved your hand, like my friend did, and the teacher hit himself on the leg, look out! The next would come with a little more zip in it. We invited him and his wife to our daughter's wedding. I could see the proud look on his face as my wife and I greeted him at the church ceremony.

During those elementary days, I found myself getting into fights often on the playground. He came up to me one day and said, "Alfred, why don't you join the local wrestling team? You would do well at that." I'm grateful for the many people God used in my life who helped in my development in my formative years. Those acts of kindness would remain with me in my heart, mind, and soul. In spite of all my problems and challenges being raised by alcoholic parents and facing racism, violence, and suicidal tendencies, God had a plan for my life and a purpose for my existence. I want you to know that in spite of all you've been through, God will never leave you or forsake you. His goodness and mercy will follow you all the days of your life. The psalmist said in Psalm 23:

> The Lord is my shepherd; I shall not want. He makes me to lie down in green pastures; He leads me beside the still waters. He restores my soul; He leads me in the paths of righteousness for His name's sake. Yea, though I walk through the valley of the shadow of death, I will fear no evil; for You are with me; Your rod and Your staff, they comfort me. You prepare a table before me in the presence of my enemies; You anoint my head with oil; my cup runs over. Surely goodness and mercy shall follow me all the days of my life; and I will dwell in the house of the Lord forever.

The Bible says that generational sins follow to the fourth generation. I didn't realize it at that time, but my parents, grandparents, and no doubt my great-grandparents, were all alcoholics. I will come back to this subject later in another chapter, when I deal with generational sins and curses in the family.

The story I'm about tell you has been on my heart for many years. I believe the Lord has put the desire in my heart to write this book. In doing so, I hope to encourage you. My personal prayer is that those who don't know the God of the Bible will come to know that nothing is impossible with God. I believe that what the Lord has done for me and for countless others, He can do for you. I've been reluctant to write this book because I have to look back and recall unpleasant memories of a former life that was filled with hurt and pain; however, God has given me the grace to help me with the past and put my confidence in Him totally.

I believe the other reason I was reluctant to write the book is that I didn't want to hurt or embarrass my mother. She loved the Lord and invited Jesus into her heart. There was a real transformation in her life and a desire to do whatever she could before her death. In her late seventies, she volunteered for a local food bank. She was always helping the down and out. I miss her dearly and regret not being at her bedside the day she went on to heaven to be with her Lord and Saviour Jesus Christ.

My sister and I met with Mom's doctor, who informed us that Mom's stage of cancer was serious and she only had a few months to live. The doctor's timeline was a mistake; she died earlier than we expected. I was doing missionary work in northern Alaska at the time I received the call from my wife, Lynda, that Mom had passed on. My brother and sister were at her bedside when she died.

Before I'd left for Alaska, my older sister and I had gone to visit my mom, and we had a difficult assignment. We had to go over her funeral arrangements. Her sister Kay was there helping her move around in her tiny apartment because she was in so much pain. She refused to go to the hospital, especially Riverview Hospital. She knew that people never left once they were admitted.

We managed to get through the planning, and she said, "I don't want flowers when I'm dead."

We said, "Okay, no flowers."

"If you want to feed people and spend your money, go ahead."

The family had to make the arrangements, so my brother and sister contacted the funeral director, burial place, caterers, etc. They chose a beautiful white coffin with flowers sketched into the corners. We felt we slipped one in there. It was agreed to by Mom that her pastor would do the service and I would do the eulogy.

On the way to the gravesite, a police car provided an escort and held back traffic. They only do that for the mayor or someone high in government. They did for my mom, one of those unsung heroes just doing what came naturally to her—helping the down and out. A lot of people attended her service whom we didn't know, but my guess is that they were the down and out. She was always a champion for those people, including her own children. Before Mom passed in the hospital, she told my brother Dennis, "Let Alfred know I love him." This book is dedicated to my mother, my dad, and all those men and women who sacrificed their lives in World War Two.

As the apostle Paul said in Philippians 4:13: *"I can do all things through Christ who strengthens me."* Without the Lord Jesus Christ, I would be eternally lost and without hope, but since Jesus has come into my heart, I'm a new creation in Christ Jesus and now have a living hope. He has forgiven me and removed my sins as far as the east is from the west: *"for all have sinned and fall short of the glory of God"* (Romans 3:23); *"there is none righteous, no, not one"* (Romans 3:10). For the wages of sin is death, but Jesus took all my sins upon Himself and has redeemed me by His precious blood. I'm able to put all things behind and press on by His grace, power, and might. Jesus has removed the shame and guilt, and I am set free by the power of the Holy Spirit living in me.

"For I know the thoughts that I think towards you, says the Lord, thoughts of peace and not of evil, to give you an expected end" (Jeremiah 29:11, KJV). Perhaps you're struggling with your past right at this moment. You can call on the name of the

Lord and He will save you; ask and He will forgive you of your sins and remove them as far as the east is from the west:

> ... if you confess with your mouth the Lord Jesus and believe in your heart that God has raised Him from the dead, you will be saved. For with the heart one believes unto righteousness, and with the mouth confession is made unto salvation. (Romans 10:9–10)

Never build your future around your past. Jesus was born with a terrible stigma. His mother, Mary, was pregnant with Him before she was married to Joseph, her betrothed. The Bible says that they had not had a sexual relationship, but that which was conceived in her was of the Holy Ghost (Matthew 1:20). Jesus never looked back. He never discussed the situation with anyone. There's not a single scripture in the Bible where He brings up His background or limitations.

Perhaps you're like me. My parents were never married. I was born an illegitimate child. The thought of my parents never marrying caused me a great deal of hurt and grief. I know it's not uncommon in Indigenous families or society in general for children to be born into such a situation. Perhaps your situation is even worse and you don't even know your parents, or someone else has raised you.

I remember as a young boy going shopping downtown with my mother. We often went to the Eaton's store in Winnipeg. At that time, the bus terminal was right behind the Eaton's on Graham Avenue. I was curious and puzzled to see so many Indigenous people coming and going. As a young child, I wondered why so many were coming to the city. They seemed so innocent to me. Little did I realize that many of them had given up their children to the residential school system.

This system was formulated by the government of Canada and implemented by the churches of Canada. Children were taken supposedly to be educated, but the intent was to eradicate their culture and assimilate them into the Canadian lifestyle. Perhaps this is the greatest mistake the government of Canada ever made. Government leaders have apologized to the Indigenous people, but the damage had already been done. They systematically took away the language and culture, our way of life, and put our children in places that would harm them physically. There was abuse, including sexual abuse, and many lives were lost at the hands of an institution that totally disregarded their way of life. Much has been written on the subject, so I would encourage you to purchase a book on Truth and Reconciliation. This book will give you a better understanding from the perspective of the Indigenous people themselves.

I worked with a pastor one time in northern Manitoba. He told me of his experience in the residential school system. At the age of eight years old, he was taken away from his parents and didn't see them until he was in his teen years. He experienced physical abuse at the hands of a cruel system designed to eradicate Indigenous culture. They were humiliated and punished for speaking their language. The government thought that if children were kept away from their parents, they would lose the Indigenous way of life.

History has proven that the system failed the Indigenous people and all Canadians in this horrible crime against humanity. Some of these precious children in the care of those institutional religious organizations never returned home but died and were buried next to these religious-run schools. In some cases, the parents were never notified of the death. The Truth and Reconciliation Committee went across the nation of Canada and heard firsthand from the parents and survivors of the residential school system. In some cases, if not in most cases, the children were taken away and the parents didn't fully understand what was taking place until years later.

The Bible says in Psalm 27:10: *"When my father and mother forsake me, then the Lord will take care of me."* God will take care of you. He cares a great deal about you and knows your very situation. In Matthew 11:28, Jesus says, *"Come to Me, all you who labor and heavy laden, and I will give you rest."*

Let me encourage you stop looking at where you've been and start looking to where you're going. Jesus saw a scared and weary woman at the well who had been married five times. He saw beyond her failures and reputation. He saw her heart; He saw a desire to be changed. People saw Zaccheus as a conniving, deceptive tax collector. Jesus saw a confused man who longed for a change of heart and life. Jesus sees your own desire for a changed heart and life. God never consults your past to determine your future. The apostle Paul wrote a letter to the Corinthians and said: *"Therefore, if anyone is in Christ, he is a new creation; old things have passed away; behold, all things have become new"* (2 Corinthians 5:17); *"As far as the east is from the west, so far has He removed our transgressions from us"* (Psalm 103:12). God can and does heal us from our past. We may still remember the past, but the hurt will be healed: *"He heals the brokenhearted and binds up their wounds"* (Psalm 147:3).

Perhaps you've experienced pain and hurt in your life. Why don't you give it over to Jesus and let Him bring healing to you. He will put His arms around you and minister His love to you. The Bible says that God is gracious to all who call upon Him. That includes you. No matter what you've done in your past, God can heal and forgive you right now. All you have to do is call upon Him. The Bible says if we call upon Him, he will save us from all our sins. The Bible says that God has come to heal the bruised, that which has been completely shattered, and He will heal the broken-hearted.

Even as I write this book, I sense a great deal of emotions beginning to stir within me regarding the years of growing up in what I call a dysfunctional family. The word "dysfunctional" means impaired or abnormal. The Bible calls it sin; the cycle of alcoholism and the endless parties all seemed to end in violence. The violence was the most painful thing to witness, especially when your own mother was a victim of physical and emotional abuse. As a young Indigenous boy witnessing violence at home, I felt a deep sense of helplessness, confusion, and anger in my own life. I realize today that much of the alcoholism and violence was a byproduct of those who went and fought during the Second World War and sacrificed their own lives, and others came back broken men and women.

My mother's first husband, Mr. Flett, never returned from the battlefield. He lost his life and left behind a young bride whom he would never see again. My mother's loss left a deep hole in her heart that took years, if not decades, to heal. She turned to alcohol, like so many others who lost loved ones in the Second World War. I never really witnessed her grief until the alcohol was consumed and then violence followed. She made many bad decisions in her life regarding men who did not honour or respect her. Most of the men she dated ended up being abusive people. That created a great deal of confusion and hurt in our family. My mother's memories of her first husband would remain with her all of her life. That was the main reason why she would never marry again and would continue being Mrs. Flett, in honour of her husband, a man she loved dearly.

Mr. Flett earned a Silver Star for sacrificing his life on the battlefields of Europe. That Silver Star was on display in the hand of my mom as she lay in that coffin, still carrying the name Mrs. Flett. My mother made the biggest sacrifices of her life when news came that her husband had died. Mr. Flett's parents gave up their son and would never see him again or visit his gravesite, as he was buried overseas.

When it was time to obtain my own birth certificate, the lady working the counter said that on my birth certificate my mother's name was Irene Flett and my father was Alfred Sinclair. She asked me which name she should register me under. I thought for a moment and then said, "My mother raised me, so I'm going to choose the name Alfred Flett." It has been an honour and privilege to carry on his name; in my mind, he was a brave young man and a warrior.

The Bible says to honour one another, and I honoured my mother and my dad, Alfred Sinclair, as well. So many times I hadn't honoured them, but they still had a lot of love for me. Although my dad wasn't around much because of his lifestyle, he was always generous and gave us many gifts. But I would have loved him to be on the sideline cheering me on in my many sporting activities. Sometimes I wonder if I could have gone further in hockey. I had the potential, but God had other plans for me. My friends had their dad or mom cheering them on.

But my God was working in my life because the prayers of my grandma, Caroline Sinclair, would one day be answered. She died when I was young, but I heard from her close friend that she prayed that God would one day raise up a preacher in her family. In spite of all the hardships and trials, she prayed; her young son, my dad, came back from the war wounded and broken, but she still believed God in an impossible situation. Please raise up a preacher! God heard and answered her prayers. It may have taken decades, but God answered. Through trials, fire, and the darkest moments of history, God heard my grandma. I am so glad He heard and answered her prayers of desperation.

> The righteous cry out, and the Lord hears, and delivers them out of all their troubles. The Lord is near to those who have a broken heart, and saves such as have a contrite spirit. Many are the afflictions of the righteous, but the Lord delivers out of them all. (Psalm 34:17–19)

Don't give up! Don't quit! God is about to answer your prayers; call upon Him in the day of your troubles. Call upon Him for your prodigal sons and daughters; believe that nothing is impossible with God and all things are possible for them who believe.

There is good reason Jesus would often require someone in need of a miracle to demonstrate an initial act of faith.

To the man with a withered hand, Jesus said, *"Stretch forth thine hand"* (Matthew 12:13, KJV).

To the man at the pool of Bethesda, He said, *"Rise, take up thy bed, and walk"* (John 5:8).

To the blind man, the Master said *"Go, wash in the pool of Siloam"* (John 9:7).

Peter walked on water after he obeyed the Lord's command to step out of the boat (Matthew 14:29).

The message behind every command to stretch forth, rise up, step out, was simply this: if you are willing to tolerate something, it will never change.

To tolerate misery is a missed opportunity.

At some point, one must stop and take an honest assessment of his or her surroundings and situation and then ask the question: Why am I still sitting here?

> By faith Abraham obeyed when he was called to go out to the place which he would receive as an inheritance. And he went out, not knowing where he was going. By faith he dwelt in the land of promise as in a foreign country, dwelling

in tents with Isaac and Jacob, the heirs with him of the same promise, for he waited for the city which has foundations, whose builder and maker is God. (Hebrews 11:8–10)

God's call to Abraham was no doubt a frightening thing for a seventy-five-year-old man. At that age, people are settling down for retirement; nevertheless, Abraham walked, not knowing where he was going. All he knew was that he was being obedient. Abraham had faith. There were no maps, no GPS, and no written instructions from anyone. All Abraham had was God's promise that He would be his guide and navigator. God basically said, "Go! I will lead you." What would you do? Go or stay? Abraham obeyed God, and so shall you. Never allow fear of the unknown to paralyze you and stop you from stepping out in faith.

Sometimes in your walk of faith, all you receive from the Lord is a directive; the destination will come later. My grandma, Caroline Sinclair, believed in her heart that God would save her household. She prayed and believed God for the impossible, for nothing is impossible for them who believe. Raise up a preacher from my family! Save my family!

Then there's Enoch. The Bible says in Genesis 5:24, *"And Enoch walked with God; and he was not, for God took him."* Our life's journey as followers is often referred to as a walk. Walking before God must be our priority as children—His children.

Isaiah the prophet said, *"Remember now ... how I have walked before you in truth ..."* (Isaiah 38:3). Anyone who walks with God is exercising a living faith.

My father, Alfred Sinclair, knew Mr. Flett. They were from the same area. My dad had nothing but praise for him; he was a good man and fellow soldier who never returned home but died on the battlefield. My dad said that the German soldiers, their enemies, were fighting a war they didn't understand "and neither did we. We were young men fighting a senseless war."

My parents' generation grew up with people who never learned how to cope with grief and loss, so they turned to alcohol to numb their feelings and emotions. Over many years, I witnessed so many adults unable to process grief and loss. As a result of their decisions, our generation would also have to deal with our own grief. Many of us had to grow up in an environment that was often hostile and unforgiving.

Here are some tips to help you deal with grief: Contact caring and supportive people. Ask a pastor for help; reach out for help; call Non-insured Health Benefits for Indigenous people, as they can refer you and help you connect with professional counsellors. Don't be afraid to ask for support. If there's one thing I learned about the Indigenous people, it's that we are resilient in spite of all we've gone through. You can and will overcome.

What traumas have impacted Indigenous communities? For all Indigenous peoples, the word "trauma" brings up painful experiences—not just in the present, but conscious or unconscious memories of grief, loss, and deep hurt passed on from generation to generation. Native peoples, collectively, have gone through many devastations, including mass disease, enslavement, massacre, relocation, stolen lands, forced removal of children from families by boarding schools and adoptions, and loss of languages and spiritual practices. Researchers call this "historical trauma" or "the soul wound."

Historical trauma sounds like these hurts have only happened in the past, but Indigenous people experience many ongoing harms that impact us daily. Current problems include racism, threats to our land and environmental abuse, uncovering the wound around boarding school experiences, and knowing that our relatives are often missing and murdered without answers. Some of our communities face high rates of drug and alcohol addiction, violence, poverty, and inadequate schooling. Even our current physical and mental health reflects the challenges we have faced across generations.

Many Indigenous people are still disconnected from their cultural knowledge, practices, and language. But this connection can come with feelings of sadness, anger, shame, and grief. We may feel lost without purpose or try to cope with these feelings in both helpful and harmful ways.

Sometimes children can be the cruelest with name calling, I went to a predominantly White school in the north end. There was a lot of name-calling by the White kids. They would call me names like "a dirty Indian." It felt awful and left me feeling ashamed. I think I lost count of how many physical encounters I had because of being called a dirty Indian. Proverbs 18:21a says, *"Death and life are in the power of the tongue."* The racism and hatred were meant to beat me down and destroy my self-confidence. But it only fed into my anger and unforgiveness! Perhaps this is one of the other reasons why I excelled in sports. I'll show you what I can do, so I became better than most kids my age in sporting activities. It only fed my pride and ego, but I got even. But I was already damaged and bruised on the inside from what was happening at home. In my adult life, I also experienced racist and prejudiced attitudes.

I went into a bank one day. Back then you had to stand in line and wait for the teller to call you. In most cases, they would call the White person before you, even if you were there before them. But my mom didn't raise us for other people to treat us that way. I would say, "Hey, I was here first." Racism ran deep within the Winnipeg culture. You would be denied employment and property rentals on the basis of the colour of your skin.

I would be called "Chief" in the workplace and confront these racist people and tell them my proper name. They not only disrespected me as an individual but the honour of leadership in our communities. It has taken decades and there are still ongoing the racial comments and struggles for respect. To this present generation: never forget those who were willing to stand up against the bullies of racial prejudice. Perhaps you're reading this book and are struggling with unforgiveness. You can call upon Jesus. He can and will heal the bruised. Jesus died so we could be saved and healed from these tormenting thoughts; He came to heal the bruised!

> The Spirit of the Lord is upon Me, because He has anointed Me to preach the gospel to the poor; He has sent me to heal the brokenhearted, to proclaim liberty to the captives and recovery of sight to the blind, to set at liberty those who are oppressed. (Luke 4:18)

Chapter Two

The 1960s

OUR FAMILY MOVED to what is known as Jig Town. We'd never lived in a brand-new place before; it was always rentals that were old and in need of much repairs. However, in Jig Town everything was brand-new, but it was still a rental. I remember my brother and I had our own room, and my sisters had their own room. Of course, my mother had hers. That may not be impressive to you, but in the past, we'd lived in a two-bedroom place, and I think we children were all jammed in one room together.

While living in one of those homes in the inner-city, my mother was dating a man who eventually moved in with her. He was a violent person who would often beat my mother. His violence would spill over onto the children, and he would hurt us—if not physically, then emotionally. One time, I must have triggered his anger, and he was about use his belt on me, but I was able to outrun him. I slipped under a car and stayed in the middle where he couldn't reach me. I have no recollection how long I stayed under that car, but I knew I had fear in my heart. My mother would eventually leave him, but things didn't get any better for her.

In those early years, my mother would often take me shopping in the downtown area, and after the shopping was over, we had lunch together. When our meals were finished, my mother would often have the teacup reader come over and read her tea leaves. I would listen in on what the person was saying, which always included meeting a special person. I believe this opened the door in her life to what the Bible calls sorcery or witchcraft or the occult.

When God gave Moses the Ten Commandments, He spoke all these words:

> I am the Lord your God, who brought you out of the land of Egypt, out of the house of bondage. You shall have no other gods before Me. You shall not make for yourself a carved image—any likeness of anything that is in heaven above, or that is in the earth beneath, or that is water under the earth; you shall not bow down to them nor serve them. For I, the Lord your God, am a jealous God, visiting the iniquity of the fathers upon the children to the third

and fourth generations of those who hate Me, but showing mercy to thousands, to those who love Me and keep My commandments. (Exodus 20:2–6)

God was pronouncing a curse upon people who would disobey His commandments. Whenever we seek a source other than God, we worship idols: *"There shall not be found among you anyone who makes his son or his daughter pass through the fire, or who practice witchcraft, or a soothsayer, or one who interprets omens, or a sorcerer"* (Deuteronomy 18:10). Practising these forms of the occult opens us to the realm of the demonic evil spirits. My mother's grief caused her to look toward the occult practices, not realizing the harm she was bringing on herself and family, perhaps thinking that Prince Charming would eventually show up. But the devil eventually shows his real colours, and his real nature would be exposed. Often he was a violent person, once alcohol was consumed, which brought the violence out of him. But some of those men were just plain evil and violent; they didn't need alcohol to bring out the violence in them.

People expose themselves to the occult in many forms. As children we'd often play with the Ouija board, seeking advice from the other side, meaning the invisible world of evil. There was a fascination that we, as children, could call upon evil forces. This fascination with the occult is present not only in my immediate family but among my relatives. You mix that with alcohol and drugs and it becomes a lethal dose to everyone involved in it.

I think of the present generation around us today and how exposed they are to occult practices in violent videos and on the Internet and social media. The temptation seems much greater today. We didn't have social media growing up. As a matter fact, we had no Internet and no cell phones. We only had the television stations CBC and CTV. If we wanted to socialize with our friends, we had to get up, walk down the road, and knock on the door. Friday night we met at the local community centre for dance night. There were no shopping malls to meet up at. But today's generation has so many evil things coming against them: the drugs, pornography, idol worship, and many other evils of the world. Just one press of their finger and they're connected to a world of evil. They're growing up lacking social skills because they're hooked up to the Internet.

One would think that after we moved into this new place, the violence and alcohol would cease. But it only seemed to get worse, and the parties seemed to be endless. My mother and her sisters would often go down to the local bars and then show up later with all the band members from the hotel, and then the party was on. The band members brought their instruments with them. These parties lasted the whole weekend! The instruments would be playing, along with the laughter and the dancing, and it would always end in violence.

The sixties were the turbulent years of our lives. So many things unfolded in that decade: John F. Kennedy's assassination, Robert Kennedy's assassination, and Martin Luther King's assassination, and the riots in major cities of the US and the Vietnam War were live on TV. And with the accomplishment of man landing on the moon, one would think that our society would get better. It didn't get any better; it just got worse. Paul says in Romans 3 that we have all sinned and there is none righteous.

In spite of the household situation, my mother insisted that we go to Sunday school, so every Sunday there was a knock on the door for us children to get up and get on the bus to go to Sunday school. Often we went on the bus without having breakfast, and there were times we stepped over people who were passed out on the floor from the night before. They either had a bleeding nose or black eye. We'd get on the bus and head out to Calvary Temple, a church we had some affiliation with. I believe that before we went by buses, someone picked us up in vehicles and taxis and took us to church.

I wonder why we were sent to the church, as our home had no resemblance to Christianity, but my mother insisted that we go. I knew she had a Bible in the house, but it was never read or practised. It was a place for her to keep important documents. My guess is that because we weren't Christians and likely wouldn't look into a Bible, she thought it was the safest place for her documents.

I remember reading John 3:16 in the Sunday school class, attending during the Christmas season, and going to summer picnics. The early years of attending Sunday school didn't last very long. Once we became older, we no longer attended. Attending Sunday school for forty-five minutes a week wasn't enough; it's the parents' responsibility to teach their children the Word of God: *"Train up a child in the way he should go, and when he is old he will not depart from it"* (Proverbs 22:6). It was impossible to live out your Christian faith in such a hostile environment. Opening the door to the occult led to demonic powers of the unseen world. I believe these demons had been unleashed upon my family because of the alcohol, violence, and occult practices.

A Demon Is a Person without a Body

Three objectives of demons: 1. torment and torture, 2. keep you from knowing Christ, and 3. keep you from serving effectively

The characteristics of demons are to entice, harass, torment, create pressures in early childhood, and cause emotional shock.

A well-known former General from the Assemblies of God, who was an overseer in Great Britain, told me about the deck of cards. King Charles of France wanted his soothsayers and magicians to invent a game that would amuse him. So they came together and invented a deck of playing cards used at gambling events and played inside the home.

The King represented Satan.

The Queen represented Mary, Jesus' mother, as a prostitute.

The Jack represented promiscuity.

The ten of clubs represented breaking the Ten Commandments.

The Joker represented Jesus Christ.

And what do you do when you started a game of playing cards? You throw away the Joker.

There were many other things to do in the sixties. It was the age of rock 'n' roll, of the hippie movement in the drug culture, and free love and everything that goes with it. Promiscuity was running rampant among most young people; we were experimenting with sex. There was Elvis Presley, the Beatles, the Rolling Stones, and more rock bands getting much attention. The counterculture was in full swing. Some of the songs were pop songs, and others more in the rebellion and counterculture stream. It was easy for many of us young people to get involved in a countercultural revolution. Every decent and good thing was dropped—that's if we even had any in the first place.

In the sixties, my cousin and I began to sneak alcohol out of the house of the party-goers. We began drinking our beers in the back yard as preteens. Eventually, the addiction slowly moved in, and we were both addicted to alcohol by the time we reached our teens. That was the drug of choice back then; besides, it was free, but it would come at an awful cost. Nothing's free. The Bible says the wages of sin is death. Jesus said in John 10:10, *"The thief does not come except to steal, and to kill, and to destroy. I have come that they may have life, and that they may have it more abundantly."*

This sinful action almost left me for dead many times. This addiction will take you farther then you want to go; it will take you so low and to dark areas of life. It affects your thinking, your health, and your relationships. Everything you have cherished in your heart is now distorted and warped. I believe that behind every addiction there's a demon at work in your life. Proverbs 25:28 says, *"Whoever has no rule over his own spirit is like a city broken down, without walls."* Inside that city is who we are, our personality and our emotions. But like a city, there are many entrances. When the demons show up, they have access because the walls are broken down. Any sense of morality or good characteristics are broken down, like a wall broken down. The enemy has access to your life and your emotions. Remember what Jesus said: the devil comes to steal, kill, and destroy!

During my preteen years, school became less important. What became more important to me was living the lifestyle of rebellion. In the late 1960s, my sister and I would often attend dancing and drinking parties. We'd meet at the Indian and Métis

Friendship Centre on Princess Street. Those who had lived on the reservation and had to attend school in the city often found this a place to meet new friends. The musical bands were local, and all of them were of Indigenous background. So there was a place to meet for identification with our Indigenous people from across Manitoba and Northwest Ontario.

During the evening, we'd dance to rock 'n' roll music and then be off to some drinking party. Keep in mind that the legal age for drinking alcohol was twenty-one at the time. No alcohol was allowed in the Friendship Centre, but eventually it would make its way in. By this time, I was already addicted to alcohol. If I couldn't sneak it into the Friendship Centre down the street, there was a local bowling alley where I would go and stash my booze behind the toilet bowl. During breaks in the music, I'd go down to the local bowling alley and consume my cheap bottle of wine, 4 Aces. I'd make it back just in time for the next set of music, usually more intoxicated. By the time the evening was over, I had already drunk a full bottle of wine. Thinking back, that was cheap wine—I mean really cheap wine that cost a dollar and five cents.

Most of our summers were spent at the Friendship Centre, and the party scene just got bigger. Although I was the youngest of the group, the older ones allowed me to hang out with them. It wasn't long before the group began to form, perhaps one of the first Indigenous street gangs in the city of Winnipeg. We had a president, a vice president, and a Sergeant of Arms. We weren't a motorcycle club; we were a street club. Besides, of all the people we ran with, only one had a motor bike.

We tossed around several names to call ourselves. I don't know if we ever called ourselves any particular name, but we belonged to one of the first street gangs. Back then the gang consisted mostly of Indigenous people and our Métis brothers and sisters. The bands that would play the weekend were mostly Indigenous people, and some of them were part of the gang. There were also non-Indigenous people involved. Back then the gangs formed because of the violence on the streets. It wasn't like the gangs of today, whose main purpose is to sell drugs, traffick humans, and fight over turf.

There was a mixture of gang members: some of them were hippies, some were from the foster system or a dysfunctional family, and some just had a mean streak in them. Some were into drugs other than alcohol; some were using hallucinogenic drugs, called acid back then.

The violence usually occurred when other groups of people would come against someone in the club, whether it was in the streets, hotels, or other places. Violence was often dished out, so at the age of twelve, I was a young gang banger. I guess that's why the older members of the club allowed me to stay in the gang, because I was willing to fight. I was just as violent as any other member and would challenge men to fight. The president of our group was a tough street fighter. His girlfriend at the time was married; her husband refused to the sign the divorce papers, so our leader took him to the back lane and beat him until he said he would sign them.

Proverbs 22:24–25 says, "*Make no friendship with an angry man, and with a furious man do not go, lest you learn his ways and set snare for your soul.*" I had already learned his way before reaching teen years! Violence became a snare to my soul. I was bound up with anger, unforgiveness, and resentment. I was trapped and bound up with a demonic spirit of violence. I learned that was the way to resolve conflict—you either win or lose by violence. At times, this rage would consume me.

As a preteen, I wanted to kill the man who was beating my mother. Had I had access to a gun, I would have shot him. I wasn't even a teenager at the time, but murder was in my heart. This man was also very destructive. During one of his violent outbursts, he totally destroyed every window in our kitchen. He had gone ballistic, and anything he got his hands on was thrown through windows until every pane of glass was broken. My mom's brother was sitting in the kitchen, and the glass was flying everywhere. He was also intoxicated, unable to move from his seat. Amazingly, he never got hurt physically. He'd been a sergeant in the Second World War, and my guess is that he was thinking this outburst was nothing compared to the battleground of Europe.

My uncle was a nice man when he was sober. He always dressed in a white shirt and suit. He worked as court advocate in those days, but when he went on his binge from drinking too much or too long, that white shirt would be dirty and stained. He tried staying sober, sometimes for a few years, and we were all proud of him. But some of those people were ruthless and didn't give up until he gave in to their demands to drink alcohol with them.

The windows were eventually repaired and replaced, but there was a sense of shame. And I wanted to get revenge. I felt a deep hatred toward this man who'd caused so much harm. I truly wanted to kill him, and had I had the chance, I would have. This outburst of anger and destructive behaviour created a deep sense of fear in the hearts of our family. Although he was told to leave many times, he would come back at night and try to crawl through the living room window. My mom had a friend who worked as a security guard at Stony Mountain Penitentiary. He would come and sleep on our couch for what seemed like days or weeks. He was willing to engage the bully and defend our family. He carried with him what looked like a long, hard rubber hose. If the bully showed up, he'd be met with the rubber hose and a man who was not afraid of him.

At that time, to get into the hotels you needed to show your identification. I was only fifteen, and I walked into the hotel beverage room. To my surprise, I saw my mother sitting there with this violent offender who had abused her for years, so I walked up to him. I said to him, "Okay, I'm a man now. Let's go outside and settle the score." I was surprised that my mother denied that he'd ever hit her. That didn't change my mind. I was an eye witness to the facts. It amazes me how some people will stay in an abusive environment because that's all they know. But in my heart, I wanted to kill him. I believe the hotel bouncer escorted me out of the hotel.

"The heart is deceitful above all things, and desperately wicked; who can know it? I, the Lord, search the heart, I test the mind, even to give every man according to his ways, according to the fruit of his doings" (Jeremiah 17:9–10).

"Do not be deceived, God is not mocked; for whatever man sows, that he will also reap" (Galatians 6:7).

> When your terror comes like a storm, and your destruction comes like a whirlwind, when distress and anguish come upon you. "Then they will call on me, but I will not answer; they will seek me diligently, but they will not find me. Because they hated knowledge and did not choose the fear of the Lord, they would have none of my counsel and despised my every rebuke. Therefore they shall eat the fruit of their own way, and be filled to the full with their own fancies. For the turning away of the simple will slay them, and the complexity of fools will destroy them; but whoever listens to me will dwell safely, and will be secure, without fear of evil." (Proverbs 1:27–33)

That violent way of thinking led me to believe that I was invincible, or at least when I was intoxicated by the consumption of alcohol. The parties back then seemed to be endless: the violence, rock 'n' roll music, rebellion, immorality, lack of restraints, thoughtlessness, carelessness, evil, and the list goes on. And I haven't even reached my teen years.

At times in those younger years, life at home became unbearable, so I found myself couch surfing at relatives' homes or whoever. Sometimes I would leave home and be gone for weeks at a time, because I just hated living in that violent environment.

There was a rooming complex on Kennedy Street in downtown Winnipeg, and some of the band members stayed there. I'd stay with one of them in a one-room apartment and then be gone during the day. At lunch time we could go to he Indian and Metis Friendship Centre for soup and bannock. We had to walk through Central Park to get there from Kennedy Street. Then we had to walk by Calvary Temple, the very church where I'd attended Sunday school in my earlier years. But I didn't make the connection at that time. Back in Jig Town, the Sunday school bus and the bus captain came by and picked us up for Sunday school. By the time I walked by the building, I forgot that I ever went there. I may have forgotten, but then I read in the Word of God that the God of the Bible never forgot me.

> For as the rain comes down, and the snow from heaven, and did not return there, but water the earth, and make it bring forth and bud, that it may give seed to the sower and bread to the eater, so shall My word be that goes forth from my mouth; it shall not return to Me void, but it shall accomplish what I please, and it shall prosper in the thing for which I sent it. (Isaiah 55:10–11)

God had not forgotten about me; His Word was planted in my heart. I don't know who my Sunday school teacher was or who taught me John 3:16: "*For God so loved the world that He gave His only begotten Son, that whoever believes in Him shall not perish but have everlasting life.*"

I didn't realize it back then, but God's Word was planted in my heart, in spite of my foolishness and rebellious ways. God was pursuing me all those years I was running from Him. Those years were the most troubling of my life. I led a life of violence, gang banging, and alcohol abuse, but God still loved me. He didn't love my rebellion or my sin, but He loved me.

The apostle Paul writes in Romans 5:6–11:

> For when we were still without strength, in due time Christ died for the ungodly. For scarcely for a righteous man will one die; yet perhaps for a good man someone would even dare to die. But God demonstrates His own love toward us, in that while we were still sinners, Christ died for us. Much more then, having now been justified by His blood, we shall be saved from wrath through Him. For if when we were enemies we were reconciled to God through the death of His Son, much more, having been reconciled, we shall be saved by His life. And not only that, but we also rejoice in God through our Lord Jesus Christ, through whom we have now received the reconciliation.

In Ephesians 2:8–10, Paul writes:

> For by grace you have been saved through faith, and that not of yourselves; it is the gift of God, not of works, lest anyone should boast. For we are His workmanship, created in Christ Jesus for good works, which God prepared beforehand that we should walk in them.

"Blessed be the God and Father of our Lord Jesus Christ, who has blessed us with every spiritual blessing in heavenly places in Christ" (Ephesians 1:3).

The apostle Paul unpacks three significant elements of God's favour: the source of favour, the scope of favour, and the sphere of favour.

1. The source of favour. God Himself is the source and resource, the provider and provision.

"Every good gift and every perfect gift is from above, and comes down from the Father of lights, with whom there is no variation or shadow of turning" (James 1:17). God is our source of everything we need to experience the abundant life that effectively advances His kingdom.

2. The scope of favour. We are given every spiritual blessing. Our physical blessings in life are first connected to the spiritual blessing, and the spiritual realm is more real than the physical realm.

> That Christ may dwell in your hearts through faith; that you, being rooted and grounded in love, may be able to comprehend with all the saints what is the width and length and depth and height—to know the love of Christ which passes knowledge; that you may be filled with all the fullness of God. Now to Him who is able to do exceedingly abundantly above all that we ask or think, according to the power that works in us. (Ephesians 3:17–20)

3. The sphere of God's love and favour toward us. How wide is His favour? David says in Psalm 18:19: *"He also brought me out into a broad place; He delivered me because He delighted in me."*

How long is His favour? *"But the mercy of the Lord is from everlasting to everlasting on those who fear Him, and His righteousness to children's children"* (Psalm 103:17)

How deep is His favour?

> I waited patiently for the Lord; and He inclined to me, and heard my cry. He also brought me up out of a horrible pit, out of the miry clay, and set my feet upon a rock, and established my steps. He has put a new song in my mouth—praise to our God; many will see it and fear, and will trust in the Lord. (Psalm 40:1–3)

Favour digs its way through the dark holes of man's dilemma. Favour reached Joseph even in the pit. Favour rescued Daniel from the lion's den.

How high is favour? *"And raised us up together and made us sit together in the heavenly places in Christ Jesus"* (Ephesians 2:6).

Joseph went from the pit to become prime minister of Egypt. An orphan named Esther was made a queen, and David the shepherd boy became king over Israel. All raised up out of obscurity.

I heard a song by Jason Crabb, and I can certainly relate to the lyrics. As I was attempting to write this book, this song had a profound impact on me and helped me to continue writing. The opening lyrics are particularly meaningful to me: "People say that I would never make it …"

Thank you, Jason, for that little nudge of encouragement, needed at the right moment! Thank you, Lord, for using your servants behind the words, the instruments, and the years of preparation. Lord, truly you love your Body! We are the body of Christ!

There came a day when my older sister got married, somewhere in the middle of 1960. I'm not quite sure the day, but I know it was summer time. She was always the closer one to me in our family. When she got married and left, I was devastated. I thought to myself that surely she'd be coming home soon. I sat on the doorstep and watched and waited with endless tears, but she never came home.

In the background you could hear the partying, the laughter, the arguing, and then eventually the violence. In my days of roaming the streets of Winnipeg and finding no place to rest or eat, I would often reach out to my sister and brother-in-law, and they would make a place for me to sleep on the sofa and provide food for me. Today my sister remains the closest to me.

The day when she and her husband were born again and became part of the family of God, I rejoiced greatly and said, "Thank you, Father." He had given me a promise that my household would be saved. I held on to that promise until my mom, my dad, and my brother and sisters were saved and born again.

The crisis continued and then I became suicidal. The pain seemed overwhelming in my mind, and I felt tormented by an invisible force. At that time I began to self inflict harm and cut myself. I was in the bathroom when I took that razor blade and cut my wrist. It usually happened when I had consumed alcohol or some other drug. I sat in the bathroom as the blood poured out of my wrist, and I heard a voice that I believe was demonic. It said to me, "I have you now; you belong to me." These demonic spirits were controlling the cutting and intended to kill me. The pain felt so overwhelming. I lived in a sense of hopelessness and didn't see any way out of it. The environment in my household wasn't changing. The people who kept coming weren't changing; my mother wasn't changing, and the brutal and violent men she lived with weren't changing.

Sometimes I defended my friends at school when the local bullies tried to intimidate them. I would often intervene and took upon myself to fight the bully. I was learning the rules of the street; one would always find someone bigger and meaner than them. So if you couldn't defend yourself by your own means, you'd need to arm yourself with a baseball bat, a knife, or a gun.

There were three brothers who moved to the neighbourhood in Jig Town. Back then, they were big men; all of them were at least six-foot-three or taller. It isn't uncommon to see men at that height today, but not back then. They were big men in my eyes, and they were violent and much older. They came from the Weston area and no doubt were real gang bangers from the fifties and sixties. One would learn really quick that you don't mess with these people.

Unfortunately, they brought violence that we hadn't seen before. When one of the brothers had an issue with the other, he just walked over to his house and stabbed him. His brother nearly died, and he ended up in prison for many years—and these men were our neighbours! The younger of the three didn't seem to be as violent as his older brothers. He would often play hardball catch with me. I believe he played semi-pro baseball back in the day. He was throwing that hard ball at least ninety miles an hour and aiming for my head. I was either going to catch the ball or get hurt severely. It helped me with my eye and hand coordination and flexibility. Besides that, I liked him, and he seemed to be a nice man. I don't know if he had any children or if he considered me a son or friend, but he was always happy to throw those fastballs at me.

A mixture of people lived in our part of Jig Town. Our neighbours were Jewish, Métis, Black, Indigenous, Ukrainian, and other nationalities. We were the United Nations of the north end, and each member had their own challenges and issues. Some had to deal with violence and alcohol and racism. We were in grade school, and there was an overweight boy there who would often be teased or abused by his schoolmates. Then one day he was no longer around, and the rumours began to flow throughout the neighbourhood that he'd gone home after school one day and committed suicide. It was devastating news for the neighbourhood and for those of us who knew him from school. Little or nothing was said about it at school, and there was little help at all from counsellors, or any material provided about the issue of suicide. Back then, schools were facing challenges and restraints due to low budgets and were just getting by.

Suicide is a tragic outcome of many factors, which differ from person to person. Feeling a sense of burden or a lack of belonging are common feelings that increase risk. Mental illness also plays a role in suicide, including depression, anxiety, psychosis, and substance abuse. According to Statistics Canada, 4,500 people die by suicide every year, equivalent to twelve people taking their lives every day. For every death by suicide, at least seven to ten people will attempt suicide or grieve the loss of someone who took their own life.[1]

Those of us who lived in Manitoba Government Housing, or Winnipeg Housing, called it Jig Town. I'm not sure how the name came about, but I have some ideas. The local bootleggers would sell a shot of whiskey in a small glass called a jigger, or the other idea was a jigging contest in public. We definitely had a lot of jiggers in our family! And when the booze was flowing, it was jigging time! When Uncle Peter took to the dance floor, it was his style that got the clapping going. But when it was Mom's time, we would move the table aside and the fiddler would reach for his fiddle. Things were going to the next level. I think it was those White settlers from Scotland that brought that style to the New World, or they just got so drunk they couldn't lift their legs as high as their Highlander style, the Scottish traditional dance. So they just kept their ankles close to the ground. And then us kids brought in a little of R & B and rock 'n' roll.

One of my childhood friends who lived across the street was Black; I believe his family was originally from Eastern Canada. We would often hang out together. One day I joined him to go visit his mother, who lived in the Deer Lodge Centre. She lived inside an artificial lung machine. That meant she would never be coming home again, so my friend's older brother was taking care of him. His brother was much older than us, and whenever I went to see my friend when his brother was home, he would always be playing his soul music, R&B. They would be moving their feet to the music of Sam Cooke singing "Bring It on Home to Me." I have to admit, they were pretty cool dancers, moving and swaying. They were killing it! And when his friend was over, they'd sing and dance, lifting up their voices. I think that's where I learned to dance, by dancing to R&B and rock 'n' roll. And without fail, they'd always try to rough us up. We were little guys compared to them, and they were in their late teens, maybe into their early twenties. Over the years, we lost touch with one another, as with many of my childhood friends.

A time came when I decided to try to change the course of my life and get back to my education and friends. One of my friends said that when I came back from the streets and tried to re-adjust, I had changed. I did not change for the better, but for the worse, living a lifestyle of a gang banger. You learn the language of the street and some forms of slang. None of my childhood friends spoke the same language, nor could they identify where I had been. The sixties were coming to a close, and I was more restless than before. I left home at the age of fifteen and would not return again. My mother and I had a falling out, but this was more serious than previous ones.

---

[1] "Suicide in Canada: Key Statistics," Statistics Canada, accessed June 30, 2024, https://www.canada.ca/en/public-health/services/publications/healthy-living/suicide-canada-key-statistics-infographic.html.

I have an older sister whom I'd never met, as she had left home, but she came to visit us sometime in the 1960s. She brought her children and visited with my mother for a short time and then left again. This would be the only time I'd meet her, as she would never come back again. Apparently they had a falling out and she too left when she was young, and they never really reconciled or settled their differences. Hurting people hurt others and never reconcile. It's unfortunate they never reconciled and enjoyed each other as a daughter and mother.

Back in the late sixties, it seemed like everyone was moving to Vancouver. I'm not quite sure of all the reasons, but it was a destination for many. I thought that perhaps I should make that journey as well, because I had a bicycle I could ride. I had a bicycle but not a whole lot of common sense. My friend asked me how much money I had in my pocket to make such a long ride, and I replied that I had $0.25. He laughed at me and said that wouldn't get me very far; thinking back, neither would my bike. It wouldn't get me outside Winnipeg.

I was always restless, trying to find something to fill the void inside of me. I was young but was already experiencing drugs and alcohol and sex. Nothing and nobody could fill the void or emptiness I was feeling. I had this longing for something that could bring me satisfaction, like Mick Jagger and the Rolling Stones sang in one of their hits of the sixties: "I can't get no satisfaction." That song resonated with me because I was feeling the same way. Nothing seemed to fill the void that I was feeling on the inside.

Life's labels can often be more difficult to deal with than life's circumstances. It could be that you've had to deal with a label all your life. I'm amazed at how easily we get them and at the damage they can do.

Maybe you acquired you first label in grade school—you failed, or someone called you stupid, or a school teacher humiliated you in front of the class. As you get older, life's labels become more complex. Maybe it's a divorce, moral failure, alcoholism, or a false accusation and no one chooses to believe your side of the story. People have wrapped you with labels before they get a chance to know you, the real you.

In Acts 3, the man sitting outside the gate beautiful was brought there every day to beg. He had no name—just a beggar labelled by all who passed by the temple. He could hear the prayers and listen to the music but could never get inside the temple. Like the man at the gate, you have a name, but no one knows it or they chose not to learn it. It's easiest to refer to you as the lame man or woman. Throughout our life we're given labels that influence what people think about us and how we view ourselves; they're stereotypes based on assumptions. Those assumptions influence our perception of our identity, and we often can't control someone's opinion!

Your heavenly Father feels much differently about you than those who pinned life's labels to you. In the Bible, the name Jacob means heel catcher, trickster, or deceiver. Isaiah referred to him as a worm, but God called him a prince when he changed his name to Israel.

Gideon was a coward, hiding from the enemy, but God called him a mighty man of valour. When Jesus met Simon, he called him Peter, meaning small stone, but He also called him a rock. Saul was a murderer chasing down Christians and throwing them into the jail, but Jesus changed his life, and his name became the Apostle Paul, who wrote nearly one-third of the New Testament. I want to encourage you to rip off that label; you are not someone's opinion of you. Like the man in Acts 3, rise up in the name of Jesus; like Lazarus in John's Gospel, come forth and remove all the death clothes.

For some reason, our family and relatives all had some type of labels put on them. We were all given nicknames; mine was Punch! It means violence, and all my friends knew me by that name back then. This name got me into more trouble and almost cost me my life. When we left Jig Town and went to see other girls in another neighbourhood, the local boys took it upon themselves to find out who was coming to see the girls. What name came up? Punch! My friend and I were on their turf in the Weston area, and they were looking for me. They found us in the local park with their girls, and one of them yelled out "Punch!" All of a sudden, about thirty of them showed up. I already had street smarts and had to make a decision to flee or fight! We were outnumbered and would certainly have our butts handed to us. At that time I always carried a six-inch knife on me. You learn to calculate risk on the streets, when to flee or fight. I thought for a moment, *I am not going to flee*. Besides, the girls were telling them to get lost. We decided to stand our ground and see what happened. I had hold of the handle of the knife in my hands and thought, *If I'm going down tonight, some of them are going down with me*.

That name Punch almost cost me my life; it was a label of violence and put a target on my back. This would play out over the course of my teen years and adult life, as I was labeled as a troublemaker or brawler. In the street gang, my name played itself out again and again. That label was wrapped around me so tightly, it was killing me. I was bound in prison, shackled to chains, unable to free myself.

That name was so entrenched in me that when my close buddy came knocking on the door and asked for me by my real name, Alfred, my mom replied that no one lived there by that name. I came from the living room and asked my mom who had come to the door, and she said some boy looking for Alfred. I said, "Mom, that's me." She giggled!

Most things that were connected with that name had me in bondage. When the devil comes knocking at my door trying to get at me, I don't answer to that label. I have a new name! It is no longer me. I have been crucified with Christ. The person you tried to kill no longer lives here. He is under the blood of Christ. Devil, you are a liar and a loser! You failed.

A demon-possessed man was healed when Jesus came to the other side of the sea to the country of the Gadarenes.

> And when He came out of the boat, immediately there met Him out of the tombs a man with an unclean spirit, who had his dwelling among the tombs; and no one could bind him, not even with chains, because he had often been bound with shackles and chains. And the chains had been pulled apart by him, and the shackles broken in pieces; neither could anyone tame him. And always, night and day, he was in the mountains and in the tombs, crying out cutting himself with stones. When he saw Jesus from afar, he ran and worshiped Him. And he cried out with a loud voice and said, "What I have I to do with You, Jesus, Son of the Most High God? I implore You by God that You do not torment me." For He said to him, "Come out of the man, unclean spirit!" Then He asked him, "What is your name?" And he answered, saying, "My name is Legion; for we are many." Also he begged Him earnestly that He would not send them out of the country. Now a large herd of swine was feeding there near the mountains. So all the demons begged Him, saying, "Send us to the swine, that we may enter them." And at once Jesus gave them permission. Then the unclean spirits went out and entered the swine (there were about two thousand); and the herd ran violently down the steep place into the sea, and drowned in the sea. So those who fed the swine fled, and they told it in the city and in the country. And they went out to see what it was that had happened. Then they came to Jesus, and saw the one who had been demon-possessed and had the legion, sitting and clothed in his right mind. And they were afraid. And those who saw it told them how it happened to him who had been demon-possessed, and about the swine. Then they began to plead with Him to depart from their region. And when He got into the boat, he who had been demon-possessed begged Him that he might be with Him. However, Jesus did not permit him, but said to him, "Go home to your friends, and tell them what great things the Lord has done for you, and how He has compassion on you. And He departed and began to proclaim in Decapolis all that Jesus had done for him; and all marveled. (Mark 5:2–20)

The curse of that name was broken the day I received Christ as my Lord and Saviour. Just recently a friend at church came up to me and used that name. He knew that name because he had married a girl from Jig Town. She knew me by that name, and so did the rest of the neighbourhood. When he called me that name, it seemed really strange to me. Even after my conversion to Christ, my mother still used that name until my older sister told her that it wasn't my name anymore. My name was Alfred. She had to lecture my mother many times about referring to me as Alfred, then Pastor Alfred, and now Reverend Alfred. That label is no longer me. I am a new creation in Christ Jesus; my identity is found in Him and Him alone. He is my rock and my salvation in whom I trust.

In the passage from Mark's Gospel above, the man is sitting in his right mind. Oh happy day! He is sitting in his right mind. I believe that throughout the many years of my rebellion, God healed my mind, touched my heart, and made me a new creation. He took this mess that I was in and turned it into a miracle. They say in professional sports that if you suffer three concussions, that can end your career. I can tell you that I suffered many concussions through those early years of violence in the street life I was living. By all indications, my brain should have been permanently damaged, but God in His grace and mercy healed and restored every brain cell that was damaged through alcohol and violence.

Jesus told the man who was demon-possessed to go home to his friends and tell them what great things the Lord had done for him and how He had compassion on him. The man departed and began to proclaim in Decapolis all that Jesus had done for him, and all marvelled.

My prayer has always been, "Lord, help me reach my family and childhood friends with the gospel." The Lord has answered that request many times and in many different ways. One of my childhood friends was John. He came from a large French family, about a total of twelve in the family living in Jig Town. There was a lake on Inkster Boulevard, a good walking distance from Jig Town. It had a deep end and a shallow end. One day everyone was jumping off the dock and springboard. I said to myself, "I can do that as well." Without having had any swimming lessons, I jumped into the deep end. That was just me, my nature—take the plunge and count the cost later. My parents never enrolled me in swimming lessons. There was a pool across the street from where we lived, but it was only ankle-deep.

Well, I took the plunge, but this time I panicked and two people tried to save me from drowning—John and someone else. I panicked and tried pull John down with me, but he pushed me toward the dock. Then I went down and my feet were touching the bottom. I opened my eyes and could see the dock, so I just started walking toward it. John, in his attempt to help, pushed me toward the dock. I finally made it onto the dock, but not before swallowing gallons of water.

I lay there for what seemed like a long time, with water coming out of my mouth. I heard some kids laughing at me. After swallowing from this man-made water system, we headed back home. I was so sick and told my mom how I was feeling and what had happened. She called the doctor and he came over to our place and checked me out. I was sick and throwing up, but I survived the near drowning because my childhood buddy jumped in and tried to save me.

In November 2009, John died and passed from this world into heaven to be with his Lord and Saviour Jesus Christ. I had only seen John off and on over the previous thirty-five years. I would usually run into him at the local shopping mall and we'd greet one another. I already had given my life to Christ and been a Christian for many years, and it just so happened that John had been my drinking buddy before I met Jesus. I changed the course of my life after I became a born again believer. My prayer had always been, "Lord, open the door so that I can speak to my childhood friends about you."

One day I received a phone call from John. He said he was struggling with an illness and had throat cancer. He'd been looking through his night table and just happened to find my phone number, so he'd decided to call me. I hadn't had a conversation with John over the telephone for decades. Once I quit the party scene, we no longer socialized. He'd held on to my telephone number all those years. That was a God moment. He told me that he was going to start chemotherapy soon, so I suggested that we get together the following week, and he agreed to do that.

When I called him back the following week, his condition had gotten worse and he had very little energy. He said that when he talked to me, he felt peace and strength. A week went by and I received a phone call from his girlfriend, who said that John had been admitted to Riverview Hospital and had stage four cancer. He didn't have very long to live, so I immediately went up to the hospital to see my childhood friend.

When I arrived at the hospital, I went to his room. There he was lying in bed, not aware of anything, unconscious, hooked up to an IV, and waiting to die. I could barely recognize him; his body was wasting away quickly, his face seemed shrunken (perhaps due to his dentures being removed), and most of his hair was gone. His girlfriend was standing in the room along with his two sisters. John's sisters knew me from Jig Town. One of them had been in the same class as me. We exchanged greetings, and I told him that I was there to pray for him. It seemed awkward at the moment, seeing old friends and now saying goodbye to their brother and my childhood friend. *Lord, I need your help*, I was thinking.

Just as I said that prayer, in walked the doctor. He greeted us and then went to John's bedside and looked at his chart. He said he would increase his pain meds. Then he turned us and said, "You can still talk to him, because the last thing to go before we die is our hearing."

I thought this was my opportunity to speak over his life. I said, "John, this is Alfred. You're going to be leaving this world and entering into another realm." I told him that God loved him and that He wanted to reassure him that he was not forgotten. I said, "John, with the last breath you have inside of you, call upon the name of Jesus. Jesus said He is the way, the truth, and life. Jesus said that He is the resurrection and the life, and whoever believes in Him, though he may die, he shall live again. And whoever lives and believes in Him shall never die. Do you believe this? "[Martha] *said to Him, "Yes, Lord, I believe that You are the Christ, the Son of God, who is to come into the world"* (John 11:27).

> "Let not your heart be troubled; you believe in God, believe also in Me. In My Father's house are many mansions; if it were not so, I would have told you. I go to prepare a place for you. And if I go and prepare a place for you, I will come again and receive you to Myself; that where I am, there you may be also. And where I go you know, and the way you know." Thomas said to Him, "Lord, we do not know where You are going, and how can we know the way?" Jesus said to him, "I am the way, the truth, and the life. No one comes to the Father except through Me." (John14:1–6)

I stood at his bedside quoting scripture after scripture. I read Psalm 23 and told him that to be absent from the body is to be present with the Lord. I said to John, "Just reach out to Jesus and tell Him that you're sorry for your sins and acknowledge Him as your Lord and Saviour. He will forgive you; He will receive you, and He will never leave you." I took the doctor seriously when he said that John could still hear me, and I made sure that he could hear me and, most of all, the Holy Spirit speak to him. By the looks of his condition, he had little time left on the earth.

I led him into the prayer of Romans 10:9–10:

> that if you confess with your mouth the Lord Jesus and believe in your heart that God has raised Him from the dead, you will be saved. For with the heart one believes unto righteousness, and with the mouth confession is made unto salvation.

For the Scripture says that whoever believes on Him will not be put to shame: *"For there is no distinction between Jew and Greek, for the same Lord over all is rich to all who call upon Him. For 'whoever calls on the name of the Lord shall be saved'"* (Romans 10:12–13).

As I finished praying with him, he lifted his left arm into the air and then put it down. I knew he was left-handed from our childhood days. A miracle happened; he was born again and from an unconscious state had called upon the Lord. How is it possible that he could still hear in that condition? That's what the people said about Lazarus, who had been in the tomb for a number of days, but Jesus stood at the entrance of that tomb and called him forth, and he came out from that tomb alive.

The next day, John's girlfriend called me with the news that John had died. His death really shook me, but I knew that he had called upon the Lord. I came to lead the young boy who had saved me from drowning to the only one who could save Him, and that was Jesus.

The memorial was held the following week, and many of his former co-workers attended the service. He had worked for Motor Coach Industry for many years. He would often say to me, "You got me that job." At that time, Service Canada had a list of potential jobs available. You could walk in and look on the board for available jobs. As we scanned the board, I found this particular job that John would be suited for, so I handed him the note and encouraged him to apply. He applied and got the job. He must have worked there for over thirty years. I think about him often, but I know he is in a better place. He was my childhood friend and the only one who jumped into the water to save me from drowning.

When we reached adulthood, he was my drinking buddy. There came a day when I decided to no longer live that lifestyle, and I started attending church. Then I gave my heart to Jesus Christ. When John called and suggested we go out to the bar, I told him that I was no longer living that lifestyle and had given my heart to Jesus Christ. He laughed at me and said, "If God is real, I'll come and kneel at your doorstep so that He can show Himself to me." Well, God revealed Himself—not at my doorstep, but in the small room in Riverview Hospital where my dear friend was dying. Oh happy day when I'll see my friend again where there is no more pain, no more sickness, no more death, no more sorrow. What a day that will be when I see my King Jesus. I will lay my crowns at His feet and say to Him, "Thank you, Lord, for saving a wretch like me and making me your child. I will worship you forever and forever."

During the course of the memorial service and luncheon afterwards, all his family members were there, except his parents. They had already passed away. Each of John's siblings came and greeted me. They all knew me by the name Punch, and they were all aware of my former lifestyle before Christ. They were aware of my new life and that a transformation had occurred. Each member came and greeted me, and I spoke with each one of them for a few moments and explained John's conversion and how he'd called upon Jesus. What an opportunity.

Remain faithful to God, and a day will come that one of your childhood friends will need your prayers and help. A year later, John's older brother passed away, but not before he heard about Jesus. I'm not sure how he died, but he heard about Jesus. You could be the catalyst God uses to bring someone to the Lord.

In the final years of the sixties, the Indian and Metis Friendship Centre was no longer the meeting place. The bands now played the local hotels. Those places would eventually become our new meeting places. The gang life was coming to an end as we knew it. By then, some of the older people were moving on and finding jobs. Others no doubt headed to prison. But some of the other members remained connected with each other.

We often met at the local hotels to listen to live music, and we were still into drugs and alcohol. There was still plenty of partying and barroom brawls and house parties. Our new dance floors were now the hotels, and we danced to rock 'n' roll music. I think I counted at least a dozen hotels on the Main Street drag. If you got kicked out of one, you had many choices. Back in the sixties, the Main Street was lined with hotels and many small businesses down both sides of the streets. We called it the Drag, which was slang for the meeting place. There was the pawnshop, meat market, grocery store, fruit stands, vegetable stands, movie theatres, barbershops, jewellery stores, clothing stores, and footwear stores. Anything you needed, you could find it on Main Street. As preteens, we often went down to Main Street and had no fear of anyone. Parents brought their children to shop there without any hesitation. But today in 2024, it bears no resemblance to what it used to be. Now most of the hotels are closed down, and you'll find many social agencies that help the homeless, the marginalized, the forgotten, and those struggling with addictions and homelessness.

During those days when I was running from God, my life didn't improve but was always a struggle. I had a deep void inside and longed for something to fill it. I would sit on our steps in Jig Town gazing up the stars and say to myself, "There must be a God who made these stars, His creation." I realized that God had given us two witnesses of His existence: His Creation and our conscience.

One day I was travelling from Toronto, Ontario to the United Arab Emirates into Dubai on my way to Africa. A man sitting next to me was travelling back to Saudi Arabia. He'd come to Canada for an interview to further his education and increase his skill level. He'd worked as a neurologist for many years in his country and was head of the department. For the next three and a half hours, we had a variety of conversations. I told him I was going to East Africa on a mission trip and that I was a Christian. He was a surgeon and a Muslim. I asked him many questions about how the brain functions. It was very interesting, and I learned a few things. I asked him how brain injuries and head trauma respond to treatment. He said that depending on the severity of the injury, sometimes the brain can heal itself, and some injuries respond to rehabilitation if detected early.

I also asked him where our conscience is located in our brain, and he pointed to the top of the head. Then I asked him how the conscience came into being and who put it there. He replied that God put it there. So here's this practising Muslim, who is a brain surgeon, telling me that God put the conscience inside the brain. God is in the putting business. He put this doctor next me! He put in me a new heart; He put joy unspeakable and full of glory into me.

Chapter Three

The 1970s

BY THE 1970s, the gang life was more or less behind me and not as important to me as it had been in the sixties. The gang just moved inside of me; remember, demon are persons without bodies. I think one of the reasons I got involved in the gang was for a sense of belonging. I'm sure that if I'd had a stable home life, that would never have been my lifestyle. My dad and my mother would get along, but once alcohol got involved, the arguing started. My dad wasn't a violent man; he had seen enough violence on the battlefield. He would just disappear. Whenever alcohol was consumed, the anger, rage, and unforgiveness would surface. And the cycle would just continue.

My sister was dating an Indigenous man who would eventually become her husband. We often attended parties with him and his family members. These parties would sometimes last for the whole weekend. When we ran out of liquor, we'd make one phone call to the bootlegger, and the booze would arrive within the hour and then the party was on again. The parties would last late into the night and to the next morning, and you'd sleep it off for a bit. And then back to the party—endless partying.

At one of those parties, I met a beautiful young lady who was knockout gorgeous. She was a bit older than me, but that didn't matter. I had dated older women before. But this person had an edge about her and still had the hippie vibe. She was smart, and I thought that she must be a model, and she was—among the local Indigenous ladies. Apparently she'd been in a local pageant showcasing young, talented Indigenous ladies. She was close to graduating from high school. She came from a community of Fisher River, among the Cree people. She'd left the reservation at the age of fifteen to attend high school in Winnipeg because there was no high school education on the reservation back then, so most Indigenous children had to come to school in Winnipeg or other cities within the province.

We were both Indigenous and our fathers were alcoholics. Unlike me, she didn't allow the alcohol or partying to get in the way of her schooling. As matter of fact, she excelled in school and finished at the top of her class. I couldn't care less about it. Staying focused on school was a challenge because of a lack of sleep due to the wars that went on in the home. This resulted in poor concentration. But because of my good memory skills, I advanced. My mom bought a twenty-four-volume set of encyclopedias, and it was good reading. She knew we needed to educate ourselves about the things around us. It's amazing how many volumes of information you can store on your smart phone today.

My mom had a running account with the bakery man, the milkman, and the furniture man from Selkirk. The other salesmen would often come and have a beer or two. On those hot summer days, even the mailman came in and had cold beer.

I had quite the entrepreneurial ambition back then. I had my lemonade stand and sold bags of popcorn to our neighbours. One day my mom told me that I wasn't actually making any profit. In her mind, I was using all her butter for my popcorn. My guess was that I made the best popcorn in the neighbourhood because I had plenty of butter and salt on it. I sold it in small bags and went throughout the neighbourhood knocking on doors and selling until my mother shut down my enterprise because it was cutting into her grocery budget.

After that, someone offered us a job delivering flyers door-to-door to make a few dollars. As a ten-year-old, I thought I could make some big money, so my buddy and I went down the streets delivering flyers. We were given the route down Burrows Avenue from Jig Town to Main Street. We were just young guys, so we couldn't carry a lot of flyers. We misunderstood the older teenager who had given us the route. We were under the impression that once we finished our deliveries, we'd meet him at Main Street and collect our money. Before we ever reached Main Street, we were already out of flyers. Then he came looking for us and found us heading east on Burrows Avenue and asked where we were going, as we still had flyers to deliver. We had to backtrack many blocks to resume our route. We eventually got all the flyers delivered and made a few bucks.

Then he had another project for us. We were to deliver flyers in the Brooklands area of Weston. There were gang members in Brooklands who noticed that we were not from their hood, so they were going inflict some violence on us. We were just pre-teens, maybe ten years old. My hair was long back then. Almost everyone had Beatle haircuts. So they threatened to put a beating on us and they were going cut my hair off. We managed to get away and told the older teen what had happened. He took his tire iron and went looking for them. That was the end of delivering flyers in that area of the city. No way they were going to cut my hair.

My mom decided that I needed to be her personal banker, so when she went out partying and had extra money, I was to take care of it, so I hid it where no one could find it, except me. Of course, there was a surcharge involved, since I was the banker. The boys and I would head out to the Red River Exhibition. When it was time to return the money to my mom, she'd say that there was twenty dollars missing. Caught red-handed! At least the boys and I had a good time! We saved money by jumping over the fence at the Ex, and with twenty dollars of my mom's budget, the boys and I had a little bit of fun.

One night I met a young lady, Lynda, at a party, and I wanted to see her again. So before the party ended, I was able to get her address. At that time she was living on Langside Street with her sister, who was also very pretty. Later I decided to head down to Langside Street and see her. I was still somewhat intoxicated from the night before. I knocked on the door, and Lynda's sister answered the door and said she wasn't home, but I could come in and wait. I went in and waited and waited until I fell asleep or passed out. I certainly wasn't making a good first impression. I woke up and gave her sister my number and asked her to have her call me.

Our telephone at home was out of service, so our Jewish neighbour allowed us to use their phone. Whenever a call would come for one of our family members, they'd just knock on the wall. When I heard the knock, I thought it could be the call I'd been waiting for. The voice that came over the phone belonged to the girl I'd met at the party.

"Hi, this is Lynda; we met at the party."

At that time she was finishing up high school. Not only was she smart, but she was beautiful. I had dated local girls and sometime girls with street smarts. But this young lady was different! Over time, we mostly talked over the phone, and whenever the knock came from the wall, my family would say, "It's for you." The neighbour was always generous with the use of their phone; besides, I was their babysitter. His wife was addicted to bingo. I made $5.00 an evening and could to talk to Lynda at the same time.

Back then we'd meet at Memorial Park downtown and sit by the fountains smoking rolled tobacco. We were weekend hippies. I think my hair was just as long as hers. She was good at rolling paper, and we'd sit for hours talking. The last bus leaving for Jig Town left close to midnight. If you missed it, the second option was to take the bus to McPhillips and walk the rest of the way. And if you missed both, it would be a very long walk home from the downtown area, but that wouldn't be new to me. I'd done that many times before in the late sixties. I had no fear, and nobody bothered me.

I decided to invite Lynda to met my mom, so she came to Jig Town. When she came through the doors, my younger brother said, "Mom, Alfred brought home a hippie." Not just any hippie but my future wife. We've been together for fifty-four years and married for fifty-two. We were both young teenagers at the time we met and had a child before marriage. It was a challenge back then. I was now a father and hadn't even finished school. Lynda moved in with me when she was pregnant with our beautiful daughter. My brother moved out of the room.

We were living with my mom in Jig Town, trying to find work and leaving school. Our beautiful daughter was born in the middle of the night at the Health Science Centre, or Women's Centre. That was a special moment for both of us! It was getting late, so I had to get home. It was around 3:00 a.m. No buses were operating, and I had no money in my pocket for a taxi, so I just skipped all the way home—sometimes leaping and, of course, running.

I found work in a boat manufacturing company. It was just a job but it paid me at the end of the week. I was working as a fibreglass worker forming the hull of boats. It was hot and hard work, bending over most of the day, and breathing in the fumes from the chemicals left you with the headache. Every day I went home with a headache.

Several people were assigned to the fibreglass role. One day somebody messed up their assignment, and because I was the youngest person, the others blamed me. So I was fired from a job that gave me a headache. The chemicals were the worst thing to breath in, even though we had a mask to cover our mouth and nose.

We knew back then that living with my mother was not ideal. She always had a nasty attitude when the booze started flowing, so we had a plan to save up some resources and move out to eventually move on with life. I had several nowhere jobs that didn't last long. I'd make a few dollars then quit. We saved up enough funds to start buying Kmart furniture, and we finally found an apartment and moved out of my mom's place. Just like with my older sister before me, I had a fallout with Mom and just left. There was never any apology from either party. The devil comes in and creates these division among family members. He comes to conquer, divide, and separate family members. I still don't know to this day what caused the rift between my older sister and my mother. It must've been really serious, considering that they never talked out their differences. I believe it was because of their immaturity and self-pity that they could never reconcile, and they no doubt had unforgiveness in their hearts.

Lynda and I eventually married. We were still both teenagers, but we believed that we should get married, considering we were already parents. We were married at a local Roman Catholic Church. Our family never practised any religious faith. The priest was more interested in converting Lynda before our marriage, so she was required to attend classes to become a Roman Catholic. It didn't matter to me because I didn't know what a Roman Catholic was. The only thing I knew from my childhood was that when I went inside that religious building, I saw candles burning and those confession booths. To me it was creepy.

My best man was nowhere to be found on our wedding day. He'd been out partying somewhere the night before, but we eventually found him. He cleaned himself up and made it to the wedding. After the wedding ceremony, several guests and family members attended the reception. Our family members were at the head table, and for some reason my mother was intoxicated and arguing and trying to fight other people. It was embarrassing but predictable. I leaned over and told her that if she couldn't control herself, it was best for her to leave. I heard later that a fight had broken out after Lynda and I left the reception. When I heard the news the following day, I headed to my mother's place and gave her a piece of my mind. She never said, "I'm sorry, son, for being rude and unkind; please forgive me." I don't think those words were ever said. Conflicts were always resolved through violence!

Lynda was working and I was still trying to finish school while working part time. A few of my high school buddies and I had a cleaning job at a garment factory after school and then we'd clean a Jaguar dealership on Main Street. I'd move that mop back and forth and say to myself, "One day, I'm going to own a luxury car." Well, my first car was not a Jaguar; it was a 1963 Ford, and it was black and red. For the day, it looked nice: besides I was the only one among my high school friends who actually owned a car. It was our McDonald's car because that's where we headed at lunch time.

By the time I would get home, it would be close ten, and then up early the next day for school. When I got my license, I began delivering groceries for Champs Chicken. I was trying really hard to be responsible, but the street life had a hold on me. I was married in high school and needing permission to use the bathroom. That's it for me. I just walked out of high school. My attitude was, "Just give me the final exam."

I had a high school teacher who was a no-nonsense type of person. She had a big King James Bible on her desk. We often got rowdy, and sometimes I'd show up with a hangover or had been smoking something during break. I'd sit in the classroom paying no attention to what was being said. She'd stand up with her big King James Bible and say, "If you want to know the truth, this is the truth." I guess she never thought that anyone was listening, but I heard her because I had attended Sunday school at one time. When I contacted her by phone, I said, "You don't remember me, but I was a student in your classroom in high school." I told her that I'd found the truth and was a born again Christian. "I heard you say that Jesus was the way, the truth, and life."

She invited me to a banquet at her Baptist church, so Lynda and I went and met with her. It was a short visit, but I could see that she was rejoicing in her heart that she'd had an impact on at least one of her students, the one most likely not to succeed in life. She made more of an impact than she ever realized. I attended her funeral, and before the service I had a chat with my pastor, H.H. Barber. I told him, "The lady you're doing the funeral for today was my high school teacher." He told me that she'd never had a teaching degree but was hired because of her skill set. I told the pastor that she was not ashamed of the gospel of Jesus Christ and that she would stand up and hold up her King James Bible. Pastor Barber shared that story during her memorial service. She was quite the lady. I don't think she was ever married or had children.

After leaving her classroom, we'd go to the science teacher's room, and he taught us evolution and how we evolved from apes. My buddy and I challenged him and asked if he really believed we had evolved and were not created by God. He answered, "I don't believe in evolution. I believe in God, but I have to teach it as a science teacher. That's what the school requires of me, so I just do my job." Sometimes I wonder if higher education really helps people. Some people don't need higher education, as they already have the ability to learn and teach.

A number of years ago, Lynda and I were invited to a church in Eastern Canada. They wanted a teaching on the deliverance ministry. So we headed to this church and held our meetings. In one of the sessions, one church member stood up and shared that she had a master's degree in education. Then she said, "When I stand up to speak, words won't come out of my mouth. It seems like there's something holding my throat." That morning we prayed for her. As we were praying, we saw that the secular and humanistic teaching had a stronghold on her. It was like cord wrapped around her from the top of her head and down to her body parts, especially her throat. We prayed over her and anointed her with oil, and God set her free that morning from the spirit that was trying to strangle every word that came out of her mouth. I'll leave that with you.

I'm not suggesting that we don't further our education but that we don't make an idol out of it. Paul says in 1 Corinthians 2:6–16:

> However, we speak wisdom among those who are mature, yet not the wisdom of this age, nor of the rulers of this age, who are coming to nothing. But we speak the wisdom of God in a mystery, the hidden wisdom which God ordained before the ages for our glory, which none of the rulers of this age knew; for had they known, they would not have crucified the Lord of glory. But as it is written: "Eye has not seen, nor ear heard, nor have entered into the heart of man the things which God has prepared for those who love Him." But God has revealed them to us through His Spirit. For the Spirit searches all things, yes, the deep things of God. For what man knows the things of a man except the spirit of the man which is in him? Even so no one knows things of God except the Spirit of God. Now we have received, not the spirit of the world, but the Spirit who is from God, that we might know the things that have been freely given to us by God. The things we also

speak, not in words which man's wisdom teaches but which the Holy Spirit teaches, comparing spiritual things with spiritual. But the natural man does not receive the things of the Spirit of God, for they are foolishness to him; nor can he know them, because they are spiritually discerned. But he who is spiritual judges all things, yet he himself is rightly judged by no one. For "who has known the mind of the Lord that he may instruct Him?" But we have the mind of Christ.

After I left school, I decided that I wanted full-time employment. Back in the seventies, there was plenty of employment to be found. By that time, some of my cousins were working at a variety of jobs. My cousin called me and said that they were hiring down at the steel mill on Logan and Arlington, where he worked. Apparently the pay was good, but it was hard and hot work. So I applied and got the job. Because it was a union shop, I could move up quickly to a variety of working stations. They gave me a position forging steel; it was hot and dirty work. It was quite a complicated machine to operate that required the ability to set the forging machine to a particular job. All those days of playing hardball catch would be helpful, because this machine required hand and eye coordination. I had to remove the steel from the furnace when the metal was red-hot and then insert it into a die machine that was moving three to five seconds at a time. It was complicated, but I was able to figure it out. I didn't plan to stay in the position for long, although the money was good. There was an older man there operating a cutting machine who'd been working at the mill for forty-five years! I said to myself, "I am not going to stay in this position for forty-five years and be an old man."

A hotel was located on the corner of Arlington and Logan. Sometimes during our lunch break, which was around seven in the evening, some of us guys would head over there and wouldn't make it back to work. The foreman would come the next day and ask us where we'd gone; he already knew where we'd been, as the hotel was the meeting place. I didn't get fired, but he told me to close my machine down and shut down the furnace next time I went.

I took my playbook from the sixties into the seventies. The endless partying, the endless binges never stopped. The devil wasn't finished with me yet. He'd already made several attempts to kill me through the thoughtless and careless life I was living. During those sixties moments, I'd pass out outside during the winter and wake up in a snow bank, but alive. Dead spiritually, but still breathing. The days of suicidal tendencies became more frequent. After binge drinking, I always felt ashamed of my behaviour and didn't like the person I'd become. The guilt was unbearable. I was hurting my family and wife and child. I had no peace. Isaiah 57:21 reads, "*'There is no peace,' says my God, 'for the wicked.'*"

Restless with no peace! Bound up with addiction! Bound by invisible chains! There were good times both in childhood and adult life, but most days there was no peace! I was running from God and trying to outrun Him. But you can't outrun Him. He will seek and still find you! Jesus said in Luke 19:10, *"for the Son of Man has come to seek and to save that which was lost."* I was lost in torment and horrible bondage until I met the man Jesus!

The party scene exploded in the 1970s of rock 'n' roll, and with that came the increase of violence on the streets. Some of those places just became more dangerous. You'd engage with also sorts of people, some just as mean, if not meaner and more violent, than you. In order to prepare ourselves, we'd carry a knife, baseball bat, or gun. At one time I carried any one of those weapons with me. I had semi-automatic 22 rifle that I could disassemble and put all the parts in the butt end of the gun. I carried it underneath the front seat of my car, not knowing if I would ever use it or not.

One time I was attending a party at a house and a brawl broke out. Fists and metal objects were flying. I was so intoxicated that when someone hit me from behind on the back of my head, they almost knocked me out. I was dripping blood from the head wound. I staggered to my car to look for my gun and tried to assemble it and put bullets into it. I went back into the house to take care of the person who'd hit me with a metal object. By God's mercy and grace, and my stupidity, I wasn't able to assemble the gun or put the bullets into the chamber.

I eventually found myself at the hospital. The cut on my head was quite long, and the doctor said he could stitch it closed but would have to cut my hair. I said, "No way, let the wound heal itself; no way am I going to cut my hair."

I eventually sold my gun to the pawn shop. It was a good thing I got rid of it, because one time I put the barrel of it into my mouth and was going pull the trigger. I didn't want to live any longer, but my family came into my mind, and I had newborn daughter. I was so intoxicated, I put the gun away and eventually sold it so that I could party on.

You'd think that after suffering so many concussions the party scenes would end, but they just intensified throughout the seventies. I was still trying to change my life by my own efforts. I tried to quit drinking and stay working and going to school. I thought I needed to be more physically active because I'd always enjoyed sports, and with the sports came discipline, so I decided to take up amateur boxing and did it for some time. It definitely helped me in my discipline and to blow off some steam on occasion. But it was only equipping me for more of the same acts of violence that I learned in my childhood.

At that time in my life, I should have been attending university or at least furthering my education. I was learning from the hard knocks of life, getting a master's degree in stupidity and a PhD in how to survive the mean streets. Those mean streets led me to a path of destruction from many vehicle accidents and street brawls. My life was going nowhere. I was searching for something to fill the void inside of me. But the street life had me bound up with chains, and it was almost impossible to break the chains. The days after the party and drinking, I'd feel a lot of shame and regret over my actions. People do very strange things when they lose the capacity to make right judgements and decisions because their brain is confused and off balance. It left nothing but a fog. Even if you black out and can't remember your actions, you're still responsible for them.

There was a lot of racism back in the day, and the police were looked upon as racist. I was standing in line to purchase beer in one of those Main Street hotels. Two police officers walked into the lobby with their guns drawn and told me to put up my hands. I did what they requested of me and lifted my arms in the air. They were pointing their guns at me. I said, "Man, I'm only here buying beer." They asked for identification, so I showed them my driver's license and then asked what the problem was. They said someone had broken out of prison and I looked like him. I said something smart, and then they put their guns back into their holsters. There was profiling and racist attitudes in the police departments back then; years later, an Indigenous man was shot and killed on the streets of Winnipeg. The police were put under scrutiny and many deep-seated racist attitudes were revealed. But there were some decent guys on the force. The police officer who shot and killed J.J. Harper would commit suicide years later.

I was in my teen years when I had a run-in with a police office who physically beat me. I didn't trust them nor did I respect their authority. Crazy thing is, I wanted to be an RCMP officer in my youth. I had no interest in being a career criminal or in selling drugs, stealing other people's property, or deliberately hurting anyone. Back then there was a strange, self-righteous attitude in the streets regarding certain criminal activities. One could be a murderer, but if he didn't abuse children, he thought of himself as better than others. Some of the career criminals enjoyed the title of being a lifer and doing hard time. I was doing ministry once in northern Manitoba, in Shamattawa, and I stayed at an RCMP officer's place. She told me that once murderers taste blood, they will kill again. The warped attitude and condition of the heart is deceitful and desperately wicked.

One time I was surrounded by a local street gang outside the hotel on Main Street, outnumbered thirty to one. They called me by the name Punch. Someone in their gang falsely accused me of saying negative things about their two leaders. It was amazing that I was able to walk away and not get harmed. The two leaders of that particular gang caught me off guard in the bathroom at the same hotel. One of them sucker punched and knocked me out; someone from the hotel came into the bathroom and helped me up off the floor. I went back into the hotel and sat down, and these two thugs were at the next table. I knew we were outnumbered, so I didn't react. I just left it. Both leaders eventually died violent deaths. One of them was stabbed to death in a hotel in Vancouver, British Columbia, and the other one died in a car accident. The way of the transgressor is hard; no matter how tough you think you are, the streets and that lifestyle will always break you.

We are created in the image of God:

Then God said, "Let Us make man in Our image, according to Our likeness; let them have dominion over the fish of the sea, over the birds of the air, and over the cattle, over all the earth and over every creeping thing that creeps on the earth." So God created man in His own image; in the image of God He created him; male and female He created them. Then God blessed them, and God said to them, "Be fruitful and multiply; fill the earth and subdue it; have dominion over the fish of the sea, over the birds of the air, and over every living thing that moves on the earth." (Genesis 1:26–28)

And the Lord God formed man of the dust of the ground, and breathed into his nostrils the breath of life; and man became a living being. The Lord God planted a garden eastward in Eden, and there He put the man whom He had formed. And out of the ground the Lord made every tree grow that is pleasant to the sight and good for food. (Genesis 2:7–9)

Then the Lord God took the man and put him in the garden of Eden to tend and keep it. And the Lord God commanded the man, saying, "Of every tree of the garden you may freely eat; but of the tree of the knowledge of good and evil you shall not eat, for in the day that you eat of it you shall surely die." (Genesis 2:15–17)

When God created man, He made him in His own image and likeness. Man was given spirit and life; he was given a free will to serve God. But in Genesis 3, we read in one verse that the serpent was more cunning than any beast of the field the Lord God had made. The serpent tempted the woman to eat of the fruit of the Tree of the Knowledge of Good and Evil, which God had forbidden. She ate the fruit and gave some to her husband, who also ate. In their free will, our first parents, Adam and Eve, disobeyed God and were banished from the garden. They would eventually die, not only spiritually, but physically, because of their disobedience. As a result of that, all of humanity is born in sin.

The Bible says it's appointed once for man to die and then the judgement. We all have an appointment. Throughout life we have appointments: appointments with doctors or any other health practitioners. You made an appointment with the minister on the day you got married. You have another appointment with death, and you never know when that could happen. That appointment is with your Creator, and you will stand before Him and give an account of your life. He'll ask you what you did with His Son, Jesus. Did you receive Him or reject Him? You're only given two choices: to receive Him or to reject Him, to build your life on sand or upon the rock, to walk on the broad way or the narrow way. That narrow way is Jesus: *"I am the way, the truth, and the life. No one comes to the Father except through Me"* (John 14:6).

God's purpose for man was to be a ruler, a ruler of the whole earth. A triune God created a triune man; the three persons make up the one: God the Father, the Son, and the Holy Spirit, three yet one. The key word is triune (three), and man was created in the likeness of God. A triune man is one person but has three elements: spirit, soul, and body. We have a triune man made in the likeness of the triune God to represent God and be His ruler in the earth. We are made in the image of God with a purpose and destiny.

What is man? *"And the Lord God formed man out of the dust of the ground, and breathed into his nostrils the breath of life, and man became a living soul"* (Genesis 2:7). He had the breath of life put in him by God, a perfect personality, divine energy of that clay that actually became a human personality. God's breath from above and the clay from below produced a soul personality, a living human personality. In 1 Corinthians 15:45, Paul writes, *"'The first man Adam became a living being.' The last Adam became a life-giving spirit."* Spirit has life in itself, a given life. But the soul must first receive life from the spirit before he can live. God breathed into that clay, and he became a living soul. What changed man from being a ruler to a slave?

All human problems ultimately go back to one root cause: Rebellion against God. *"All we like sheep have gone astray; we have turned, every one, to his own way; and the Lord has laid on Him the iniquity of us all"* (Isaiah 53:6). In man's rebellion, he became self-willed and turned his back on God.

The soul is the self, the ego: I want. I don't want. I will or I won't. Decision-making as a function of the human personality, self-will or rebellion, originates in the soul. Man made a decision in his soul to disobey God, and as a result, he would die. Adam lived nine hundred years and then he died. In man's disobedience, he cut himself off from the only source for his life.

Life rolled along without any purpose or clear direction. I felt like a ship, and the waves were just coming against me, tossing me here and there, and I could never arrive at my destiny.

"*But your iniquities have separated you from your God*" (Isaiah 59:2a).

And you He made alive, who were dead in trespasses and sins, in which you once walked according to the course of the world, according to the prince of the power of the air, the spirit who now works in the sons of disobedience. (Ephesians 2:1–2)

The root problem is disobedience, the result of turning away from God. We are spiritually cut off from the life of God: "*having their understanding darkened, being alienated from the life of God, because of their ignorance that is in them, because of the blindness of their heart*" (Ephesians 4:18). There are four key words in this passage: darkened, separated, ignorance, and hardened. That's the condition of man. In his rebellion, he is spiritually dead—dead in trespasses and sin, dead as a result of disobedience or rebellion.

As a result of man's disobedience, the soul became infected with rebellion, and every succeeding generation has been infected. Man no longer needs to be tempted from the outside; there is an interrelating rebellion in his soul. Temptation of man came from another source, and we now have perverted desires and souls. We are the sons of disobedience (Ephesians 2:2). James says that each one is tempted when he is drawn away by his own desires and enticed by his own inner lust (James 1:14).

The third element of man is his body, which as a result of his rebellion is subject to corruption and ultimate death: "*The sting of death is sin*" (1 Corinthians 15:56a). Man's lower elements, his soul and body, are united in rebellion against God's appointed inner ruler. God appointed the spirit to rule the body. But the soul and body, tempted by Satan, united against the spirit.

Here was I living my life in rebellion against God Himself. You cannot break God's law; it will break you! My lifestyle grew out of control; the farther I ran from God, the worse I became. The endless parties, the endless attempts of suicide left me broken, and my life was in shambles with a deep sense of hopelessness!

I thought that if had more money, it might fill the void. I didn't have a lot of money, as I worked to party! I always rented other people's houses and owned used cars, but I never prospered. A local trucking firm needed city drivers, so I applied to get some quick cash. The foreman asked me how much experience I had driving a truck in the city, and I told him I could drive. He gave me a set of keys and said, "Here, drive that three-ton truck over to St. Boniface for deliveries."

Well, I never got out of the yard. I'd never driven a truck that size. I sat in the truck and looked at the gear shift. I knew how to work it, so I put it into action. The truck was sitting on an angle, and the clutch wasn't working properly, so I tried to get it out of the position it was in but I couldn't. I went back into the office and told the foreman that the truck wouldn't move forward. He asked if I knew how to drive a truck, and I said yes. Then he told me to release the clutch slower and give more gas on the pedal.

I was heading for more problems. I didn't know that most of the guys working there were in similar situations as me. They were big drinkers and loved to party. We could all disappear for days or weeks from the job and we'd be hired again without any questions asked. The party was on and the binges lasted longer; you just worked hard, and they paid cash at the end of the week. I don't think the company paid any CPP or taxes on my behalf. Money in your pocket and broke, then a hangover to prove it!

The owner would show up at one of the local drinking holes or bars. He also was a boozer. Perhaps that was the main reason we all had jobs after long absentees. At this time, I was getting physically bigger, but not because I was going to the gym. My route often required loading heavy beef to be delivered to local butcher shops. The beef sometimes weighed between 200 and 230 pounds. Not only did I have to deliver them, but I had to go into the butcher's cooler. With the hind of beef on my shoulder, I had one chance to drop into my arms and then hook it. If I missed, it became more challenging. Looking back, it really was a two-person job; it just allowed us to be more irresponsible. I have no doubt he was billing the meat company for a two-man job. We did it so that we could get the bonus of being irresponsible.

I was still trying to find peace in my heart but always had this inner emptiness. The parties of the seventies and the lifestyle of the late sixties were catching up to me and putting strain on our marriage. Lynda was always the more responsible person, and I would always be irresponsible. I just had a mean streak and couldn't-care-less attitude.

She also had her own issues. I was living such a reckless and careless life, I nearly died in a serious car accident. The last thing I heard was the ambulance attendant saying, "We lost him." No doubt I died that day, but God in His grace and mercy gave me another chance. I was at the gate of death many times because of my own recklessness and lifestyle. I could have drunk myself to death or killed myself with a loaded gun or a sharp razor, but the psalmist says in Psalm 9:13b, *"You who lift me up from the gates of death."*

On one of my many binges, I ended up in Las Vegas, Nevada. Perhaps what I'd been looking for could be found here; besides, all the booze was free as long as you were feeding the slot machines with your money. Nothing is free. There's a cost for everything. I just roamed the streets to see what was happening. I walked into one particular restaurant and bar that was filled with Black people. I have some Latino features, but I slowly turned around and walked out of restaurant. I'd just walked on someone else's turf and didn't realize what I was doing, but I had enough street smarts to know it was not a good place to be.

I made a second trip to Las Vegas with the same results and the same empty feelings, trying to fill myself with whatever I could be filled with. The night clubs and casinos couldn't fill the void. So I rented a car and headed toward California, not sure of where I was going, but I was driving. I had no GPS, no map, and absolutely no common sense. I recognized the street names Hollywood and Vine, and I pulled over and got out of the car. I found myself walking on Hollywood Boulevard, where famous people had their names and a star laid on the sidewalk near the Chinese theatre. I'd heard about them on television, but here I was walking there.

The next day I drove to San Diego, California and took a tour bus to Tijuana, Mexico. Well, wouldn't you know it but I found a Mexican bar and went inside and tried their tequila. Not quite sure how much tequila I drank, but I don't know how I made it back onto the bus. When I made it back to San Diego, I was intoxicated from the tequila. It was more powerful than I thought.

I didn't have a lot common sense. It reminded me the time I was delivering Champs Chicken to the inner city and was offered a drink of home brew. What the heck, why not try? He was going to give me a $50.00 tip. I never got the tip, as his partner thought it was too much money. Back in San Diego I had this overwhelming sense of guilt come over me; I'm not sure why, but I know now it was the Holy Spirit pursuing me. He came into the dark bar in Mexico and wouldn't give up on me. I couldn't run fast enough or far enough away. He was always pursuing me no matter where I ran or how deep in sin I was living. He was there.

That night in San Diego, I called home and spoke to Lynda. I was crying but I didn't know why, nor did I understand that the Hound of Heaven had me on His radar.

In one of those neighbourhoods in Los Angles, I went out to buy some beer. I was walking in a Black neighbourhood, and it seemed like everyone in the store was looking at me, like "Man, don't you have your own neighbourhood to buy your booze in?" Keep in mind the streets gangs and turf wars of the 1970s. I thought I better head back to the hotel real quick. You would think after I'd had that encounter with the Holy Spirit, I would give up and surrender my life to Him. No!

The party scene only intensified with more street drugs, booze, and opioids. I was on a collision course with death. I was searching to fill the emptiness, and nothing could fill it. I thought that I'd head out west to see if I could make a new start, find some type of job and get out of the Winnipeg scene. My buddy and I headed out west and partied all the way, making stops in western cities until we found ourselves in Vancouver. My funds were running low, and I needed to find work or head back to Winnipeg. We slept in my car and found ourselves in the famous Stanley Park. No direction or purpose and running low on funds with no credit card or cell phone. Just a couple of dumb guys.

We woke up the next day and heard that Elvis Presley had died; at first I couldn't believe it. I liked his smooth voice, and he was a huge celebrity. That was August 16, 1977, and my idol had just died. That kind of took the wind out of my sails. There I was sitting in Stanley Park some ten years before I was going to attempt to ride my bike to Vancouver. Where were the hippies? It wasn't what I thought it would be. I was disillusioned and still trying to fill the emptiness in my soul. The drugs, booze, and prescription opioids were no longer filling it.

I knew a friend back in Winnipeg who was a heroin user, but I stayed away from those types of drugs. I tried to keep myself aware of my surrounding at all times. That didn't work, and I lost track of how many blackouts I experienced. It was crazy, the things that happened to me. That's what happens when your perspective of life is narrowed down to your street smarts. But those drugs also impacted my mind, leaving me paranoid. The drugs today are so much more potent and lethal than in my generation. Drug users in this generation are putting things into their bodies that they're not aware of, such as fentanyl and other lethal drugs. Marijuana has been legalized in Canada, and I believe this drug just opens the door for the next drug. The high you get from these drugs only makes you want to go to the next level of abuse.

The devil is a liar and always has something and someone available to harm you and take advantage of you. He takes great delight in binding people with addiction. I was at a house party, and an old friend from the sixties was there. He gave me a hit of acid, which is a hallucinogenic drug that takes you into deep places of darkness. I was trapped in a dark room and couldn't get out. A creature was visible and talking to me.

He even takes a greater delight in bondage to religion, and billions are in bondage to good works. If he can't deceive with substance abuse, he'll deceive with a false religion of good works, and he will transform himself into an angel of light. He just gets his kicks out of the addiction of drug abusers. I'm writing this book in Mexico, the largest exporter of drugs globally. The vast majority of Mexicans are also in bondage to a religion that gives no hope!

By the end of the decade, things weren't going well. The tragic news that followed would have an impact on our family and leave many of us traumatized. My five-year-old nephew was playing in his back yard along with his friends. He was told under no circumstances to leave the yard. Well, he and his buddies didn't listen and left the yard. They made their way by themselves to Omand's Creek. It was springtime, and a lot of snow had fallen that winter. The boys were playing alongside the creek, and the water was moving swiftly in the direction of the Assiniboine River. The ditch was full of fast-moving water, and apparently my nephew reached into the water to retrieve a stick that had fallen in. Immediately the family heard the news, but it was impossible to find him.

The family immediately put a search party of friends and relatives in place, walking down each side of the bank. The water was moving extremely fast. We launched boats and used ropes with attached hooks, hoping to find the body. The water was very cold, and you could feel the coldness from the aluminium bottom of the boat freezing your feet. It was dangerous going up and down the creek. We went to the Assiniboine and Red Rivers, but the current was so strong, our little boat and motor could hardly move across the freezing water. At that time the search and rescue team said it was too dangerous to make any attempts to search the rivers.

Days and weeks went by and still no body was found. One man heard what happened, so he and his dog would show up every day and walk up and down the creek. By this time a whole month had passed, and it had made front page news. Most of the public had heard of the accident. We would gather together as a family, but we had little to offer one another. My sister called Calvary Temple, although none us were Christians at that time. Pastor H.H. Barber arrived at my sister's place and offered his condolences and prayed.

The man who walked up and down the creek with his dog found the body one month later. It was caught on a grocery cart. Had his body missed the cart, it might have ended up in the river and may have never been found. This brought relief to the family, but the grief was overwhelming. Many family members helped, mostly on my brother-in-law's side. He had a large family from Fisher River, and they were a major help in the search party. At some point during this tragic event, my sister who had lost her son started attending church at Calvary Temple. It was a turning point in her life, and a change was about take place that would impact many, many lives.

I still wasn't interested in religion or Jesus. I thought my sister had gone overboard with this Jesus stuff. My lifestyle didn't change. I just continued partying.

My sister who joined the church had once liked to party as much as anyone else. Although she was a bit older than me, she kind of watched my back during those hellish moments living in the sixties and seventies. My other older sister never abused alcohol or drugs.

My life continued to spiral downwards. You never fall up; you always fall down. There's not a whole lot of loyalty on the streets, and you'd think that your friends had your back. Not so! They would turn on you really quick! Back in Jig Town in my preteen years, my friends stole a car and came to pick me up. We didn't make it very far before the police had their lights flashing as we headed down the highway. We abandoned the car on the side of the road and ran for what seemed like forever across the field, heading home. We made it back, and before separating, I said, "Nobody snitch."

The following day, the police arrived at my house and arrested me, but I told them I had only been a passenger. They said it didn't matter, since I'd been in the car. We went to youth lockup in the old Vaughn Street building. At about midnight, I heard a loud banging at the door. It was my mom; she demanded that they release me, and they did. The next day I went looking for the snitches, the two who originally stole the car, but they didn't own up to it. One of them was going to get their butt kicked. That was my last time riding with those two snitches.

During the seventies I was into bar hopping and more violence. I was like the prodigal son in Luke 15 running off to the far country, wasting my life away. It seemed like I'd already lived a lifetime, yet I couldn't shake the feeling of being empty on the inside. Around this time my sister who had lost her son was picking up our daughter for Sunday school. We were okay with that and didn't think much about it.

Lynda had come to point in her life that she was running away from God. Back on the reservation of Fisher River, she'd attended family Bible camp as a child, and her mother was trying to live out her faith. What seemed very challenging at the time was that my father-in-law liked his booze. The daughters left for Winnipeg, and the sons stayed on the reservation. Lynda and I often went out to the reservation with our daughter to visit her parents. In spite of all the challenges before my mother-in-law, she remained steady. She must have thought that her baby girl had married a teenager who was a heavy drinker like her husband. The problem was that we were never the type to have a couple of beers. Once we started, it would just go on and on until we couldn't drink anymore or we ran out of liquor. Back in the city, at times I'd start on Friday night and go until Sunday or Monday. Then back to work until it started again on Thursday night.

I thought that my sister who gave her life to Christ had gone off the deep end. Lynda was also under conviction, and one day while riding her bicycle she was praying and asking God where she could go to church. As she looked up, she saw Calvary Temple. "That's the one you will go to," He said.

Lynda eventually started attending Calvary Temple, but I couldn't care less; besides, the party life was still in full swing. I am amazed at the devil's schemes and lies and how he captures the thinking of the ungodly. He builds a wall around their minds and blinds their eyes to truth. No wonder he's called the god of this world. I was in total blindness to the life I lived, and my friends—at least, who I thought were friends—were just as blind as me. Over time, their lifestyle and thinking would be exposed. People who I thought were solid were actually losers. So I started distancing myself from those bad characters, as that's the way things worked.

Lynda was making changes to her life by Bible reading and Bible studies, and more praying and more Bible reading. I have to admit, I gave her hard time for at least a year about this Jesus stuff.

She was having minor surgery and had to stay in the hospital, so I decided to record a Billy Graham show for her. I knew she liked watching him. I pulled out my tape recorder and put a chair in front of the television and made sure nothing happened to the recording. I stayed close by and heard Billy Graham give his sermon. At the end of his program, the mass choir came on and sang that song "Just as I Am." *Just as I am, without one plea, but that thy blood was shed for me.* So off to the hospital I went with tape in hand. I don't remember what Billy Graham spoke on, but that song kind of hit me!

One year went by, and my wife and daughter were both going to church with my overboard sister, always talking about Jesus. When going to church, must you always be talking about Jesus? Jesus this and Jesus that. I don't know how Lynda survived that first year of her Christianity, as I gave her such a hard time. I even threw her Bible on the floor at one time.

It was one of those usual Friday evenings drinking beer at a local bar. I was sitting there thinking about my life. I knew once I started with one beer it always led to another and another. But that night the first beer tasted terrible, so I decided to push it away and returned home before 10:00 p.m. This never happened on a Friday night with cash in my pocket.

Not too long after that I decided to go to church with Lynda. The placed was packed with Christians everywhere. It seemed like I was the only one dressed in blue jeans and a black leather coat. I thought to myself, *These people look nice, but really boring*. I remember the preacher on the platform, H.H. Barber. He didn't realize the impact of his prayer when my nephew died. That room had been filled with prodigal men and women who were running from God. I just happened to be one of those persons in that living room that day.

I liked his preaching and his conviction in what he was preaching. The street life gave you insight and discernment into people. I sensed he was sincere, and the words that came out of his mouth were from the Bible. I sat and listened, and it seemed like he was reading my mail or my mind. I was feeling somewhat uncomfortable with what he was saying and where I was in my life. I thought that if I sat in a different pew, maybe he wouldn't be speaking about me.

After several attempts at different views and angles, I was still feeling uncomfortable on the inside. Then one Sunday I said to Lynda, "Let's go to church this evening." I think that really blew her away or astonished her. I could see the expression on her face! Attending two services on Sunday never crossed my mind before. Back then, one service was hard enough. I couldn't imagine going to another service, and in the evening.

Eventually we made it to the evening service, and I thought that if I sat in the balcony, that preacher wouldn't be reading my thoughts. In the back of my mind while I was testing this Christianity stuff, I thought that perhaps I'd go to one more party before giving Christianity a try. The evening service had fewer people, especially in the balcony. So we headed upstairs and sat in the balcony. The evening service was much different than the morning service. H.H. Barber seemed to come alive, and his preaching seemed more powerful. And he was speaking to me. I didn't think he was aware that I was even in the church that night, and then he made a comment: "No sir, you may not have another party." That really got my attention. I knew it would be my last party.

At the end of the service, he closed with "Just as I Am." He will accept you just as you are! Really? Just as I am? I raised my arm that night and walked from the balcony to the front of the platform. I was shaking and crying uncontrollably. The pastor led us in a prayer of repentance and faith in Jesus Christ, and then the counsellors led us into the prayer room. There were only two men at the altar that night: myself and a person named Bill.

Ted Bradford spoke to me in the prayer room. He had such a kind voice and calmness about him. He gave me a Bible study guide and the Gospel of John to take home to read. He said, "Alfred, there is going to be a voice that will sit on your shoulder and speak condemnation over your life. Don't listen to him; it's the devil lying to you." Boy, was he right!

The moment I left the prayer room, I saw Lynda waiting for me. We hugged and cried and went home. We were both Christians, and Ted recommended the New Life class that he taught on Sunday morning before the main service. There must have been thirty or more people in the class. This was no seeker-friendly environment and no back-door Christianity. This was where you made a decision for Christ and grew in your faith. Jesus said in Matthew 10:32–33: *"Therefore whoever confesses Me before men, him I will also confess before My Father who is in heaven. But whoever denies Me before men, him I will also deny before My Father who is in heaven."*

If you can't stand in the house of God and make a confession of your faith, how can you stand in the world.? As the apostle Paul says in Romans 1:16: *"For I am not ashamed of the gospel of Christ, for it is the power of God to salvation for everyone who believes, for the Jew first and also for the Greek."*

Now a certain ruler asked him, saying, "Good Teacher, what shall I do to inherit eternal life?" So Jesus said to him, "Why do you call Me good? No one is good but One, that is, God. You know the commandments: 'Do not commit adultery,' 'Do not murder,' 'Do not steal,' 'Do not bear false witness,' 'Honor your father and your mother.'" And he said, "All these things I have kept from my youth." So when Jesus heard these things, He said to him, "You still lack one thing. Sell all that you have and distribute to the poor, and you will have treasure in heaven; and come, follow Me." But when he heard this, he became very sorrowful, for he was very rich. And when Jesus saw that he became very sorrowful, He said, "How hard it is for those who have riches to enter into the kingdom of God! For it is easier for a camel to go through the eye of a needle than for a rich man to enter the kingdom of God." And those who heard it said, "Who then can be saved?" But He said, "The things which are impossible with men are possible with God." (Luke 18:18–27)

"Then Peter said, 'See, we have left all and followed you'" (Luke 18:28). So Jesus said:

Assuredly, I say to you, there is no one who has left house or parents or brothers or wife or children, for the sake of the kingdom of God, who shall not receive many times more in this present time, and in the age to come eternal life. (Luke 18:29–30)

I thought to myself, *I gave the devil 100 per cent of my life, and now Jesus is asking me to give 100 per cent*. You may think that you've not fallen to that degree of immorality, but the Bible says that at the foot of the cross, we are all equal, whether you're down and out or up and out. We all have sinned and fallen short of the glory of God. There is no one righteous. You may have attended church all your life, but that doesn't make you a Christian. The rich young ruler was sorrowful in his heart because he had many riches. Nowhere in scripture do we see this young man come back and acknowledge Christ as his Lord and Saviour. You can have all the riches of life yet miss heaven.

Chapter Four
The Restoration of the 1980s

THE SEVENTIES WERE coming to a close and the eighties had begun. Now I was going to church and sitting in three services a day, and I started attending Wednesday night Bible study and prayer night. That was four services a week and a home Bible study on my own reading the Gospel of John. During one of those Bible study evenings, I was reading in the kitchen and came to 1 Corinthians 6:19–20:

> Or do you not know that your body is the temple of the Holy Spirit who is in you, whom you have from God, and you are not your own.? ... For you were bought at a price; therefore glorify God in your body and in your spirit, which are God's.

I was doing my personal Bible study and smoking a cigarette at same time. When I read the scripture, I felt a conviction come on me: *My body is the temple of the Holy Spirit, who is in me.* I immediately put that cigarette away and then went to the refrigerator, where I kept my cigarettes. I grabbed them and threw them into the garbage. No way was I going to defile the temple of God. Well, that was an easy breaking of a nicotine addiction. The worst was yet to come.

For the past fifteen years, I'd been addicted to many different types of drugs and alcohol, and I felt like my body was broken up. Well, my body was broken—literally. I had enormous back problems from all the heavy lifting and street life, car accidents, and life in general. So my body felt the withdrawal from the liquor and drugs. I realized that the painkillers I'd taken during my life brought the bondage, and I was determined to shake free of it. My body, my back, was in such horrible pain.

I sought out a chiropractor to help me with my back pain, and for years I struggled with it. The chiropractor was puzzled and had never seen a condition like mine before. He actually brought in his coworker to help with the adjustments. In the meantime, I was going through withdrawals from the years of substance abuse. In most cases, people in my condition would end up in a recovery program. The months that followed were the most challenging I'd ever gone through. I'd wake up in the morning with an overwhelming sense of shame and guilt, and my body was racked in so much pain. I didn't want to take any pain medication, because in the past I'd been addicted to them. I wanted to avoid anything that would put me back in the bondage and lifestyle of addiction.

Some mornings I'd wake up weeping because my body was in so much pain. I'd go right to my knees and cry to God, "Please help me, Lord. I don't know if I'm going to make it through. I know that you've forgiven me, because your Word says you remove my sins as far as the east is from the west, and you will remember them no more." God did not remember my past, but I did, and with the guilt and shame there were times I felt like giving up and going back to that same lifestyle, but I persevered through the withdrawals. I had opened my life in my rebellion to the demonic realm. I was actually demon-possessed and didn't realize that I'd invited them in my life. But Ted told me I was going to face my enemies! Thank God for his godly advice!

Follow these steps to be delivered from demons:

1. Be humble.
2. Be honest.
3. Confess faith in Christ.
4. Confess any known sin.
5. Repent of all sin. Proverbs 28:13 says, *"He who covers his sins will not prosper, but whoever confesses and forsakes them will have mercy."*
6. Break with occult/curses/secret societies.
7. Forgive others.
8. Expel.
9. The devil is not your destiny!!

Those early years were challenging, but I didn't realize back then that I was enlisting in an army! This army and conflict don't end. My pastor back then said that we may lose some battles, but in the end, we win the war. Sound advice! I've learned over the years in the deliverance ministry that it's like peeling an onion, layer after layer. Just remember what Jesus said in Matthew 12:43–45:

When an unclean spirit goes out of a man, he goes through dry places, seeking rest, and finds none. Then he says, "I will return to my house from which I came." And when he comes, he finds it empty, swept, and put in order. Then he goes and takes with him seven other spirits more wicked than himself, and they enter and dwell there; and the last state of that man is worse than the first. So shall it also be with this wicked generation.

At some point in my childhood, I thought I'd made a decision to follow Christ, but I never followed through with it. I believe that behind every addiction there is a demon! And the list goes on and on. As a young believer, I certainly didn't know my authority or position in Christ. I was just learning to walk out my faith! Now the demons were influencing areas of my life that hadn't been surrendered to Jesus.

We were living in the north end at that time and both sensed that we needed a new location and a new beginning. We had some money saved up, and we found a townhouse complex in Garden City. We applied for the rental unit and got it. We were the second people to ever live in it, so it felt brand-new, and it was farther away from the north end and the bad memories. It was like we were getting a new start, and things were looking up, but the battles continued.

I thought that maybe AA could help me, so my next-door neighbour invited me to their talk therapy sessions. I sat and listened, and all they talked about was how much they'd lost. This seemed to go on forever—living in the past and thinking of all the things you've lost because of your addiction. I didn't want to live in the past, and I certainly didn't want to live in addiction thinking anymore. So I stood up at one of the meetings and told them that I'd made a decision to live for Jesus Christ. The man overseeing the program came up to me later and said that we couldn't speak about religion there. But they could speak of a higher power. I'm sure some people got sober, but I wanted more than sobriety. I wanted to live as an overcomer. I had no desire for alcohol, but I had a lot emotions going through my mind.

Once I stood up and confessed Christ to this AA club, I sensed a breakthrough in my life. Chains were breaking off me; human wisdom couldn't do it, just sitting around and saying that I am an alcoholic for the rest of my life. No way. I am a new creation in Christ Jesus. Unknown to me, every time I fell to my knees to pray and then stood up, the spirit realm heard chains breaking off of me. There were still issues in my life, but something began to change.

Now with the new place to live, things were looking better for us, and I started to look for work. I certainly wasn't going back to the trucking firm because I knew what that would lead to. One of the men in our New Life class was employed in management at a steel mill. I applied and got the position. The work was hard and heavy, but I always had a good work ethic when I applied myself. There was a great deal of conflict at the workplace. Some of the workers were attempting to bring a union shop into the factory. There was division between those who wanted it and those who rejected it. It didn't really matter to me. I had a job and was making a decent income. My body was starting to heal, and I was getting the exercise I needed. My mind was clear and making right decisions. But I didn't want to stay in that position for long. I knew I had more potential within me, and I wanted to go in a different direction.

During a coffee break at the steel mill, I was sitting outside on a bench and looking up into the sky when I saw an airplane gaining altitude. As I looked at the plane, I said to myself, "One day I'm going to get on a plane and fly around the world and preach the gospel." I felt the Holy Spirit touch me at that very moment and put that in my heart—the desire to serve the Lord and preach His message. It was a prophetic moment; I just spoke a word over my life. When I looked at my circumstances, it looked impossible. I was sitting there on a hot summer day wearing long coveralls that were dirty, greasy, and grimy. But something came over me, and it was the Holy Ghost anointing. Just as I was experiencing this wonderful encounter, back in the plant the machines broke down and the foreman asked me to sweep the floors. I'd swept factories and car dealership floors, and now he wanted me to sweep another floor. I picked up the broom and for the next eight hours walked around sweeping the floor and quoting Philippians 4:13: *"I can do all things through Christ who strengthens me."* I had to let go of my ego and pride to submit to authority.

Within a year I bought my first brand-new car, a 1981 Monte Carlo, in a beautiful jade colour. I desired to do something different. One summer back in the 1970s, I had a job working as a youth counsellor and also in group home for boys. I saw a position advertised with a group home with Jewish Child and Family Services. They wanted someone to do night shifts in their group home, which could lead to a position as a behavioural counsellor. I applied for the position and was called for an interview.

The management asked the typical questions: How do you handle stress? I told them I pray. Why do you want to work for a Jewish organization, as you're a Christian? I don't remember my answer, but I got the position. I told my foremen at the plant that I'd found another position but could still work evening shifts. He said that would work, so now I had two jobs, evening and night. I was also working for Winnipeg Child and Family Service on the weekends.

Now we were saving money to buy a house. I was more involved at church, as I wanted to help in some way. I started praying with people in the prayer room and taking leadership sessions with Ted Bradford and Ron Michalski at Calvary Temple. Church life was busy, as we were both involved with a home Bible study. It was located quite a distance from where we were living. The people were new in the faith, and we hungered for the Word and enjoyed the fellowship. The couple who led it were professional, so it was easy to relate to them. Lynda and I eventually opened our house and held Bible studies in the Garden City area.

Holding those three jobs was getting to be too much for me, so I informed my foremen at the steel plant that it was time to quit. At the plant, I was a hooker, meaning the forty-thousand-pound crane operator needed eyes below to direct him to move bundles of rolled steel to the cutting machine. The rolls weighed between ten thousand and forty thousand pounds, and my task was to move the bundles from one aisle to the cutting machine. The plant was at least the size of a football field.

As I was giving direction to move a bundle one time, a voice said loud and clear, "Move now." I walked away from where I was standing, and at that moment the crane operator dropped a ten-thousand-pound bundle of steel at the exact location where I was standing. Had I not moved, it would have killed me instantly. I found out later that this operator would show up for work drunk.

Now I was focusing on my task with Jewish Child and Family Service. They gave me a full-time position, but it was still shift work. I did three days of twelve-hour shifts and rotated. I wanted to improve my skills, so I took college and university courses related to my position. The work was more than challenging. I worked with newly-graduated students out of university, and this would be a mission field in itself. The children in care were overall good; they just happened to have problems with their parents and, in some cases, were rejected or abandoned. My night shift duties were to make sure everyone was safe, had taken their meds, and got up the next morning for school. And I'd make muffins from scratch, meaning from the beginning. The night shift was really hard at times, but I always brought my Bible and prayed when all the children fell asleep.

Besides working staff, there was a presence of evil over the place. A place where I was learning spiritual warfare! I have to admit that there were some nights I just didn't want to go back to the night shift, as I knew what awaited me — the evil powers of darkness. I was still learning the first principle of growing in my faith: *"As newborn babes, desire the pure milk of the word, that you may grow thereby"* (1 Peter 2:2).

I said to my wife as I was writing this book that I was grateful for Pastor Barber, who fed us the Word of God. He was an expository preacher, and you received a full meal and aways felt the presence of God. He preached the whole counsel of God and would preach on difficult topics. It was those Wednesday night Bible studies and prayer and fellowship with other believers that helped and encouraged me.

Another Indigenous person, Grace, was always at those Bible studies, and over the forty-four years, we often ran into each other. She would remind me that we were the only Indigenous people who were faithful to those Wednesday Bible studies. There are no shortcuts to spiritual growth; one must be diligent and read and pray to grow in their faith. It seemed to me that I was on an accelerated growth plan and faced spiritual warfare. Mr. Bradford was right on the night that I gave my life to Christ when he said there would be a voice on my shoulder condemning me: *"There is therefore now no condemnation to those who are in Christ Jesus, who do not walk according to the flesh, but according to the spirit"* (Romans 8:1).

> But I see another law in my members, warring against the law of my mind, and bringing me into captivity to the law of sin which is in my members. O wretched man that I am! Who will deliver me from this body of death? I thank God—through Jesus Christ our Lord! So then, with the mind I myself serve the law of God, but with the flesh the law of sin. (Romans 7:23–25)

The battle in the spiritual realm was quite intense, so there was a war raging not only with the powers of darkness but with my old carnal nature. The apostle Paul describes this in Galatians 5:16–26. The old nature needs to be crucified daily, and we need to walk in the Spirit, which gives us the liberty and the power to overcome the old nature and put on the new man, who is created in Christ Jesus.

A few years after I had resigned from the Jewish Child and Family Services, I found out that some of the staff were also into drinking and using marijuana. Although I was desiring this sincere milk of the Word of God, I realized that for me to overcome, I would have to become more disciplined.

> For though by this time you ought to be teachers, you need someone to teach you again the first principles of the oracles of God; and you have come to need milk and not solid food. For everyone who partakes only of milk is unskilled in the word of righteousness, for he is a babe. But solid food belongs to those who are of full age, that is, those who by reason of use have their senses exercised to discern both good and evil. (Hebrews 5:12–14)

> I beseech you therefore, brethren, by the mercies of God, that you present your bodies as a living sacrifice, holy, acceptable to God, which is your reasonable service. And do not be conformed to this world, but be transformed by the renewing of your mind, that you may prove what is the good and acceptable and perfect will of God (Romans 12:1–2)

In Ephesians 6:10–18, Paul writes about putting on the whole armour of God. He is referring to a Roman soldier equipped for battle. He reminds Christians that they are also in the battle against an unseen force of evil. As he closes this letter, Paul gives these believers great doctrine as a foundation for their faith, and then he also gives them a practical application:

> Finally my brethren, be strong in the Lord and the power His might. Put on the whole armour of God, that you may be able to stand against the wiles of the devil. For we do not wrestle against flesh and blood, but against prin-

cipalities, against powers, against the rulers of the darkness of this age, against spiritual hosts of wickedness in the heavenly places. Therefore take up the whole armor of God, that you may be able to withstand in the evil day, and having done all, to stand. Stand therefore, having girded your waist with truth, having put on the breastplate of righteousness, and having shod your feet with the preparation of the gospel of peace; above all, taking the shield of faith with which you will be able to quench all the fiery darts of the wicked one. And take the helmet of salvation, and the sword of the Spirit, which is the word of God; praying always with all prayer and supplication in the Spirit, being watchful to this end with all perseverance and supplication for all the saints. (Ephesians 6:10–18)

This generation of preachers today need to preach doctrine and the whole counsel of God and not just their favourite Scriptures. All the scriptures are needed to equip the saints for the ministry God has called them into. Be a shepherd that is fearless to preach the whole counsel of God. There are some pulpits across this nation that feature their favourite teaching. God has not called us just to preach our favourite scriptures. He has called us to preach Christ and Him crucified.

In 1 Corinthians 2:1, Paul is writing to a church that was having a lot of problems: division among themselves, misuse of spiritual gifts, fornication, and all sorts of evil. Some of these church members were following their favourite preachers and weren't submitting to the Lordship of Jesus Christ, so Paul wrote a letter about his authority in Christ:

And I, brethren, when I came to you, did not come with excellency of speech or of wisdom declaring to you the testimony of God. For I determined not to know anything among you except Jesus Christ and Him crucified. I was with you in weakness, in fear, and in much trembling. And my speech and my preaching were not with persuasive words of human wisdom, but in demonstration of the Spirit and of power, that your faith should not be in the wisdom of men but in the power of God.

So at the beginning of our Christian walk, a good foundation was laid for us by men and women of God who knew how to live out their faith. God put these people in our lives to help us in our faith.

This new life in Christ was an exciting life. The moment we were born again, we were new creations, and old things had passed away. I had a new beginning, a new start in my life, pointing in the right direction. We were saving up funds and aiming to buy a new home. We opened our home to Bible studies, and people were coming, like old friends who were born again and had faith in Christ.

At least fifty people who started attending our Bible studies came as a result of our nephew's tragic accident. Many lives turned around on my brother-in-law's side of the family. At one point, we all celebrated birthdays and special occasions. We had at least thirty-six people attending one night of fellowship. The people we used to party with were now celebrating our new-found faith in Christ.

Those early days of our Christian faith were challenging, but we had a new life. Now I knew why my sister was always talking about Jesus. We felt the leading of the Holy Spirit many times to give out Bibles, and we often did to our family members. My older sister and brother-in-law moved into Garden City, into the same townhouse complex as us. At that time they weren't Christians, but we always had time for one another. My sister noticed the change in my life and the joy I now had. She knew how I'd lived before and now saw the transformation in me. No way was I perfect and never would be, but my life had been transformed by the power of God. People would say today of their conversion that they had a Saul encounter with Jesus.

> Then Saul, still breathing threats and murder against the disciples of the Lord, went to the high priest and asked letters from him to the synagogues of Damascus, so that if he found any who were of the Way, whether men or women, he might bring them bound to Jerusalem. As he journeyed he came near Damascus, and suddenly a light shone around him from heaven. Then he fell to the ground and heard a voice saying to him, "Saul, Saul, why are you persecuting Me?" And he said, "Who are You, Lord? Then the Lord said, "I am Jesus, whom you are persecuting. It is hard for you to kick against the goads." So he, trembling and astonished, said, "Lord, what do You want me to do?" Then the Lord said to him, "Arise and go into the city, and you will be told what you must do." (Acts 9:1–6)

In 1 Timothy 1:12–17, Paul writes to Timothy:

> And I thank Christ Jesus our Lord who has enabled me, because He counted me faithful, putting me into ministry, although I was formerly a blasphemer, a persecutor, and an insolent man; but I obtained mercy because I did it ignorantly in unbelief. And the grace of our Lord was exceedingly abundant, with faith and love which are in Christ Jesus. This is a faithful saying and worthy of all acceptance, that Christ Jesus came into the world to save sinners, of whom I am chief. However, for this reason I obtained mercy, that

in me first Jesus Christ might show all longsuffering, as a pattern to those who are going to believe on Him for everlasting life. Now to the King eternal, immortal, invisible, to God who alone is wise, be honor and glory forever and ever Amen.

Working those long overnight shifts was a time of growth personally and spiritually. Part of what we did for the children was teach practical life skills. The grocery store was always a challenge when buying food for twelve people or more. The Jewish community always provided extras, unlike Winnipeg Child and Family Services. Eventually, I let go of the other position and now had extra time for more work for the Kingdom of God.

One of my old friends from our drinking days called to ask if I was interested in volunteering with Youth for Christ in my old hood, Jig Town. I prayed about it, but I didn't feel that I was able to take on the task. I was a new Christian and had barely memorized the names of the sixty-six books of the Bible. So I prayed, "Lord, what should I do?" I went through a very long list of what I couldn't do for the Lord. He answered me very clearly: "Paul said he must go to Rome to testify of the grace of God." God was saying to me, "You can testify of my grace." Yes, that's easy. I can testify about the grace of God. For by grace we are saved through faith in Christ Jesus! Yes, I can tell them about you!

So began my busy life in church and now back in the old hood. When I started the with the group, it began to grow in numbers. We were playing street hockey once, and things were getting a bit rough with pushing and shoving. The boys thought I would back away from the rough stuff. Not on your life! Remember, I was a new Christian and still dealing with the old man. Once the boys realized that I wasn't a pushover, they began to show more respect.

Over time, new YFC leadership came on the scene with a different approach to reaching the youth. So it was my time to step away and let them lead. Besides, we were busy with church life and had met some wonderful Christians who helped us. Ted was such an encouragement; he lived what he taught.

We had our challenges in the church world. Outside of church, you knew exactly who your enemy was, but not so in the Christian world. I never let anybody bully me in the world, and I certainly wouldn't allow the Christians to bully me. There were plenty of Dr. Pharisees and Dr. Sadducees in the crowd. Don't take me wrong, we should take care of the house of the Lord, but the building is not the church. We are the body of Christ, the church, the called-out ones.

Back to Youth for Christ. We took these young boys on adventures they never would have experienced otherwise. We took them for a weekend of camping on Lake Winnipeg. They had a wonderful time. Many years later when I was pastoring at Calvary

Temple, one of the young men who'd been in the group reached out to me and asked if I could perform a wedding ceremony for him. It was my first wedding ceremony, and they were as nervous as I was. Instead of looking at each other during the vows, they were looking at me. I tried to give a facial message to the groom to look at the bride. Well, we got through it, and he got to kiss his bride. All those years later he reached out to me. I still had the same phone number.

The other leader in the group was Alvin. He was such a genuine guy—no street smarts, but a big heart to reach out to the boys from the hood. He was 100 per cent committed to reach those boys for Christ; he even moved his family into Jig Town. I thought that was pretty serious. Most people are trying to get out of the hood, but Alvin wasn't your ordinary Christian. He was living out his Christian faith. He'd actually moved to Winnipeg from southern Ontario and ended up in the hood.

Eventually he realized he'd made a mistake moving into Jig Town, as it was too dangerous for him and his family. He once tried to intervene with a family in crisis. He went over and someone threw a bottle or ashtray at him. He moved out of Jig Town, but he didn't move far, just over to the next housing unit across the street. This was not Manitoba Housing but a co-op type place.

He eventually introduced me to his father-in-law, who'd been a missionary in West Africa for thirty-five years. Brother Berg had to leave the mission field for health reasons. He was a teacher and had this canvas cloth that he'd placed on the wall. It was quite wide and displayed colourful illustrations of the end times and the history of the church. He taught us about the rapture and many other subjects. He had such an influence on me. I admired his zeal for the Lord. I now know how he influenced his son-in-law with his faith; it was something you felt whenever you were around him, He was a humble man.

Once when we were still living in Garden City, he came over to our home to attend our Bible study. I was teaching and didn't feel in any way intimated by his presence. Here was this thirty-five-year veteran missionary listening to this young preacher, still wet behind the ears, a rookie. But he was a gracious and loving soul of a man; he was a humble man, just like my friend Ted. These men demonstrated humility, and you felt blessed to have them in your life.

Behind these godly men were godly women, and that demonstrated biblical headship. That is much needed in the body of Christ today. Ladies, let your husband be the head over your marriage. It's a biblical and good foundation. He may be imperfect, but so are you. That may sound old fashioned, but it's biblical. I would rather be old fashioned than miss God's best for my marriage and family.

Alvin moved back to southern Ontario to help his dad on the farm. I was attending workshops in Orilla, Ontario one time and decided to visit him and his family. Alvin had a vision to plant green peppers and make a few dollars. Most of the farmland around the area was being used to grow tobacco. Alvin asked me if I'd like to help him. I am in no way a farm boy, but I will try. So we went to the field to plant his crop. We were sitting on a machine side-by-side, like a motorcycle carrying passengers, while being pulled by a tractor. This piece of machinery must have been one hundred years old. There was a plant tray between us and a wheel moving around in a circle as we went up and down the fields. We had to place the plant on the moving circle, and the machine would push it into the ground. I don't think I was all that helpful, but we managed to put the crop in. It was just like our days together in Youth for Christ planting seeds of the Word of God into the hearts of young people. The Word of God tells us that some plant, some water, but God gives the increase.

Back in Garden City, we were so grateful, and still are today, for the work of the Lord in our lives and the lives we touched in our Bible study group. Although there were some real challenges to overcome, most of the bad habits had been broken off me—or at least I thought so. But there were still some things God wanted to remove from my life. In the old life of rock 'n' roll, I had accumulated many albums, and the Lord was convicting me. I was no longer playing or listening to them, but I had spent a lot of money on them. I had sold some of them, which I regretted later.

John, writing his love letters to the church, says:

Do not love the world or the things in the world. If anyone loves the world, the love of the Father is not in him. For all that is in the world—the lust of the flesh, the lust of the eyes, and the pride of life—is not of the Father but is of the world. And the world is passing away, and the lust of it; but he who does the will of the Father abides forever. (1 John 2:15–17)

The musical bands I had listened to were now appearing in Winnipeg. I thought to myself, *I could go and just listen to them and it won't harm me.* At least that's what the devil was wanting me to believe. I was just new in my walk with the Lord. Before that, I had walked after the god of this world, the devil. What seemed harmless at the time was actually a door I had left opened from fifteen years of my life. The Holy Spirit was searching my heart and revealing what still had a grip on me. That demon was trying to influence me, as that door hadn't been totally surrendered to God. How did that come about? I worshipped and prayed my way through these temptations. Before the popular teaching were popping up about intercessory prayer, the Lord was already leading me in that direction. Those long nights of prayer and worshipping God were helping me to be a worshipper. He then put a burden on my heart to pray for nations. I had such a burden to pray for Vietnam.

So one day I grabbed my remaining rock albums, walked across the parking lot, and threw them into the garbage bin. Their stronghold on me was broken and the chains fell off. The memory bank of this music also needed to be broken from my mind. I had the ability to memorize so much music, and I could easily quote lyrics by memory. Back in the day, those party bands came to my mom's house, and I'd spent all those days and nights dancing at the Indian and Metis Friendship Centre and the many bars and night clubs. I had downloaded so many lyrics. You would think I could sing and play an instrument. Not so. I tried, but it just didn't happen. What I had to do was found in the Word.

> I beseech you therefore, brethren, by the mercies of God, that you present your bodies a living sacrifice, holy, and acceptable to God, which is your reasonable service. And do not be conformed to this world, but be transformed by the renewing of your mind, that you may prove what is that good and acceptable and perfect will of God. (Romans 12:1–2)

My former life had been conformed to the music of the world.

We attended church during those early years, and the music was mostly hymns. I have to admit, the music was kind of boring. I was used to high intensity, high volume, and upbeat music that moved your feet to dancing. I enjoyed the preaching; it fed my soul. The hymns were full of doctrine, such as there is power in the blood of Jesus! Wonder-working power! I have been redeemed by the blood of Jesus. I have been forgiven by the blood of Jesus, and I am being sanctified by the power of the Holy Spirit. Wonder-working power!

Contemporary Christian music has some good stuff and some not so good. I never had any musical training, but I can tell when a musical instrument isn't tuned properly, or when the band isn't in harmony, or when the song leader isn't depending on the Holy Spirit. Some depend on their talent and skill set rather than the Holy Spirit.

> You worship what you do not know; we know what we worship, for salvation is of the Jews. But the hour is coming, and now is, when true worshipers will worship the Father in spirit and truth; for the Father seeking such to worship Him. God is Spirit, and those who worship Him must worship in spirit and truth. (John 4:22–24)

When you worship God, something happens and things begin to change: chains break, walls are torn down, hearts are mended, and spirits are renewed.

"The garment of praise for the spirit of heaviness" (Isaiah 61:3). We will wrap ourselves with that garment of praise and leave no openings through which hostile elements can penetrate. The garment of praise repels and replaces the heavy spirit. Believe me, there was a heavy spirit that seemed to be over my mind until Jesus broke it off.

> But I will sing of Your power; yes, I will sing aloud of Your mercy in the morning; for You have been my defense and refuge in the day of my trouble. To You, O my Strength, I will sing praises; for God is my defense, my God of mercy. (Psalm 59:16–17)

Keep praising Him who is the King of kings!

> But at midnight Paul and Silas were praying and singing hymns to God, and the prisoners were listening to them. Suddenly there was a great earthquake, so that the foundations of the prison were shaken; and immediately all the doors were opened and everyone's chains loosed. (Acts 16:25–26)

Keep praising, because He is worthy of all our praise. I pray that the chains of the enemy of your soul will be broken in you, in Jesus' name!

> Then I looked, and I heard the voice of many angels around the throne, the living creatures, and the elders; and the number of them was ten thousand times ten thousand, and thousands of thousands, saying with a loud voice: "Worthy is the Lamb who was slain to receive power and riches and wisdom, and strength and honor and glory and blessing!" And every creature which is in heaven and on the earth and under the earth and such as are in the sea, and all in them, I heard saying: "Blessing and honor and glory and power be to Him who sits on the throne, and to the Lamb, forever and ever!" (Revelation 5:11–13)

Before we moved to our new home, I had left behind a room full of broken chains. Whom the Son sets free is free indeed!

Often the children from the Jewish Child and Family Services who had been abandoned were adopted and then abandoned again. This spirit of rebellion was upon them, as well as upon the staff who secretly were living a double life. They were trying to lecture these young people to live a moral life, but they were just as rebellious as the children. Some of them were breaking the law and using marijuana while trying to be morally upright. Their empty philosophy of life made them parrots, just repeating their professors from university days.

They all knew of my Christian beliefs, and we often had long discussions. I wouldn't allow these intellectuals to bully me. I knew the one who had broken the chains off me; I'd had a supernatural experience of being born again, and the addiction was broken. Jesus set me free from fear and from the bondage of suicidal thoughts.

I was respectful in the workplace. It was a Jewish organization that practised dietary laws, so we had to remove the meat and dairy plates. They marked their Jewish festivals, and in many cases, the children received special gifts. Some of the children were mentally challenged but could function with more instruction. I felt connected to them, especially one particular boy who always wanted hugs. Once on my day off I was sitting in a coffee shop, and who came in with another staff member but the one who always wanted hugs. He noticed me sitting there and yelled at the top of his voice, "Alfred!" Then he ran over to me for his hug.

There was something special about these mentally challenged boys. When I had to take them for doctor appointments, they would ask questions like: What does Christmas mean? They'd heard about Jesus. Many years later, one of the boys, now a man, walked into Calvary Temple, as he had become a Christian.

I enjoyed working at the Jewish Child and Family Services. The work was rewarding, and I learned so much, but the shift work was becoming too much. It was like a long flight overseas, and when I got home, I felt jet lagged. That's what it felt like after you worked the evening shift and had one day off and then started the night shift.

We had saved enough to purchase our first home in 1984, so we moved to Tyndall Park, not too far from Jig Town. My time at the group home was coming to end, as the shift work was getting more difficult to deal with. I needed more of a challenge as well. I did apply for a supervisor position, but they gave it to the Jewish person.

The possession date for our new home was in July, but the contractor was behind schedule. The house was finished on the inside but not completely finished on the outside. They still needed to complete work on the stucco. It was terribly hot that summer, and we spent the weekends in an air-conditioned hotel room.

During summer vacations, we spent a week at family Bible camp, and there were many Christians from our church in attendance. The atmosphere was much more relaxed. The Christians raised their hands in the air, giving praise and worship to Jesus. But back at our home church, it was much different. Those believers were no longer lifting up their hands to worship King Jesus. They actually seemed somewhat subdued. They weren't free to lift up their hands or speak in tongues like they did at camp. At camp when their children and teenagers spoke in tongues, they acted like they had won a lottery. It was certainly odd to me.

I was hungry for the baptism of the Holy Spirit with the evidence of speaking in tongues. Some people in our Bible study had received the baptism by attending different churches. I had been watching Jimmy Swaggart on TV, and he was always talking about Pentecost and speaking in tongues. Lynda and I decided to take a vacation and headed down to Indianapolis to attend one of brother Swaggart's crusades. It was the same summer we moved into our new home. Our daughter came with us to Indianapolis. I was hungry and thirsty for more from God.

Our pastor was on the airplane, heading out to be the speaker at a family camp. We exchanged greetings, and I told him we were heading for Jimmy Swaggart's crusade. It was powerful and amazing there, and the anointing seemed to be everywhere. Near the closing of the crusade, perhaps the last day, I received the baptism of the Holy Ghost with the evidence of speaking in tongues.

I came to realize that our home church was called a classical Pentecostal church. The emphasis in the evening service was on evangelism, and the prayer room was open for any hungry, seeking believers. Many were baptized in the Holy Spirit, but it seemed the church was more or less nondenominational. Back then, people were becoming disillusioned with their denominations when they started to ordain those living lifestyles contrary to the Word of God. Many left their denomination and landed in Calvary Temple, and they were welcomed with open arms. Others were exiting their churches to get away from legalist attitudes. These people told me that their parents and church believed that bowling was worldly, as was swimming in the same pool with the opposite gender. We preached the Word of God, but little was said about the Pentecostal experience or being baptized in the Spirit. That was left for the camp setting, where many people experienced the baptism of the Holy Ghost. I believe that we need to put Pentecost back into Pentecost.

We continued holding Bible studies in our new home. We were grateful for this new chapter in our lives. My sister was encouraging us to undertake the work of evangelism and outreach to our Native people. We already had our people involved in Bible study. We took them through first things first and then we ran a two-year, more in-depth Bible study.

Our Bible study group was growing, and my sister kept asking us for more involvement to reach our people with the gospel. I was reluctant to add more work to my already busy life. Besides, I knew the challenges of working with our people. I didn't want to take on that work. I prayed about it and sought the Lord for an answer. He spoke clearly to me and said, "Didn't I show you my grace?" He had to break my heart even more, because I didn't want a difficult assignment. When you pray for

God's will to be done, He takes you seriously and says, "Okay, let's start the process, and we'll begin in you first."

Had I said no, I'm not interested, I would have missed God's best for me and my ministry. I would have missed reaching our Native people in North and South America. I would have missed the Philippines, Mexico, and the East African countries of Uganda, Kenya, Sudan, and Tanzania. I would have missed Russia, Korea, Jamaica, Hawaii, Argentina, England, Germany, Denmark, Hong Kong, Brazil, Chile, and London. These are just some of the places I either passed through or preached revivals in. I also travelled Canada and Alaska, and I spoke to millions through radio in the Philippines. This reached 25 million Roman Catholic listeners. In the many years of travelling around the world several times, I saw first-hand tens of thousands give their lives to Jesus Christ. I witnessed many miracles, from blind eyes seeing and deaf ears opening. People were healed from cancer and broken backs. Thousands of people were freed from addiction. People bound in wheelchairs would rise up and walk. I am so glad I said, "Yes, not my will but your will be done!"

> The hand of the Lord came upon me and brought me out in the Spirit of the Lord, and set me down in the midst of the valley; and it was full of bones. Then He caused me to pass by them all around, and behold, there were very many in the open valley; and indeed they were very dry. And He said to me, "Son of man, can these bones live?" So I answered, "O Lord God, You know." Again He said to me, "Prophesy to these bones, and say to them, 'O dry bones, hear the word of Lord! Thus says the Lord God to these bones: "Surely I will cause breath to enter into you, and you shall live."' (Ezekiel 37:1–5)

Now that takes courage and faith to stand over the valley of dry bones and speak to the bones to come alive. Sometimes it takes courage to speak the word of the Lord.

> After the death of Moses the servant of the Lord, it came to pass that the Lord spoke to Joshua the son of Nun, Moses' assistant, saying: "Moses My servant is dead. Now therefore, arise, go over this Jordan, you and all this people, to the land which I am giving to them—the children of Israel. Every place that the sole of your foot will tread upon I have given you, as I said to Moses. (Joshua 1:1–3)

> Be strong and of good courage, for to this people you shall divide as an inheritance the land which I swore to their fathers to give them. Only be

strong and very courageous, that you may observe to do according to all the law which Moses My servant commanded you; do not turn from it to the right hand or to the left, that you may prosper wherever you go. This Book of the Law shall not depart from your mouth, but you shall meditate on it day and night, that you may observe to do according to all that is written in it. For then you will make your way prosperous, and then you will have good success. Have I not commanded you? Be strong and of good courage; do not be afraid, nor be dismayed, for the Lord your God is with you wherever you go. (Joshua 1:6–9)

A leader's courage develops as a fruit of encouragement. Moses revealed this leadership role well in shaping the young leader Joshua. He encouraged him in leading God's people into the Promised Land, emphasizing the seriousness of his task. Then the Lord Himself encouraged Joshua after Moses died, telling him not to fear but to be strong and courageous. The officers of Israel's army also encouraged Joshua, promising their loyalty and urging him to take the leadership. Those who would shape leaders encourage them. Those who would follow should do the same: Be strong, courageous, balanced, manly, strengthened, established, firm, fortified, mighty (Joshua 1:9).

David encouraged himself, literally making himself strong in the Lord (1 Samuel 30:6). Strengthened by Yahweh, Joshua would be the leader to take them into the promised land. Our Joshua, Jesus, takes us into the land of promises. There are over eight thousand promises in the Word of God. Just like Joshua, God has promised that wherever He puts His foot will be His land. Our Joshua, Jesus, our deliverer, has given us the land of promises, and we claim these promises by putting our Amen to the promise. I can do all things through Christ who strengthens me. Amen! I don't need God's strength to pick up that broom and sweep the floor. I need His strength to say no to my pride and ego! I put my Amen to His promise! There is always a cost to walking in the will of God. But if He calls you, nothing is impossible. He will go before and make a way for you and will supply all your needs.

Calvary Temple already had many different fellowships going, but we didn't have one for the Native people. We gathered various born again people at our house for a conversation about putting a Native Fellowship together at our home church. Over the years, many Native people attended the church but would leave. I called Pastor Barber and invited him over to our home to have a conversation regarding our desire to grow as a Bible study group and have a Native Fellowship group within the church. There must have been at least twenty of us in the room when he arrived.

Pastor sat graciously and listened to our concerns. He then turned to me and said, "Alfred, I'm going to make you the president of the group, and you can all meet at Calvary Temple. I'll arrange for a room."

I wasn't expecting him to ask me to be president of the group. Most in that room had come to Christ after the tragic drowning of my nephew, so all were family and friends. I might have been the youngest one among the group.

That was the beginning of our future church plant. I'd never heard of a church plant. We just wanted our Native people saved and growing in their faith and walk with God. Some people called and said they were going in a different direction. I said, "Okay, thanks for calling." We then talked about what time should we meet. I mentioned that before the main service would be good, then they could stay and hear our lead pastor, H.H. Barber. That would mean a 10:00 a.m. start. Some thought that we'd never get them there that early.

In the 1980s, there were small Native churches in the city, and most of them had services in the afternoon. I certainly didn't want to affiliate with any of them. I wanted us to have a firm foundation and structure that would help the people. None of these fly-by-night preachers who came to town and their only interest was to collect the people's money and then leave. That seemed to be the pattern. Paul writes to Timothy:

> I charge you therefore before God and the Lord Jesus Christ, who will judge the living and the dead at His appearing and His kingdom: Preach the word! Be ready in season and out of season. Convince, review, exhort, with all longsuffering and teaching. For the time will come when they will not endure sound doctrine, but according to their own desires, because they have itching ears, they will heap up for themselves teachers; and they will turn their ears away from the truth, and be turned aside to fables. But you be watchful in all things, endure afflictions, do the work of an evangelist, fulfill your ministry. (2 Timothy 4:1–5)

Paul, in 2 Corinthians 11:4 and 13–15, writes:

> For if he who comes preaches another Jesus whom we have not preached, or if you receive a different spirit which you have not received, or a different gospel which you have not accepted—you may well put up with it! ... For such are false apostles, deceitful workers, transforming themselves into apostles of Christ. And no wonder! For Satan himself transforms himself into an angel of light.

Another Jesus.

A different spirit.

A different gospel.

Some of the people who attended these meetings seemed confused about teaching and lacked any type of discipline. It wasn't uncommon for these people to sing and share their testimony in these independent settings. My position had always been to get to know them first and then perhaps allow them to sing, play an instrument, or share their testimony. We wanted structure and accountability from anyone who had talent and wanted to share. We already had people who'd been with us for the past five years in the Bible study.

Those early days were extremely challenging and seemed impossible. Some people in leadership didn't approve of the direction; they felt we should just let the people do their own thing. At the beginning on Sunday mornings, we had a great deal of enthusiasm. To put this vision into practice and meet that early would be an overwhelming challenge. There were other Native groups that gathered at 2:00 p.m. on a Sunday afternoon. But that was not the direction in which the Lord was leading us. I wanted them to get under the teaching of our senior pastor. Besides, we were the Sunday school class for the Native people.

Over time the crowd began to grow. We had a room that could hold fifty people, and we were outgrowing it. We faced interruption and interference from the choir and band members, who didn't realize that the Native work was now using their band room. Once they realized this, they simply used the back stairs to get to the choir room.

Sometimes only two or three people would show up for those early morning services. But we were determined to make an impact and remain steady in the call to reach the Native people. As we set up chairs in the morning, we would pray over each one: "Oh Lord, fill these chairs." God answered our prayers, and the room was now being filled with broken and hurting people who needed to hear the good news that Jesus saves, Jesus heals, Jesus baptizes in the Holy Spirit, and He's coming back for His Church, His Bride.

Many times I was discouraged because of the lack of attendance and discipline of the people. It seemed the smallest detail would sidetrack them, and they didn't follow through with their commitments to church attendance and being involved with other believers. They allowed for these roadblocks that were put in front of them by the enemy, and they failed to live according to the Word of God. In many cases, it wasn't much different from the lifestyle I'd lived in rebellion and drug abuse. I knew where they were coming from, but I also needed to let them know that they had power and authority in Jesus' name.

Therefore submit to God. Resist the devil and he will flee from you. Draw near to God and He will draw near to you. Cleanse your hands, you sinners; and purify your hearts, you double minded. Lament and mourn and weep! Let your laughter be turned to mourning and your joy to gloom. Humble yourselves in the sight of the Lord, and He will lift you up. (James 4:7–10)

We began to teach the people about spiritual warfare. They already had sense of what that was like in their personal lives, so we taught them from Ephesians 6:10–20. The battle was on in all of our lives against an unseen enemy who created havoc. We as a people group were already aware of the medicine men in our communities. I overheard people talk about the power of the medicine man and how he had power over people and put curses on them. Their faces would be twisted, and they had all sorts of issues.

Some people had never had boundaries in their lives and were undisciplined because of it. They seemed to think that they could lash out at people and say nasty things. They'd been bullies in their former life, and now they wanted to be bullies in their spiritual life. They thought they could speak whatever was on their mind without any consequences. There are always consequences for our actions and words. There will be a time when people will no longer want to fellowship with you. If everyone spoke their mind, there would be many more problems. That's why Paul tells us in Romans 12:2 to renew our minds.

The mind is where we are assaulted by the enemy, who wants us to believe that everybody is against us. It's actually a spirit, a spirit of pity, a poor me attitude, and it says that everyone is picking on me. Remember, demons are persons without bodies. There is a lying spirit, and people believe those lies. They begin to peddle their words to whoever will listen. The enemy uses words to discourage you, blame you, lie to you, and eventually defeat you. An unseen evil force is working against you, and it's your old nature.

But if you are led by the Spirit, you are not under the law. Now the works of the flesh are evident, which are: adultery, fornication, uncleanness, lewdness, idolatry, sorcery, hatred, contentions, jealousies, outbursts of wrath, selfish ambitions, dissensions, heresies, envy, murders, drunkenness, revelries, and the like; of which I tell you beforehand, just as I told you in time past, that those who practice such things will not inherit the kingdom of God. But the fruit of the Spirit is love, joy, peace, longsuffering, kindness, goodness, faithfulness, gentleness, self-control. Against such there is no law. And those who are Christ's have crucified the flesh with its passions and desires. If we live in the Spirit, let us also walk in the Spirit. Let us not become conceited, provoking one another, envying one another. (Galatians 5:18–26)

Even so the tongue is a little member and boasts great things. See how great a forest a little fire kindles. And the tongue is a fire, a world of iniquity. The tongue is so set among our members that it defiles the whole body, and sets on fire the course of nature; and it is set on fire by hell ... But no man can tame the tongue. It is an unruly evil, full of deadly poison (James 3:5–6, 8)

Hebrews 12:15 reads, *"Looking carefully lest anyone fall short of the grace of God; lest any root of bitterness springing up cause trouble, and by this many become defiled."* This root of bitterness grows deeper and deeper until it crushes you and affects all those around you. It may have come into your life as result of someone harming you physically or sexually. Perhaps you went through a failed marriage, or someone in leadership, maybe your parent or pastor, failed you, and now you are bitter. The only way to become better is to forgive those who have hurt you. The parable of the unforgiving servant, in Matthew 18 is quite a long story. I encourage you to find it in your Bible and read it.

You wicked servant! I forgave you all that debt because you begged me. Should you not also have had compassion on your fellow servant, just as I had pity on you?" And his master was angry, and delivered him to the torturers until he should pay all that was due to him. So my heavenly Father also will do to you if each of you, from his heart, does not forgive his brother his trespasses. (Matthew 18:32b–35)

The reason you may have lost your joy, peace, and victory is that you might have been handed over to the torturers! Forgiveness is so important in your Christian walk. Forgive them and be set free; forgiveness is available!

We were now reaching out to our Native people in many ways. Lynda's co-workers had a baseball team, and they sent a challenge to our fellowship group. What an opportunity to reach people for Jesus by playing baseball with them! The game was set, and it was progressing along. As I was playing in centre field, a group of people exited their car and came over to talk to me. I recognized one of the men. He came off and on to the fellowship. We actually had a surprise birthday party planned for him after the game. The leader of the pack came and started yelling, asking why we weren't on Main Street witnessing to the street people. I listened to her and recognized that spirit as a legalistic one.

When the game was over, we headed over to the house that was hosting the birthday party and explained to them what had happened at the baseball field. The man whose birthday it was left with the angry crowd, so I led a brief devotion from Galatians about legalism and liberty. That legalist and unteachable attitude would surface many times over the years. Some were born into it, and others picked it up from their independent preachers. It left them in bondage. These people seemed addicted to meetings with a lot of hype and no substance. Paul writes:

> O foolish Galatians! Who has bewitched you that you should not obey the truth, before whose eyes Jesus Christ was clearly portrayed among you as crucified? This only I want to learn from you: Did you receive the Spirit by the works of the law, or by the hearing of faith? Are you so foolish? Having began in the Spirit, are you now being made perfect by the flesh?" (Galatians 3:1–3)

I read somewhere that if you only have the Word of God, you will dry up, and if you only have the Spirit, you will blow up. But if you have both, you will grow up. These people were unstable and unreliable, and when it came to commitment, you couldn't depend on them. When an emotional experience wasn't there, they seemed to come apart easily. They would call those meetings "revival meetings." There were three things happening at the same time: the Holy Spirit, the human spirit, and the evil spirit. Now which one would you take home with you and think it was the Holy Spirit? In most cases, in was the human spirit that manipulated you, and the evil spirit kept you in bondage.

One day I received a phone call from Pastor Randy from Vancouver Native Pentecostal Church. He introduced himself and told me he was travelling with group of young adults by van to northern Quebec to attend the National Native Leadership Council. He asked if they could stay the night at our home. I told him that we only had two bedrooms but we had a larger living area that they could stay in for the night. They stayed for the night, and once the young adults and youth fell asleep, Pastor Randy wanted to talk about issues he had to deal with on their way to Québec. I understood exactly what he was talking about; it was a rebellious and unteachable spirit. It would not submit to authority or take direction. The pastor was concerned about trying to bring any kind of discipline to the group, as the young men's parents were influential in the church. Sometimes as leaders, hard decisions have to be made for the unity of the group.

"The fear of man brings a snare" (Proverbs 29:25a). It traps you in their opinions, their legalist mindset, and what they want you to do. As a leader, I learned quickly not to be snared by anyone's opinions. There will be people who try to control, manipulate, dominate, and intimidate you. If that's the case, it's a spirit of rebellion, which is a spirit of witchcraft.

As a leader, this was the first time I'd heard about the National Native Leadership Council. I missed the one being held in northern Quebec, but the following year, 1987, it was held in Saskatoon. I liked what I saw. There were workshops during the day and an evening service. Excitement was in the air, and the evening services were like camp meeting time. At this time, the meetings were mostly held in Western Canada, and they had a good representation of people from British Columbia. I thought it would be a good thing to host in Winnipeg the following year.

Our superintendent was at the meeting in Saskatoon, and I spoke to him briefly at the airport and informed him we would like to host the next NNLC in Winnipeg. He said there was a protocol we had to follow by sending a letter of invitation to Missions Canada and then to the National Native Leadership Council. It kind of sounded strange to me, as the people in the room were already to committed to going wherever the next meeting would be held. I was excited for the possibilities for leadership to rise up among our Native people. The task before us was enormous—to evangelize Native Canada with the gospel of Jesus Christ. I was pleased to see the structure and accountability to advance the cause of Christ. Our fellowship was 100 per cent committed to the national vision to disciple and win souls for the Kingdom of God.

> Then the Lord answered me and said: "Write the vision and make it plain on tablets, that he may run who reads it. For the vision is yet for an appointed time; but at the end it will speak, and it will not lie. Though it tarries, wait for it; because it will surely come ..." (Habakkuk 2:2–3)

Our fellowship hosted the 1988 NNLC at Calvary Temple, Winnipeg, and the theme of the conference was Spiritual Warfare. The guest speaker for the evening service was Pastor Montana Locklear, and what a blessing he was to our fellowship. We had a taste of what it could be and where we were heading. Our vision connected and resonated with what we had already been doing. For the next ten years, I would be involved with the NNLC, travelling across Canada in the planning of the conference. Our Native director at the time wanted me to represent the Manitoba and Northwest Ontario area at the national level.

It was a privilege to work with our national leader, James Kallappa, at the time. He was a humble and patient man who helped us with the national vision. Our district already had thirty Native-pastor-led churches. Some of the men had been doing that for years. When the revival came to Winnipeg from the outpouring of the Holy Spirit on Azusa Street in 1906, which spread around the world, our Native men sought after it, and some were touched by Pentecostal power and the baptism of the Holy Ghost. Many of them took that experience back to their communities, so we already had Pentecost from those early years.

We encouraged our leadership to help more with the development and receiving of credentials in our district for the Native pastors. Then we proceeded to have our own conference, with the same format as our NNLC. From there we encouraged our fellowship not only to honour long-time pastors who didn't have formal training but to ordain them ministers of the gospel. These faithful men and women were recognized for their many years of service to the Lord and Saviour Jesus Christ.

In time, the district passed a resolution, to be moved and seconded at the district level, to have a Native leader at the executive leadership table. It only made sense, considering we had thirty churches, which made up 33 per cent of the total churches in our district. There was consent among the leadership for more Bible training for the next generation. As a result of planning and casting vision, a program was now in place in Saskatoon. There was excitement in the air, but many great challenges lay ahead.

The president of the Native college put together courses to help the next generation of believers. The college programs were hosted by a Native church in Saskatoon. Some of the students came from Manitoba and Saskatchewan. It was a challenge for students who lived on the reservation and were now living in an urban setting. Many had support from their band and community members. I had the privilege to be one of those teachers to help with the programs. I drove to Saskatoon many times to help, and I stayed at the dormitory, sleeping on a single cot and sharing the shower stalls with the rest of the young men attending the main college. It was rewarding and a blessing to be involved.

During our fellowship, we had many opportunities to reach our people with the gospel. We held many banquets and brought in guest speakers. The Antoine family was such a blessing. We had them come and do ministry several times.

One year we wanted to do a city-wide crusade with the Antoine family. It was decided with the cooperation of other Native churches from different denominations to reach our people. We planned and prayed for the project. We ran radio announcements and made up life-size posters to be placed in strategic places in the city. We also placed advertisements in bus stop areas, with full-size pictures of the Antoine Family. Over the few days of meetings, we reached four thousand people, and many were saved. Each church was given the responsibility to follow up with the new Christians. It was a challenge to work across different denominations, but we made it happen and showed respect, allowing many to participate in the services held at Calvary Temple under the leadership of Pastor H.H. Barber. He was such a big supporter of our meetings.

My role shifted from president of the Native Fellowship to lead pastor of the fellowship. Looking back, it was the call of God on my life that I had sensed when I first began my Christian walk.

I was soon elected to the board of Calvary Temple. To my knowledge, I was the first Native person elected to the board. With little experience as a board member, I put in everything I had to represent the congregation at the board level. The congregation had quickly noticed that I was faithful in small things, so I was elected. I must admit, I was a bit nervous at our first board meeting. I showed up with my Bible in hand, thinking there would be a devotional, or maybe even a Bible study at the board level. Well, it didn't turn out that way. We were down to business, planning for the church. The men who served on the board had been around Calvary Temple for many years. I was the youngest man at the table, and the only Native man on the board.

Church life became very busy, and my term as a board member was coming to an end. I was heavily involved in our Native Fellowship and travelling back and forth from Saskatoon to Winnipeg. I was also travelling across Canada, helping with the planning of our NNLC. Over the many years serving in this capacity, I met a lot of great people and wonderful Christian workers. At our first national meeting in Saskatoon, Lynda and I met this wonderful couple, Jack and Peggy Kennedy. Over the years we became good friends, and they were great encouragers.

Jimmy Swaggart was now holding a crusade in Minneapolis, Minnesota. We rented a van and took as many people as possible on the trip to hear him. We had such a great time during that weekend, and all the way back from Minneapolis to Winnipeg, there was such joy and laughter. I think we laughed all the way from Minneapolis to Winnipeg nonstop.

Some of the people were on a tight budget and didn't have a lot of extra funds. Since there was no morning service on Sunday, they encouraged everyone to find a local church to attend. Wouldn't you know it, there was a Pentecostal church right behind our hotel. So we all headed over to the service. The pastor greeted everyone and said that after the service, they would serve lunch. We were welcome to stay and eat with them. There had been a wedding the previous day, and they had plenty of food left over.

A young family in the service provided special music. They were travelling by faith from church to church and raising their family from their mobile home. For their offering plate, they had a gas-tank bank into which you could place extra funds to help them reach their next ministry destination. This young couple were living by faith. The Holy Spirit was teaching me lessons about faith. We had a group of people, including myself, who had been ministered to and now were getting a free lunch. Our needs were met, and we were helping this young couple reach their next destination. God was revealing that He is a generous God and will bless our obedience. And He continued to bless us for over forty-four years of ministry. He revealed that we as members of the body of Christ need each other to fulfill our destiny in Him.

That little Pentecostal church in Minneapolis needed us as much as we needed them, as did the young couple. They needed the body of Christ to come together to supply their need. That would be a life lesson learned over many years of ministry. We need each other to fulfill the great commission to go into all the world and preach the gospel of the Kingdom of God. When I look back at those early beginnings and the faithfulness of our God again and again for His people, I see His character and nature. He is not willing that any should perish but all come to repentance and faith in Him.

Around this time, I was still working a full-time job Monday to Friday. I was working for Big Brothers Association of Winnipeg as a caseworker while also working full-time as a pastor of the Native Fellowship. It seemed back then that my telephone was ringing all the time; calls would come from morning to night. People needed help, encouragement, and prayer. Sometimes an angry family member would call, cursing and swearing and saying all manner of evil. I'd rebuke them and hang up the phone after saying good night. We were living in our new home, and I think it made some people jealous. They didn't realize how hard we'd worked for it and the sacrifices we'd made.

That spirit of jealousy is prevalent in our Native communities. One can't seem to get ahead in life without someone trying to pull you down to their level of insecurity and immaturity. One preacher said it's like a bucket of crabs, and every one of them is trying to reach the top of the bucket and get out. But the ones on the bottom are trying to pull them down as they climb to the top. Keep climbing, brother and sister; don't let those crabby Christians pull you down. *"Yet in all these things we are more than conquerors through Him who loved us"* (Romans 8:37).

If they can't get you outside of the church, they show up inside the church among the fellowship of believers. Luke 15 contains the story of the lost son. There are two sons in the story; one is unfaithful and the other is faithful. The unfaithful son comes back to his father's house and there's great celebration. The father tells his servants to bring out the best robe and a ring for his son, along with sandals for his feet. They kill the fattened calf to eat and be merry, for his son was dead and is alive again. He was lost and is found.

Now his older son was in the field, and when he came and drew near to the house, he heard music and dancing, so he called one of his servants and asked him what these things meant. He said to him, "Your brother has come in, and because the father has received him safe and sound, he has killed the fattened calf."

But he was angry and would not go in; therefore, his father came and pleaded with him, so he answered and said to his father, "These many years I've been serving you I never transgressed your command at any time, yet you never gave me a young goat that I may be merry with my friends. But as soon as this son of yours came, who has devoured your livelihood with harlots, you killed the fattened calf for him.

And he said to him, "Son, you've always been with me, and all that I have is yours. It was right that we should make merry and be glad, for your brother who was dead is alive again, and he who was lost is found."

The attitude of the older brother can be found in most churches today.

"Then the word of the Lord came to me, saying: 'Before I formed you in the womb I knew you; before you were born I sanctified you; I ordained you a prophet to the nations'" (Jeremiah 1:4–5). In the Hebrew, "ordained" means I recognized you, I designed you, or I appointed you.

You've had a divine appointment in the mind of God from the foundation of the world. You are not an accident; you are not here just to fill up the world. The world was created so that you have a place to become your destiny. You are more important than the world. The Lord also said that before you were born, He sanctified you, or set you apart. He has a special purpose for you. He dedicated you, chose you, and secluded you. Think about this: before you were presented to the world, He had nine months alone with you in your mother's womb as He fashioned you and built you cell by cell, according to His divine blueprint. He made you ready for your destiny in every single detail. Remember, God knew your destiny before the foundation of the world. He formed you in your mother's body for that destiny. By the time you were fashioned and came forth at birth, you were absolutely, impeccably ready for that destiny. You had all the ingredients inside you necessary to be what God called you to be.

"For You formed my inward parts; You covered me in my mother's womb. I will praise You, for I am fearfully and wonderfully made" (Psalm 139:13–14a). I am made with a difference. I'm a miracle, one of a kind. David says, "I know who I am, and I know why I'm here. I know what my purpose here is. I will not follow those sheep around forever. God has a destiny for me, two full destinies of being and doing."

Proverbs 23 speaks of the way you live your life. If you believe that you're a failure, you become a failure. If you're convinced God is mad at you, you'll go through life cowering in fear and guilt. God is not mad at you; in His eyes, you are awesome and wonderfully made, His finest creation. You are made in the image of God, in His likeness. You have a body, mind, and soul. You have the ability to reason, think, and be creative. You are made in the image of God.

First Peter 2:9–10 states that you are a chosen generation. We need to know, understand, and believe what God says about us. Whatever you constantly hear is what you will eventually believe. God has made us unique and different for a reason. You are one-of-a-kind; there is no one in the world exactly like you. For this very reason, no one else in the world can do what God has called you to do. You can touch people like no one else can. By being yourself, you have absolutely no competition. That is why you should never be jealous of what someone else has or does. Focus instead on your own unique capabilities and fulfill your dreams and destiny in a way no one else can.

You need to change the way you speak, because your future is at stake. Rather than saying "I can't make it," say "I'm going somewhere." Things may not look good today, and I may be in the wilderness, but I'm coming out of this thing. I'm working my way out. If God be for me, who can be against me? With God's help, I'm going to turn my life around. My best days are still ahead. Joseph was forsaken, falsely accused, and forgotten. But finally he was favoured by God and restored to rule what God had ordained for him. Joseph reassures his brothers at the death of their father that they meant evil against him, but God meant it for good in order to save many people.

I might have been raised in the hood, but I'm coming out; I may have been raised in an alcoholic home, but I'm coming out, making my way out. My best days are ahead of me. Don't look behind you; focus on what's in front of you, which are multiple blessings. The prodigal son was restored and given back blessing and opportunities that he thought he had lost. But the father had been laying up these blessings while waiting for his son's restoration. All these years God has laid up these missed opportunities for me and you. All those missed opportunities God would restore and then bless me.

When I came to God, all I had to offer Him was a broken heart and a broken young man who'd nearly killed himself. The devil tried to kill me so many times. I lost count of how many times I nearly died and was bound in prison, bound in chains. I had nothing to offer God but my brokenness. My life was in shambles, but He took what I had to offer and made a miracle out of it. I am a wonder, a walking and talking miracle of God. Paul says in Ephesians 2:10, *"For we are His workmanship, created in Christ Jesus for good works, which God prepared beforehand that we should walk in them."* Don't quit before your breakthrough. Breakthrough is closer than you can imagine, yet in the midst of your personal struggles, it's hard to see it.

Looking through the Old Testament, you find people like Moses. He could have easily given in to temptation while standing on the banks of the Red Sea with the armies of Egypt following after him and breathing down his neck. Somehow he needed to know that his breakthrough was going to come. It was just seconds away, and the parting of the waters would prove it.

Think of Elijah, ready to give up and quit. He could have easily said, "What's the use?" His breakthrough came; he realized that God could not be found in the earthquake or a raging fire, but God was speaking to him in a still, small voice. And He's still the same today and forever. Don't give up; don't be a quitter. Press on, for you are about to receive your breakthrough. It's on the horizon. Many times in ministry you'll feel discouraged, disappointed, and betrayed, and you'll want to quit and give up. But the apostle Paul pressed onward to the high calling of God in Christ Jesus. In spite of all his trials and tribulations, this man of God wouldn't quit, for he knew in whom he believed, that He is faithful, reliable, and dependable. He is my God!

These lessons only come when you have lived through them. Nobody can teach you. You need your faith to believe that your breakthrough is coming; it may be morning or night, but it's coming. Your miracle is already in place. God already knows your tomorrow. He knows what you need, and He will supply all your needs in Christ Jesus:

"The steps of a good man are ordered by the Lord, and He delights in his way. Though he fall, he shall not be utterly cast down; for the Lord upholds him with His hand" (Psalm 37:23–24). David was anointed to reign, but he didn't until he was trained for that purpose. *"'I have found David the son of Jesse, a man after My own heart, who will do all My will' … For David, after he had served his own generation by the will of God …"* (Acts 13:22b, 36a). Instructed by God, Samuel anointed David with oil, so fill thine horn and go.

The Hebrew word for "oil" means God's character and nature and the capability of imparting it. In other words, God's divine anointing oil represents His creative ability inside a person's life. God says, "I am giving him a measure of my nature and character, my spiritual genetics, to become and accomplish that which I have called him to."

"I will send thee to Jesse the Bethlehemite: for I have provided me a king among his sons" (1 Samuel 16:1). The Hebrew word for "provided" is *rae*, and it means "to see" or "see the depths."

When God said He had provided a king, He said three primary things:

1. I have already produced myself a king.
2. I have already prepared and chosen myself a king.
3. I now am ready to present myself a king.

Bethlehem is the place of calling. The Hebrew word for Bethlehem is *beth*, meaning "house," and *lemeh*, meaning "bread." Bethlehem is the house of bread. It's your home church, the place where you eat the bread of God's Word. That's where you get the basics inside of you so that you can grow into who and what you're called to be.

Lynda and I had the privilege of sitting under H.H. Barber's ministry for a number of years. He was an expository preacher, line by line, precept upon precept. That generation produced some of the best preachers in our fellowship. They not only could hold a crowd with their oral skills, but they were also builders. He preached the whole counsel of God and kept committed to the text, even though it made some people uncomfortable. Heaven was preached and hell was preached. The Word was spoken like a hammer; it smashed idols, broke addictions, and set the captives free. When you finished listening to him preach, it was like getting fed a full meal. Not so with this generation of many lazy preachers, who preach a watered-down version of the gospel—sermons they find on social media, sermons that can't save a church mouse.

The Word had an impact on its listeners; lives were changed by sitting under the Word. If your pastor isn't preaching whole counsel of God, find a church that does. That's the only way you'll grow in your faith and walk with God. You might just have to stand up to the spiritual bullies.

Bethlehem is a place of calling, a place of anointing. It's a place of new beginning. It's a place of training. I am so grateful for all the men who helped me grow in my faith, men like Ted and Ron and so many others whom I served alongside in Calvary Temple. It was a place that confirmed my calling.

I walked into Pastor Barber's office one day and asked him about the calling of God. I was eager to serve God and needed direction in my life. My Grandma Sinclair's prayers were being answered so many years before I ever asked that question about the call. I just sensed God wanted to equip and teach me. I asked other godly men the same questions over many years. The two answers that often stood out were "faith" and "perseverance." The leadership training and equipping over the years confirmed in my spirit that God was calling me into ministry. But there were lessons to be learned in Bethlehem.

The first lesson concerned spiritual authority. David's first act after he got glimpse of his destiny and felt the touch of the anointing was to find a king to serve. He came under spiritual authority. In the meantime, the enemy was trying his best to sidetrack me. I had speaking abilities, and some of these well-meaning pastors were offering me places to preach. One of the pastors said, "You come and preach for me while I'm out of town, and you can keep the offerings." But I was serving at my home church and felt that was my place to be. I was committed to going every Sunday evening to pray with and counsel people. It may have seemed small in someone's eyes, but I was committed to a small thing.

"*So David came to Saul and stood before him. And he loved him greatly, and he became his armorbearer*" (1 Samuel 16:21). The Bible says that David stood before Saul, which means to station oneself before or offer oneself to another in service. It means asking, "What can I do to serve you?" No one can be under God's authority unless he himself comes under human authority.

In Psalm 134:1, the psalmist writes, "*Behold, bless the Lord, all you servants of the Lord, who by night stand in the house of the Lord!*" He's talking about all those who present themselves to God for service. The priest under the old covenant sometimes swept the floor to clean up the splattered blood of sacrifices. At times they had to skin the animals, remove the refuse from the area, and keep the candles lit and the wicks trimmed. David presented himself to Saul and did whatever his hand found to do.

The Bible describes Joshua as Moses' minister, valet, personal servant (Joshua 1:1). Everything Joshua became, he became through his apprenticeship to Moses. He got it by washing Moses' hands, by serving and watching his mentor.

In 1 Kings 19:19, Elijah finds Elisha plowing a field with twelve yoke of oxen. Elisha gets a glimpse of his destiny and feels a touch of the anointing.

God is saying to you and me, "I'm going to touch you with the anointing." If you don't respond, then the design will never become destiny. The Bible say Elisha slew his yoke of oxen and offered them as a sacrifice to God. Then he ran to minister to Elijah. He became Elijah's servant, the man who washed Elijah's hands, immersing himself in the vision of Elijah.

When Jesus called the twelve, they dropped everything they were doing and followed Him. They recognized Jesus' call and left their businesses, professions, daily tasks, and incomes. They left all those things at His Word. Who is the delegated authority God has placed in your life?

The first lessons David learned in Bethlehem was the lesson of spiritual authority. All of us have to learn this lesson before we go on in God.

There are a lot well-meaning preachers out there who have never learned the lesson of spiritual authority. Many have shipwrecked their faith, landing on the shores of disappointment, disillusionment, and defeat. If they could have only learned this basic lesson of spiritual authority.

The second lesson of Bethlehem is the lesson of personal integrity. David found a king to serve and came under spiritual authority. He found a giant to kill and came into personal integrity. The word "integrity" means firm adherence to a code, especially moral or artistic values, and incorruptibility. It is an unimpaired condition, soundness, or a state of being complete or undivided, completeness. It literally means to be the same thing on the outside that you are on the inside.

As soon you step into your calling, your Goliath will show up. The moment you get a glimpse of your destiny in God, Goliath is going to rise up against you! Why? He knows that the only way for you to reach your destiny is over his dead body. One of you must die for the other to live.

If you reach your destiny, he will die. You will never get out of Bethlehem without a fight. Deal with Goliath in Bethlehem! Call him out of the shadows. Do what David did: challenge and defeat your Goliath at your home church, your Bethlehem. The battlefield is the prayer room of your home church. Call out every hidden sin, every hidden hindrance, and every hidden enemy. Call those things up and out of you. Remember, demons are persons without bodies. They will try to influence the areas that have not been totally surrendered to God. Deal with them in Jesus' name. Take their heads off in Bethlehem or they will destroy you.

Whatever Goliath is, you can handle it in Bethlehem.

What strongman is shouting at you from the shadows of your mind?

What stronghold stands between you and your dream from God?

What vain and taunting imagination needs to be cast down in your life?

For though we walk in the flesh, we do not war according to the flesh. For the weapons of our warfare are not carnal but mighty in God for pulling down of strongholds, casting down arguments and every high thing that exalts itself against the knowledge of God, bringing every thought into captivity to the obedience of Christ. (2 Corinthians 10:3–5)

We pull down the strongholds by the Word of God:

For the word of the Lord is living and powerful, and sharper than any two-edged sword, piercing even to the division of soul and spirit, and of joints and marrow, and it is a discerner of the thoughts and intents of the heart. And there is no creature hidden from His sight, but all things are naked and open to the eyes of Him to whom we must give an account. (Hebrews 4:12–13)

We pull down the strongholds by the Word of God and the blood of Jesus: *"And they overcame him by the blood of the Lamb and by the word of their testimony, and they did not love their lives to the death"* (Revelation 12:11). We pull down strongholds by the Word of God, the blood of the cross, and in the name of Jesus: *"And these signs will follow those who believe: In My name they will cast out demons; they will speak with new tongues*" (Mark 16:17).

There are several kinds of Goliaths; some are internal, while others are external. The internal Goliath falls into three categories:

1. Demon spirits. Remember, demons are persons without bodies. They need to be expelled in the name of Jesus.
2. Our carnal nature. The old nature needs to be crucified.
3. Tradition, which often wears church clothes.

Internal Goliaths want to take the head off your dreams so that they can destroy the divine destiny of your life.

External Goliaths include family members. David's old brothers rose up against him with bitter anger, as did Joseph's brothers.

Another external Goliath is the temptation to substitute the world's methods for God's methods. What are the last seven words of the church? "But we have always done it that way!"

Paul wrote, "*Awake, you who sleep, arise from the dead, and Christ will give you light*" (Ephesians 5:14). In this verse, he is referring to spiritual slumber. Thank God for the training and preparation that goes with the call. But you have to reach out and go for it.

Five steps to your calling:

1. Put your body where your destiny is. "*And the king and his men went to Jerusalem*" (2 Samuel 5:6a). David put his body where his calling was. He changed his environment so that he could remain conscious of and focused on his destiny. God called me to be a minister. God called me to go to Africa. God call me to go to China, or God simply has called me. Why haven't these people ever done what they say they're called to do? It's because they have failed to put their bodies where their calling is (stuck in a rut). God will ultimately bring you to a point where either you put up or shut up. Put your body where your calling is.

It's a privilege to be a preacher. It's a higher calling than to be the prime minister. The great apostle Paul says in Philippians 3:13, "*this one thing I do!*" (KJV).

2. Don't reason with the enemy. Take what is yours. "*Nevertheless David took the stronghold of Zion*" (2 Samuel 5:7); "*And from the days of John the Baptist until now the kingdom of heaven suffers violence, and the violent take it by force*" (Matthew 11:12).

I'm not going to allow other people's prejudices, suspicion, or criticism get in the way; I am not going to allow man-made systems to hinder me. I am taking back my destiny; I'm taking back my call. I'm taking back my inheritance, and I'm going to do violence to everything that would get in the way.

David went against the Jebusites. Just knock them down and take what belongs to you. Don't argue with them. Zion is your birthright. Your destiny is yours. You've caught a glimpse of it. You've felt the touch of the anointing. Take possession of what is yours. The Hebrew language actually has two words for "inherit" or "inheritance." In the Old Testament, the legal term means something inherited as an estate, awarded as a legal heritage, or a possession. The Greek word means "authority." It means to occupy by driving out previous tenants; a day will come when you have to take possession and control of your destiny as God's child.

Jesus said, *"All authority has been given to Me in heaven and on earth"* (Matthew 28:18);

"Behold, I give you the authority to trample on serpents and scorpions, and over all the power of the enemy, and nothing shall by any means hurt you" (Luke 10:19). You have authority, but you need to take action. Paul says in Philippians 4:13, *"I can do all things through Christ who strengthens me."*

Jesus came and served the legal papers at Calvary. It is finished. He paid by His own blood. The only way to collect this inheritance is to stamp it with your faith; reach out for your destiny to possess it. God said to Abraham, *"I am the Lord, who brought you out of Ur of the Chaldeans, to give you this land to inherit"* (Genesis 15:7). He was saying, "I give you this land, this inheritance, so take possession of it." That didn't happen until Joshua came along many years later. Israel struggled to possess the land for many years, and then the people rested for many years. God spoke to Joshua: *"Now Joshua was old, advanced in years. And the Lord said to him: 'You are old advanced in years, and there remains very much land yet to be possessed'"* (Joshua 13:1); *"all the inhabitants ... I will drive out from before the children of Israel; only divided by lot to Israel as an inheritance, as I have commanded you"* (Joshua 13:6). God told his leader that the way to handle the task of helping all of Israel to cease their inheritance was to divide the inheritance by lot among them.

This is a picture of the primary purpose of the ministry of the New Testament church. The ministers of God are to help people discover their birthright and God and then teach and motivate them to seize and possess their inheritance in Christ.

> When you cry out, let your collection of idols deliver you. But the wind will carry them all away, a breath will take them. But he who puts his trust in Me shall possess the land, and shall inherit My holy mountain. (Isaiah 57:13)

If you put your trust in God, you will receive your birthright, and God will help you seize it out of the enemy's hands. We must not only put our bodies where our calling is, but we must also take our birthright away from the enemy (Ephesians 6:12).

3. Dwell in your destiny and collect your destiny. *"Then David dwelt in the stronghold, and called it the City of David. And David built all around from the Milo and inward. So David went on became great, and the Lord God of hosts was with him"* (2 Samuel 5:9–10). David was now dwelling in his destiny. There are two things involved with dwelling in your destiny: ruling and confessing. The word "dwelt" means to sit oneself, to take the proper seat, to find your place, your seat, and your rightful destiny in the kingdom of God. Every one of us has a unique design from God, a divine design from God. When each of us finds our place in the body, then we will have wholeness. Every high throne of authority in the Kingdom of God begins at a humble seat of servanthood in the church. Reach out and take that destiny through servanthood. Seek yourself in your destiny and dwell in it, as David dwelt in his. He sat down, being placed in authority, to dwell in his destiny—the wanderer, the shepherd of sheep, the captain of a ragtag army on the run—and changed his lifestyle forever. He settled himself into his destiny and prepared to stay put for life.

> Behold, how good and how pleasant it is for brethren to dwell together in unity! It is like the precious oil upon the head, running down on the beard, the beard of Aaron, running down on the edge of his garments. It is like the dew of Hermon, descending upon the mountains of Zion; for there the Lord commanded the blessing—life forevermore. (Psalm 133:1–3)

In Luke 24:49, Jesus says, *"Behold, I send the Promise of My Father upon you; but tarry in the city of Jerusalem until you are endued with power from high."*

When David came into his destiny and seated himself in Zion, he enthroned himself in his destiny. Everything came into balance and wholeness because he was totally focused on who and what he was in God. He established himself there.

Why did things happen suddenly? Acts 2:1 tells us, *"When the day of Pentecost had fully come, they were all with one accord in one place."* Each believer was in one place and one accord in the body. Each person filled his or her destiny in the body of Christ, and suddenly, God poured out His Spirit. God is still the same today. When the church gets in order, God will pour out His blessing just as suddenly.

We say we want a harvest and revival, and all we have to do is come into destined order. Once you find out who you are, where we belong, and get into proper order, revival will come. God was ready a long time ago; He is waiting on us.

The second part of dwelling is confessing. David called Jerusalem the City of David. The Bible says in Genesis 1 that God called everything into being that was not. He called for life, and He called for day. God called for the fish, and He called for the trees. God called the universe into being. Romans 4:17 (KJV) says, *"and calleth those things which be not as though they were."* David sat down in his seat of authority and destiny and boldly called Jerusalem his city. "This is my town. because it's my destiny in God." Jeremiah 29:7 says to *"seek the peace of the city."* Invest yourself in your destiny, your call, your Jerusalem—ministry, church, elders, pastor. This is my calling. I'm appointed. This is my destiny. I'm established.

4. Restructure your priorities. *"Then David dwelt in the stronghold and called it the City of David. And David built all around him from the Millo and inward"* (2 Samuel 5:9). The Hebrew word for build means to repair and strengthen and set up. David repaired and rebuilt everything around him, especially around the centre of his destiny below, meaning headquarters. This is where David heard from God and conferred with his leaders. Everything David did was built around a centre, which represents a disciplined life. He built it and ordered his life around his destiny.

You don't fit divine destiny into your current lifestyle. Don't try to make God accommodate you. You accommodate God. Some of us need to destroy old habits and lifestyles and rebuild around the centre of our God-given destiny.

5. Keep on and grow great with God. David put his body where his calling was. He took his birthright out of the enemy's hands and dwelt in it. He called it his own; he changed his priorities: *"So David went on and became great, and the Lord God of hosts was with him"* (2 Samuel 5:10).

He "went on" means that David made a ruling within his destiny, his lifestyle. David's destiny and purpose was to sit, to mark, and throne himself in his divine calling. He wasn't interested in anything contrary to his calling.

David's task was to keep on, pursue, go forward, and make his God-given destiny and lifestyle his own. God then automatically just keeps on blessing.

There were so many challenges before us as a Native Fellowship. It seemed like we took two steps forward and three back. We had our share of disappointments and discouragements. In one of my early memories, we were invited to come and speak at what was then called Indian and Metis Pentecostal Church right on Main Street. The man overseeing this missionary outreach was getting on in age. I thought I had challenges. This man was working with the homeless and addicts on the drag. There was no resemblance between his task and what we were facing. His challenge was like climbing Mount Everest.

He asked me to preach to the youth, so I worked really hard at putting my sermon together. When we arrived at the church, there was no youth group. There were young adults and older people who attended the church. The pastor was doing all that he could for these people: he was feeding them, handing out clothes, and praying for them. At the end of the service, several people came forward for prayer.

The pastor was an older Native man who was laying hands on the people to pray for them, so I went to lay hands on the pastor. I could see and sense that he was discouraged and tired in the work. As I laid my hands on him, the Holy Spirit said, "I am going to send you to my discouraged people." I didn't realize at the moment that I would also have to go through the discouragement process. Their burden would also become my burden. The years went by, the valley experiences became deeper, and it seemed it would be part of my ministry, helping discouraged men and women in ministry, believing that there would be many that were ready to give up and quit and would need encouragement.

David says in 2 Samuel 22:31, 33–35:

As for God, his way is perfect; the word of the Lord is proven; He is a shield to all who trust in Him … God is my strength and power, and He makes my way perfect. He makes my feet like the feet of a deer, and sets me on my high places. He teaches my hands to make war, so that my arms can bend a bowl of bronze.

"*Seek the Lord and His strength*" (1 Chronicles 16:11a).
"*Do not sorrow, for the joy of the Lord is your strength*" (Nehemiah 8:10b).
"*The Lord is my strength and my shield*" (Psalm 28:7a).
"*The Lord will give strength to His people; the Lord will bless His people with peace*" (Psalm 29:11).

Have you not known? Have you not heard? The everlasting God, the Lord, the creator of the ends of the earth, neither faints nor is weary. His understanding is unsearchable. He gives power to the weak, and to those who have no might He increases strength. Even the youths shall faint and be weary, and the young men shall utterly fall, but those who wait on the Lord shall renew their strength; they shall mount up with wings like eagles, they shall run and not be weary, they shall walk and not faint. (Isaiah 40:28–31)

God Himself is my strength and my shield. If He holds the shield before me, not a hair of my head can be touched, and the evil one shall not come near me. But if God is my shield, then I lift my head in the raging storm, in the midst of tribulation, and say, "God is my strength; God is my shield."

God strengthens me and is my strength. If God strengthens me, then through His grace I experience within me His anointing power to accomplish more that I could imagine: *"Now to Him who is able to do exceedingly abundantly above all that we ask or think, according to the power that works in us"* (Ephesians 3:20).

I can overcome barriers, obstacles that would hinder me; mountains can be removed and problems solved. I experience blessing in and around me; doors open and there are difficulties all around me, yet He will go with me. He will rebuke the wind and the waves with the word of His power. God is my strength, and my feet are placed upon a rock (Matthew 8:23–26).

Psalm 84:11 says, *"For the Lord is a sun and shield; the Lord will give grace and glory; no good thing will He withhold from those who walk uprightly."*

If you're facing a dilemma, praise Him. If you're in a valley, praise Him. If you're going through a storm, praise Him. As you praise Him, Jesus, the living Word of God, will walk right into your dilemma and say, "Let it be so." He will be a shield all around you. You have to trust God even when you can't trace Him, believe Him when you have no visible evidence, believe Him when everyone else has given up on you, believe Him when you're on the mountain, but more than that, believe Him when the mountain is on you.

It isn't always the one who is shouting and dancing who is most anointed. The anointing falls on those who have been through the storm and stood the test, who believe through the weeping of the night. The night eventually passes and a new day will bring forth joy unspeakable and full of glory. Weeping may endure for the night, but joy is coming in the morning! Thank God for the joy that comes in the morning after a night of weeping; joy comes in and peace like a river flows within you. Don't give up and don't quit. Your breakthrough is, coming!

"But He knows the way that I take; when He has tested me, I shall come forth as gold" (Job 23:10).

Smith Wigglesworth said, "We have to get rid of our small measure of faith because God's measure is so much greater than ours."[2] A measure that cannot be measured. Don't settle for anything less than the best. And there's nothing better than a life of faith. It brings challenge and excitement.

God has no room for a man who looks back, thinks back, or acts back.

Our little fellowship did some amazing things to move the cause of Christ forward, from visiting women's and men's prisons to visiting nursing homes to minister in song and with words of encouragement. Doors would open, and we had sense of God's favour in so many ways. From hosting special speakers to holding banquets,

---

[2] Smith Wigglesworth, *On Faith* (New Kensington, PA: Whitaker House, 1998), 2.

everything always pointed toward evangelism. Our banquets were well attended, and some of the nicest and warmest people came with their gifts. Evangelist Bruce Thumb was one of many speakers. He was such a kind and caring man, and he was proud of his Native American heritage. He also wrote the play *Heaven's Gate and Hell's Flames*. He took that drama to different cities and aimed for it to be hosted on Native American reservations.

It's amazing to look back on how many people came through our fellowship and where they land in their professional fields. Some would go on to become a doctor, an RCMP officer, a fireman, a teacher, social workers, pastors, and the list goes on. I knew if I could reach just one person within the Native family, many more would follow the life-changing message of the cross. Many would come to believe.

Our vision was to reach the whole family and see them grow in their faith. Many had been influenced either in the city ministry or back in their community church. In some cases, the pastor was doing everything, including leading music and preaching. And there was nothing for the children or teenagers. We'd be invited to some communities to speak to the youth, and most were young adults. Our vision was to grow in the grace and knowledge of the Lord. It wasn't a slogan; it was the Word of God.

The 1980s were coming to a close, and what a decade of ministry! We connected with people on a national level with a common vision to reach our people with the gospel of Jesus Christ. We had some very good preachers come: James and George Kallappa, Dobie Weasel, and many more brought their gifts to help build and equip the body of Christ.

It was clear that the Lord wanted us to move forward and take the fellowship in another direction. The vision was to move our fellowship to the north end and begin an outreach to the people. We started to look for a suitable building that would become our home church. The only way for us to grow was to step out of our comfort zone and take a risk in relocating our fellowship. We would need the help of our mother church, Calvary Temple, to make that a reality.

Lynda and I were also changing our careers. Lynda had worked for the federal government in the Department of Indian Affairs, as it was called back then. She was an executive secretary for the director of the department. The pay and benefits were good, but she wanted to work more closely with our people. She took an entry-level position with South East Child and Family Services. It was a challenge, but removing herself from the bureaucracy was worth it. She eventually moved up to the position of Human Resource Manager and worked toward receiving Certified Professional in Human Resources status. Lynda accomplished much in her position as Director of Human Resources. Sometimes having Christian principles in the workforce has its trials and persecution.

In spite of the hardship, we continued moving forward. The enemy stole much from us, but God would supply even more than what the enemy stole. Before working for the government, Lynda worked for the Manitoba Indian Brotherhood. It was the political arm for our people back in the day. So our history of outreach to our people spans over five decades.

I moved from Jewish Child and Family Services and took a position with Big Brothers of Winnipeg. Then I took a consultant position to help our people who were in various stages of dialysis treatments and, in most cases, had to move to the city for their treatment. From that involvement, a housing project came into being to help people move into the city and find accommodation. During our early days of holding Bible studies in our home and working with Youth for Christ, Lynda was helping the girls' Crusaders and was a camp counsellor. As I reflect over the many years of ministry, I see that God has proven Himself faithful again and again.

I had now been working a full-time job and pastoring our church for at least six years. It was time to make the decision to either go back to Big Brothers from one year of leave or take on a full-time position with the church. When we opened our home for Bible studies and got involved doing church work, it felt like full-time work. My phone rang all hours of the day. In addition to our Native work, I was elected to the board of Calvary Temple. This was my second attempt to be elected; my first attempt came up short because I couldn't make it to the general meeting because I was terribly sick.

The National Native Leadership Council was enjoyable work as we travelled across Canada helping local leadership. In some of these places, they had little or no structure. It had become a tradition from my first camp meetings in northern Quebec among the Cree people to be the morning speaker. The meetings were to start at 10:00 a.m. I am never late for any meeting, so I promptly arrived before 10:00, and I didn't get to preach until 2:00 p.m. The morning was full of testimonies and singing. I was taken aback by the lack of structure and discipline. This would happen again and again in those early years of ministry. Keep in mind, there was little or no urban Native ministries for people.

Pentecost had become a tradition in Native communities, and the Holy Spirit was definitely in those meetings of revival. But just like any other revival, there's the Holy Spirit, human spirit, and evil spirit at work. I began to see most, if not all, of these three things in the meetings. The White Pentecostal churches had the same issues, only a much shorter tradition. Both cultures had experienced Pentecost but moved away from it. It became in name only. The non-Native groups even changed the name of their churches to community churches. But the Natives kept "Pentecostal" on their buildings.

How do we bridge two cultures together? There were definitely differences between both groups. Our people were birthed in Pentecost from the moment of their conversion. They knew that other religious organizations didn't help them or their communities. The Pentecost message that Jesus saves, heals, baptizes, and is coming back again was embraced wholeheartedly. They got saved, and in most cases, it was a like a Saul conversion. Instantly saved and delivered from the bondages of addictions. There was good reason to shout and testify of all God had done for them. But things need to be done in an orderly manner, as Paul makes reference to in his letter to the Corinthians. So you have a White man's version and a Native version of order and conduct. The European classical version of Pentecostalism evolved from its motherland. Our storefront Pentecostal movement was moving full-steam ahead with the mainstream of their day.

I get that you want to save the up and outers. If you can do it in the classical way and with the music that goes with it, go for it. The gospel is for the down and outers and the upper and outers. Keep in mind that at the foot of the cross, we are all equal. We all have sinned and come short of the glory of God.

The music we grew up with was much different. I don't remember ever hearing Bach or Beethoven in our household. No one in our home, my relatives' homes, or in our Indigenous community listened to or played that type of music. Yes, we had instruments from various backgrounds. The Scottish and the Irish had their version of the violin. We called it a fiddle, and the Metis brothers learned it from their French heritage. So the music evolved from the classical to non-classical version. In our home growing up, the fiddler played until he got tired. After a while, it seemed much different and more spontaneous and exuberant than the classical version. However, if you ask a classical listener and a trained listener, the sound had no harmony or ending, and they weren't reading from the music sheet.

Our history had some written but mostly oral traditions passed down the family line. Our stories were in picture form and could be told in many ways in the language spoken. The English and French language evolved from their original context. There are seventy Indigenous languages spoken across Canada.

Traditions and prejudices are carried over from our life before Christ; they come with the old nature. The Greeks, Jews, Germans, English, and French see through the lens of their tradition and culture. The apostle Paul tells us to be transformed by the renewing of our mind. The old man is gone, but the old nature needs to be crucified by the renewing of our mind by the Word for the whole man, his emotions and will.

Paul expresses this truth in Romans 6:17: *"But God be thanked that though you were slaves of sin, yet you obeyed from the heart that form of doctrine to which you were delivered."* The will and emotions! The truth came, and the mind was given the ability to comprehend by the Holy Spirit, but it did not remain there. It moved the heart; it melted the individual, who then put it into practice by the will.

I was in a northern Ugandan village speaking in a small building with local people. We were about fifteen miles from the Sudanese border. I arrived in the small village by vehicle and went into a building that seemed to be made out of mud and sticks. The service started, and to my surprise they sang three hymns that were new to me but the Western missionary had taught them. After they sang the hymns, they took up their locally-made instruments and played their stringed instruments and drums. The service suddenly came alive, and they were beating their drums and playing their homemade stringed instruments. The song was full of joy and life.

They had a version of Christianity that didn't fit who they were as a people. Because the White missionary gave them religion, they believed that if you sang three hymns, you pleased God. All they left them was an intellectual vision of Christianity with very little emotion. Not much different in reaching Native Americans with the gospel message. Our Native Fellowship provided a place for people to experience the Word of God and celebrate and worship God with stringed instruments and drums.

The cultural aspect of our people had long been lost, with only a few adults who could still speak their language. The Native Fellowship provided a place of fellowship and teaching with an expression of our style of worship. But in order for it to grow in numbers and reach out to our people, we had to move to the next level. This would begin the process of moving our fellowship to the north end to reach people with the gospel. So the search was on to find a building to purchase. We had very little money to do it, but we had faith and vision to begin the search.

There were things in the spirit realm that God was to accomplish, and obedience was the key. We found a building for sale on College Avenue. It just so happened that another Native group was also interested in buying it. They had a fellowship on Main Street. Because they had already expressed an interest in the building and had met with the realtor, our district superintendent suggested that we allow the process to go ahead and see if they could raise the financial support.

Three months had passed, and the district superintendent called and said, "Okay, go ahead and make an offer to purchase." The first group wasn't able to raise the necessary support. The building itself was well-maintained, and the congregation that owned it were up in age and had no youth or children. I found out later that in the fifties, the Mennonite Brethren owned the building. The present owners had decided to join their sister church in another area of the city. The building was on the market for $165,000, and that included a piano.

To find that kind of money among our fellowship was going to be a challenge. Most of the men were seasonal workers. They tried to tithe, but it only happened when they were working. And even when they were working, some just didn't tithe at all. Our district was willing to give us a bridge mortgage, but we needed to have the funds raised and a portion of funds toward the mortgage. I sat down with our lead pastor and explained the situation. He said, "I have an investment certificate I can cash in for $95,000." Then I approached a business couple that I knew, and they gave $35,000. We were set to make an offer on the building, and we settled at a price of $160,000. Once our bridge mortgage was in place, we were able to give the funds back to our investors.

The building was now ours, but we were new to the church plant and found out later that Lynda and I were the owners of the building. Somehow our names were placed on the ownership. We had to then give the ownership back to the district, and they would fund our mortgage, and our fellowship would make monthly contributions to the district. So our church was in the status of a developing assembly.

My goal was to make a self-governing church. That would mean leadership within the fellowship would need to be raised. Easier said than done. Some people were able but didn't want the responsibility or accountability to make it happen. They wanted to be leaders, but it had to start in the home. In some cases, men were not leading in the home, and the women were in charge. That was one of the major challenges, from my perspective. Broken and hurting people in some cases are just not able to lead their families or help in the church.

They all enjoyed the new building, but on the first day of possession, half of them didn't show up. We wanted to have a family church, but some people just didn't get the memo. So we started with a vision to reach out to families and our community. We managed to purchase a bus to reach out to the children, and it grew in leaps and bounds. One of the men volunteered to drive the bus, which would require an upgrade of his driver's license.

Soon we had a youth program and mid-week service for adults and children. Of the four adults who were meeting in our Bible study days in our home, only three were still involved with the church. Perhaps we could have done what most Native works did and just focus on adult services. But that was not in my DNA, even though it would have been easier to move in that direction.

We then began having family camp at our district camp grounds. The whole family was involved for a whole week. We had ministry for children, youth, and adults. We did that for about seven years. It was a challenge for the people to come for a whole week and could be a financial hardship to bring the whole family. We were well aware of that and raised support. They had to rent units, and meals were provided. Looking back now, it was a lot of hard work. Because we knew some of the speakers from our National Native Leadership Council and Native American Fellowship, we were able to invite many of the same speakers that we had on a national level. Our friends in Bethel Assembly in Brandon were a big support, and our friends Daisy and Ella helped with the fundraising. Many families were able to come because of their contribution to subsidies from Bethel church and our friends.

At the same time, I was working with a pastor from the Korean Presbyterian Church. They were such a help and blessing. Their church often fellowshipped with us and prepared meals. The Korean food was great, and their kindness was evident. We had plans for a church plant in Sioux Valley, but it didn't work out. They brought a team of young Korean people all the way from Korea to help with our week-long camp. It was amazing! I spoke with the young people who came—or at least tried to speak with them. They were serious young people, showing up for prayer meetings in the morning. When I spoke to them and thanked them for coming, some of the young girls cried because a pastor was speaking to them. In most cases, Korean pastors are respected and held in high regard.

Their fellowship from Korea had a burden to reach Native Americans for Jesus, and a few of their executives came all the way from Korea to visit our church on College Avenue. They wanted to know if we could give a cultural presentation of our people during their visit. I apologized and told them many in our fellowship had no contact with their culture. That's unfortunate, considering we have a colourful and rich history. But the traditional people of our culture decided to exclude Jesus from their expression. The Korean church was such a help and blessing to come alongside of our vision to reach as many people as possible with the gospel. At the same time, they needed us as much as we needed them. Their congregation was getting up in age and needed a purpose.

I was in a Mohawk community, and the Indigenous elders of that area respected our Christian faith and showed up as elders to speak peace and comfort. They welcomed us and spoke in their language. We sat in a circle, and the Chief came and spoke on behalf of the members. My dear friend John was laid to rest and honoured by the Mohawk people. John knew they would hear the gospel message of Jesus Christ.

I knew we needed to pay our own bills and rely less on our home church. I received a call from our friend from Brandon, Daisy. She always seemed to know just when to call with a word of encouragement. Many times the work was discouraging, and at the lowest time, I'd want to quit. The winter was very cold, and our church heating bill was $900. Daisy said, "Pastor, our fellowship in the Native work here in Brandon is closing down, and we have $900 to send to your church." Thank you! God had supplied again.

The next largest outreach besides the tent meeting in the park and the family camp at Manhattan Beach was the production of *Heaven's Gate and Hell's Flames*. It needed at least fifty cast members, but our fellowship didn't have enough people to make it happen. Another church group outside of Winnipeg came with their youth and helped us. We now had enough people to do the drama. By the way, our West Indies Fellowship at Calvary Temple under Rev. David Rose had given us the inspiration to put on the drama. The drama team came with a director and producer, and they had the lights and fog machine.

Thousands of invitations were given out in the community. This time we printed on the invitation that everyone who came would receive a free soft drink. One of the brothers who worked as a sale distributor for the soft drink company donated the drinks. What a response we had from the community! That little church building hadn't seen that many people for decades in its pews. The drama was presented for four nights, and each night the building was packed full. It could only hold four hundred people. Someone told me that the late comers had to be turned away. There was just no room left to accommodate them.

Attempt great things for God and expect great from God. For a small group of people, we had attempted many things for God, and it was always in partnership with other groups or individuals. It's important to have a vision that sees the larger picture. Some people are just small thinkers and never accomplish much for the Kingdom of God. They're good a pointing their fingers and complaining about every little thing, just like Dr. Pharisee, Dr. Sadducee, Dr. Tradition, and Dr. Religion, stuck in their little world of legalism and self importance. The embalmers are the ones who like to start ministries and then unload them onto someone else when things get tough. They're the ones who want what you have but won't pay the price you paid to get it. They'd rather split your church and scatter the flock.

My dear friends Daisy and Ella and others would drive all the way from Brandon to Winnipeg to attend our evening service. It was a four-hour return trip. Yet people living two blocks away couldn't make it to church. They were such encouragers, and they were the anointed crowd. Hang around the anointed ones, like our friends who helped with our drama presentation.

Sister Sherry was one of the anointed ones. She brought street people to the service, and they were always a lively group. They had coloured hair, pierced bodies and tattoos, and ragged jeans, but they were alive in the Spirit. One of the young men in the group called me one day and said, "Pastor, is it okay to baptize our friend in the bathtub?" I told him to go right ahead, just not to leave him under the water too long. Those street kids had no religious background or church history. They were supernaturally touched by the Holy Spirit and were respectful in the house of God.

We had religious kids come and fall asleep in the house of God when they needed to be prayed up and ready to worship the King of kings. They were leaning on their fleshly talent and not on the Holy Spirit. They lost the touch of the anointing. They were playing church and somehow felt that the Holy Spirit had to wait on them. There are so many people like that in the body of Christ, wanting the Holy Spirit to wait on them like He's their personal waiter.

> But as it is written: "Eye has not seen, nor ear heard, nor have entered into the heart of man, the things which God has prepared for those who love Him." But God has revealed them to us through His spirit. For the Spirit searches all things, yes, the deep things of God. For what man knows the things of a man except the spirit of the man which is in him? Even so no one knows the things of God except the Spirit of God. Now we have received, not the spirit of the world, but the Spirit who is from God, that we might know the things that have been freely given to us by God. These things we also speak, not in words which man's wisdom teaches but which the Holy Spirit teaches, comparing spiritual things with spiritual. But the natural man does not receive the things of the Spirit of God, for they are foolishness to him; nor can he know them, because they are spiritually discerned. (1 Corinthians 2:9–14)

During the second half of the 1980s and into the 90s, I reached out to my dad, who was living in a rundown hotel on Main Street. The place smelled terrible, and the living conditions were just horrible. He was not in a good space mentally or physically. I thought to myself, *I have to get him out of here and move him somewhere where he can live in better conditions*. It seemed that every time he started to drink heavily, he'd have no money and have to wait until he got his small pension. His friends would come and drink with him, and they would get loud and my dad would get evicted again and again. This went on for several years of his abusing alcohol. He was a broken man. He'd served his country in World War II, which left him emotionally tormented. He had several medals but never talked about what had happened to him. He was wounded from machine gun bullets and had been held captive as a prisoner of war.

When he was sober, he was the nicest person you could met. He always had a sense of humour and would often tease or poke fun at people he knew. My dad's side of the family was soft-spoken and the hugging type. He had an older sister, but they didn't get along that well, but my other aunties and uncles were nice people. I spent several years trying to help him. The more I tried to help him, the worse he got.

One night I woke up from a terrible dream; in the dream, demons were throwing whiskey bottles at me and saying, "You cannot have him; he belongs to us." I woke up and cried out to the Lord. Shortly after, I received a call from my mom, saying that the ambulance had just taken Dad to the hospital. I drove to the hospital immediately after I heard the news. It turned out that he'd had a stroke and never fully recovered, leaving him paralyzed on one side of his body.

He spent nine months in the Health Sciences Centre and then eventually moved to Deer Lodge Centre. This is where the veterans were put for palliative care. He would never walk again. He could still speak, but he slowly lost his ability to do so. I was his caregiver and took on the responsibility, even though I was extremely busy. But he was my dad, even though he had never been there for me. I loved him and cared for him deeply.

He spent a number of years at the Lodge. I would arrange for a wheelchair van to pick him up and bring him to our family gatherings, until it became too much for him physically to travel. I had a lot of one-on-one time with him, and I told him on one of my visits that I loved him. He said, "I love you too, son." It was a healing moment for both of us. I always knew he loved me, but he never said it. He then said that when he was young, he read the Bible and knew Bible stories. My Grandma Sinclair had deposited the Word of God in his heart.

After a number of years, he developed a serious infection on his leg. The doctor wanted to speak with me about surgery, as Dad might not make it through because of his age. My friend Pastor James Barber came with me to the Deer Lodge to pray for my dad. Pastor James went immediately to my dad's bedside and leaned over and said, "Alfred, Jesus loves you." He then led my dad into a confession of faith in Jesus Christ. I was standing by the doorway and heard my dad call upon Jesus. I had tears rolling down my cheeks. At that moment, when I first believed for his salvation, it came to pass. It took me almost eleven years of witnessing and moving him and loving him before he called upon the Lord Jesus Christ. Never give up believing. The demons of hell threatened me with their evil intent to destroy my dad. But God!

Lynda and I were away once in Cancun, Mexico on well-deserved vacation. I let my sister use my car or I just left it in her back yard. My dad's health was reaching a point where his organs were shutting down. I had no knowledge that he was that sick, or my plans would have been different. I didn't think of telling anyone what hotel we were staying in. I told my sister we'd found a hotel and the colour was pink. In her desperation, she called the Mexico operator.

"I'm trying to reach my brother; he's staying in a pink hotel in Cancun."

The operator replied, "Do you know how many hotels we have that are pink?"

It was urgent that they connect with me and let me know that it was serious about Dad. The Holy Spirit led her to the back seat of my car, where she found a brochure I'd left there. I had circled the hotel where we were staying. What were the chances of her finding the brochure?

The phone rang in my hotel room, and it was my sister. "Alfred it's serious," she said. "It's Dad. He's dying and doesn't have much time left to live."

We arranged for a flight back to Winnipeg and headed right to Deer Lodge. Four days had already passed since Dad had gone into a coma. I immediately went to urgent care, where Dad was lying. I said, "Dad, this is Alfred. Jesus is with you, and He loves you."

Within eight hours of our arrival, Dad passed away. The nurse said that sometimes people like my dad just hang on until they hear that familiar voice. I knew what she meant; my dad always knew when I was walking toward him.

Our church was growing at this point, and our outreach into the community was a priority. The bus ministry was bringing children into the Sunday school program, which ran alongside the morning service. It was growing in leaps and bounds, and it needed more attention than one person could give it. We needed someone to oversee the program. One of the young ladies in the church had a burden to reach and teach the children, so we hired her to oversee the work. At one point, the highest number of children in the class reached 110. She did fantastic work with the children, and we were sad when she resigned from the position. The work was amazing and, at times, overwhelming for one person. The children often came from homes where life was just not fair. Some came from homes similar to my own upbringing in Jig Town, with alcohol, drug abuse, single parents, etc. They needed a lot of love and care.

Our adult congregation were sorting out life's issues themselves. When we come to Christ, we also bring our former lifestyle and old habits. The apostle Paul says in Romans 12 to renew your minds. Our habits are easily formed and much harder to break. If you were an argumentative person when you got saved, you will be the same in your new life until you break the old habit.

> My son, give attention to My words; incline your ear My sayings. Do not let them depart from your eyes; keep them in the midst of your heart; for they are life to those who find them ... Keep your heart with all diligence, for out of it spring the issues of life. (Proverbs 4:20–23)

What's coming out of your heart? What's coming out of your mind? Is your life lining up with scripture, or are you making the scripture line up to your life? Are you molding God in your image? What habits need to be broken in your life? Some people have no problem breaking nicotine from their lives. Others struggle with gossiping and slandering other people. At times they might make up stories and discredit people's character. They are doing the work of the devil, as the devil is a slanderer. That habit needs to be broken off, just like people who lie to themselves and lie about other people. I pray your chains will be broken off you in the name of Jesus.

Some people who call themselves a Christian struggle with pornography. Many years ago, I counselled a man who was well dressed and had a dignified looking wife. To my surprise, the man needed prayer for his addiction to pornography. By the time we left the prayer room, you could hear the chains falling off him. Jesus sets the captives free. He was sincere and wanted the addiction broken. By all appearances, it seemed he'd finally been set free from his addiction. God knew all about it, and He's patient with us.

> He who dwells in the secret place of the Most High shall abide under the shadow of the Almighty. I will say of the Lord, "He is my refuge and my fortress; My God, in Him I will trust." Surely He shall deliver you from the snare of the fowler and from the perilous pestilence. He shall cover you with His feathers, and under His wings you shall take refuge; His truth shall be your shield and buckler. You shall not be afraid the terror by night, nor of the arrow that flies by day, nor of the pestilence that walks in darkness, nor of the destruction that lays waste at noonday. A thousand may fall at your side, and ten thousand at your right hand; but it shall not come near you. Only with your eyes shall you look, and see the reward of the wicked. Because you have made the Lord, who is My refuge, even the Most High, your dwelling place, no evil shall befall you, nor shall any plague come near your dwelling. (Psalm 91:1–10)

What a wonderful promise! Almighty, all-powerful. It is "God Almighty." This name occurs about fifty times in the Old Testament. El Shaddai was a name by which God was known to the patriarchs in Genesis 17:1. Some scholars trace its origin to the verb *shaddai*, meaning "mighty, unconquerable."

Let Him reveal Himself to you as the Almighty God for whom nothing is impossible. He is an all-sufficient God, eternally capable of being all that His people need.

I stayed connected with other pastoral ministries in the city. It seemed quite hectic trying to line up our schedules. I was on a TV program called *It's a New Day*, hosted by Willard Thiessen. He was such an easy man to work with. He was always full of the joy of the Lord. I'm sure he faced a lot of challenges keeping his TV programs growing across Canada. I lost track of how many times I appeared on TV with him. I believe it was Willard who told me that I had the gift of an evangelist. Then several other people kept saying to me that I was an evangelist.

It was at this point that I sensed that the Lord wanted me to resign from the church I had guided since the early eighties. Our church had started in our living room in Garden Park City. I had no idea that it would grow into a developing assembly within the Pentecostal Assemblies of Canada (PAOC), or that I would be an ordained minister in 1997. Before that, I held credentials with the fellowship. I knew God had a call on my life, long before I even understood. That day when I sat outside the steel mill and looked up into the sky and saw that airplane, I knew that the Lord would take me places I never thought possible. Believe me, I had no idea how that process would work, but the Holy Spirit came over me that day in such a powerful way, and forty-four years later, I still remember the touch of the anointing.

Chapter Five
The 1990s

THE NINETIES WERE full of challenges, with our fellowship relocating to the north end and the purchase of the building on College Avenue. This would be another chapter of our ministry, and there were many obstacles and challenges before us. I was excited to have our own building and reach people with the gospel message. It was in my heart to have a family-type of fellowship. Most of our activities were family-based; we celebrated birthdays, had women's ministry, and held picnics in the park, attracting at one time 250 people. The ladies held wedding showers and helped with newborns. I baptized many people in Bird's Hill Park, until we had a church donate a baptismal tank.

Perhaps I was taking a direction and didn't realize that the majority of the people didn't see it that way. They were quite willing to settle for less than God's best. We have so many promises in the Bible to guide us through life, including promises and instructions on how to have better relationships with your spouse and children. But that would require a change of lifestyle, a change of attitude, and the renewing of our minds.

I had many opportunities in the 1980s for self-improvement and making adjustments to my life. I had men as mentors and a pastor who loved to win souls. These men poured their lives into me in leadership training, discipleship, and friendship.

Initially I had no real sense that getting my credentials and being ordained was a priority, but Lynda encouraged me to move forward with this. So I received more instruction in the Word of God through correspondence courses with Global University. I was now pastoring in a new location as well as studying for my ordination. After many years of travelling across Canada with the National Native Leadership Council, I sensed that God wanted me to travel full-time as a missionary-evangelist.

A local pastor friend in Winnipeg was taking a group of people from his church to Argentina for missions in 1996. They were going to do the drama *Heaven's Gate and Hell's Flames* in Santa Fe. Lynda and I were invited to join the team and travel to Argentina. Before we ever heard about the trip, I was attending a leadership conference at *It's a New Day*. The guest speaker was from Argentina, and he spoke about the revival they had experienced. The man of God, Carlos Anaconda, was used for the revival in Argentina. He was a businessman working in a nut and bolt factory. He said if you ever get a chance to go to Argentina, go. As he said that, he pointed his finger right at me. We had friends, Carol and Wayne Parks, who were interested in going as well. They'd been missionaries in Argentina years before but always felt a burden to go back and help whenever possible. I wanted to minister to the Indigenous people, so I wrote a letter to the visiting minister. He replied that there was a group working in northern Argentina with the Indigenous people. So we had an invitation in hand, and now we were going to make plans to travel with the team.

These trips require you to raise your own funding, so we had to come up with the funds. During this time, someone broke into our house while we were at work. Whoever did it knew we would be away and used a heavy hammer to break the door down. They stole many items, including Lynda's jewellery, which had a value of a few thousand dollars. We made an insurance claim and now had the necessary funds to make the trip.

This trip would change our lives forever and change our perspective for years to come. All things work for good to those who love God. Who would think that a thief would make the way for us to go on our first missionary trip to South America? We still had no idea what lay ahead of us on the trip. We both sensed a peace and calm that we were in the will of God.

Upon arriving in Buenos Aires, we were jet-lagged and tired. We finally made it to our hotel for a well-deserved rest—at least that's what I had in mind. The pastor and his wife looked like they'd had a good sleep on the flight down. They were eager to show the people downtown Buenos Aires and go to their favourite restaurant. They instructed us to meet in the lobby at a certain time and head to the restaurant. Lynda and I were dead on our feet and told them we would catch up to them later. All I heard them say was that it was a famous steak house. They gave me the name, but I forgot it.

We lay down a for few hours and then headed to the lobby to find our way to the group. I didn't speak any Spanish, and the hotel staff spoke little or no English. We tried to explain to them that we needed a taxi to head to the restaurant. They had overheard the pastor and group talk about the restaurant. I think the group all took the subway to the downtown. I ordered a taxi, and the girl at the front desk gave the driver the information for the restaurant. We arrived as our group was just sitting down at the table. To the pastor's surprise, Lynda and I showed up. The first thing the pastor asked was how we'd paid for the taxi. I replied "250," and he thought I meant dollars. I explained it was 250 pesos, which is less than five dollars.

We had already travelled across Canada, the USA, and Mexico by this time, so we knew how to find our way around cities, even though Buenos Aires had population of 15 million people. We didn't speak Spanish, nor did we have a phone with translations on it. Some of the people carried Spanish dictionaries with them. It was kind of funny when they were trying to witness to a local and find the right words.

The next day the pastor gave instruction for the young people and some adults to take the subway to the bus station. The rest of us took taxis with all the luggage to the station. The taxi driver smelled like he had alcohol on his breath, and the other driver decided that they were going to have a race to the bus station. They were travelling far too fast for my comfort level, especially when we came to four-way streets with no stop signs. Upon arriving at the bus station, some of the adults wanted to explain the gospel to the driver. They fumbled through their Spanish dictionary and tried to win their first convert to Christ. Well, that didn't go well; the man was only interested in getting paid.

We were now on the bus heading to Santa Fe. The bus was amazingly comfortable. It took us six hours to get to Santa Fe. They took Lynda and I to a hotel and the other group to another hotel. The next day, Wayne and Willy arrived to pick us up and take us to the bus station. Pastor Willy told us how to order a ham and cheese sandwich.

Now we were heading to a place called Resistencia. It would be a twelve-hour bus ride, and we would have to change buses halfway. We had this amazing sense of peace and trust in God. Whatever God had in store for us would be good.

We arrived close to midnight, and all I had was a phone number and the name of someone who would meet us at the bus station. It was a long bus ride, and the farther north we went, the less English would be spoken. We were met by Pastor Daniel and his wife, Alice. Alice could barely pronounce my name, but I heard someone trying to speak my name. They greeted us and gestured to us to come with them. They took us to Pastor Daniel's parents' place; it was a small villa with an upstairs bedroom. They kept telling us that we were going to see the witches. Lynda and I just looked at each other.

I was under the impression that I would be speaking to a gathering of Indigenous people in a large assembly, so I had packed my suits and dress shirts and ties for the occasion. Pastor said no suits, no dress shirts, and no suitcases. "We leave tomorrow to see the witches." They showed us a video of their ministry, but it still hadn't registered. Okay, we leave tomorrow in a half-ton truck that looked like it had seen better days. There were four of us in the front and at least six or more people riding in the back.

Now we were heading to a place called Formosa, another eight-hour drive north. The road was covered with red dust, and we were all covered in dust. The truck broke down halfway, and it seemed like we would be stranded. The pastor had spare parts in the truck with him, so the young men got busy repairing the truck. Then out of nowhere a bus came by, so I asked Alice when the next bus would come. I thought that if the truck wasn't repaired, we could catch the next bus. Alice said, with her limited English, "One week." Here we were in the middle of nowhere with a broken truck. We spoke no Spanish, and Alice could barely speak English. At best one word of English would come off her lips.

They finally were able to fix the truck, but we had to head to the closest town for a part to be welded. Pastor drove to place called J.J. Castelli, and the welder did his thing. This put us behind, so we arrived in a small town near midnight. At this point we'd been travelling all day. The town had no lights on, but I thought that there must be at least a Motel Six in town. The pastor said he was taking us to where they kept the mice (maize). I wondered what we'd gotten ourselves into. Witches and now mice?

We ended up in a small building with one room and an attached washroom with a squat toilet and a pipe with water coming down for a shower. They gave us a wooden pallet for a mattress and a blanket, not that we needed a blanket, as outside the temperature was still very warm. These small green bugs kept landing on me as I was trying to read my Bible with my flashlight. I got up and closed the wooden shutters so that the bugs wouldn't get into the room.

Lynda seemed to adjust to these inconvenient situations better than I did. She told me to keep the shutters open. I explained that there was no screen and the bugs were coming in. The next morning we woke up early and looked up, where we saw this huge spider web hanging from the ceiling. It was full of those green bugs. I began thanking God for the spider webs. It changed my perspective of my surroundings.

You need to know that I was far out of my comfort zone. At times God will take you out of your comfort zone just to show you how much He cares for you. We were in the middle of nowhere and hardly knew the people we were working with.

The morning arrived, finally, and we got to minister to the witches. Pastor picked us up and off we went into the jungle. We arrived in a little village and met the people. They weren't witches; they were called Wichi Indians. They lived in third-world conditions: no electricity, no running water, and little huts made out of mud and sticks. The children were barefoot and their clothes were dirty. Their faces looked dirty, and their hair was straggly and out of place. Our hearts were moved to see the pastor and his wife loving these people.

The ministry began with putting on the maize, which was mixed with corn meal. The pot must have held five gallons of this soup. Pastor and his wife then began washing the children's hair and removing the lice from their heads. Lynda took a pair nail cutters and started cutting their fingernails. After the meal, it was time to share the Word. Keep in mind, I normally speak for one hour, but not this time. My first sermon lasted a whole five minutes. My translator, Alice, could only do five minutes at a time. That's all that was needed. Five minutes and the Lord saved these precious people.

Alice told us later that she first learned English in school but never used it for years. The Lord spoke to her a year before we arrived and said that she was to learn English again. She said, "Why, Lord? The Wichi don't speak English." The Lord was preparing her before we even knew we were going to Argentina. There we were in the middle of nowhere holding outdoor meetings with these people, and I preached for five minutes. The more English I spoke, the more Alice spoke it. It was coming back to her, and she was full of confidence.

The Wichi responded to John 3:16 and gave their lives to Jesus. When they came forward, they fell to their knees and confessed Christ as their Lord. We spent a week with Pastor Daniel and Alice Lopez. What an amazing couple to work with. It was heavy lifting all the way. We moved from village to village. Alice was now up to speed with her English and asked me if we wanted a cold drink. I said, "For sure." So we pulled over to a store with Alice leading the way. She spoke to the clerk in perfect English and ordered drinks for us. She then laughed at herself, not realizing that the clerk had no idea what she'd said. From nothing and not speaking English for years.

We went back to Resistencia covered in red dust from the top of our heads to the bottom of our feet. We had so much joy and peace. It was soon time to head back Santa Fe and join the rest of the group. Before we left, I had time to sit and talk with Daniel about how we could help in the future. He gave me a list of things that would help him with his ministry. They already had a training centre for the Wichi Indians, but the building needed an extension. He also needed new guitars for the pastor and bicycles for them. He also wanted honey boxes to harvest honey, which would support the ministry. I asked him how much he would need, and he said $5,000.00 US. Without any hesitation, the Holy Spirit gave me a nudge: "Tell him you'll raise the support."

We took a plane back to Santa Fe from Resistencia. Believe me, we were extremely blessed by the whole experience. Back in Santa Fe, we caught up with the other group. They were wrapping up the *Heaven's Gate and Hell's Flames* drama. They were all pumped up and celebrating.

Lynda and I went out for coffee and ran into our team leader and his wife. He said, "You guys look pretty good considering where you've been." He must have known something of the area we'd just come from. It was a dry and very hot place. I believe one day it reach fifty degrees Celsius. Every place of shade was a place of refuge. We stopped in one particular area where there was a pond of water covered with a green slime. The Wichi children were using throwaway cans and dipping them into the pond to drink the water. The team in Santa Fe told us that they all stayed in a fancy resort with a swimming pool.

Back in Canada, our team leader wanted to get together and share our pictures. So about a month later, we all met at his church with our slide pictures and photos to share. The other group showed pictures of their fancy resort, and then we shared our third-world pictures of the Wichi Indians. Their jaws dropped. Some of them were hoping to have had that kind of experience.

It was time go and try to raise the $5,000 US toward Pastor Daniel's projects. I started calling local churches to see if they were interested in having me come and preach and show the slide pictures of our mission trip. I had a few churches lined up and began the search for donations. Well, I shared the vision and the need, but it was going to be much harder than expected. So far, I had raised $75 dollars. I didn't have time to travel throughout the district looking for funds. I was still having to take care of my own church and raise support for our needs. I said, "Lord, this is going to take a very long time. I need help!"

The phone rang and it was somebody calling from *It's a New Day*, wanting me to come on their national TV program. I went on and shared our experiences working with the Wichi Indians in their third-world living conditions. I told them about the financial need and how much I needed. I looked right into the camera, and it was like I was speaking to an individual. It turned out I was speaking to one person. Three weeks later, a phone call came in from *It's a New Day* telling me that one lady had given $7,500—exactly what I needed for Daniel's project. Thank you, Lord, for your faithful servant.

Now that the project money was raised, I still needed to raise support to cover our travel expenses. Lynda was still working full-time and would use her holiday time to come with me. We knew the living conditions, and it certainly wasn't going to be a vacation for her. For over twenty-five years, Lynda used her vacation time to come with me to various countries. Believe me, it was not a vacation at all, but she knew the sacrifice required to do missions. At her workplace they offered an extra week of vacation time for perfect attendance. Lynda achieved that five years in a row. She would have done it anyway, but it was a bonus.

One year she slipped down the stairs at home. We went to the hospital and found out she had a cracked rib. In spite of that, she drove herself to work, and she was driving a standard shift car. She mentioned that every time she shifted the gears, the pain was too much. She drove until her rib was healed, and she earned the extra week bonus.

Chapter Six

International Evangelism

WE CERTAINLY DIDN'T have it easy on those mission trips around the world, and it came at a huge cost. It wouldn't have happened without the people who prayed and gave sacrificially to make it possible. We were always mindful of the partners who helped us reach thousands and millions of souls for Jesus. Now that we had the funds in place, we would to go back to Argentina and help Pastor Daniel reach the Wichi Indians. But this time we knew what we were getting into—at least we thought we did, until later in our trip.

We arrived back in Argentina, but this time without the drama team. We made our way to Santa Fe and then flew up to Resistencia. Then we drove back up to Formosa to be with the Wichi Indians and Daniel's team. This time we stayed in another building and slept on the floor and then visited Wichi villages again. We travelled to even more remote places than before. We overnighted in a place and stayed together in someone's home. The women and the men slept in separate rooms, so Lynda and I were separated for the night, but I couldn't sleep because the men were snoring. So I went outside and then Lynda joined me. We stayed awake all night and listened to the jungle animals, and believe me, it was creepy.

The next morning, we got together and prayed with our local hosts; it turned into a forty-five-minute prayer meeting. The young men I stayed with were touched by revival. They were praying and lying face down on those dirty mattresses and crying out to God. That really touched me. In the early eighties, I would pray for the Christian church and God's people for long periods of time. I didn't realize at the time that I had been praying for revival. When revival comes, it touches God's people and they revive and become soul winners.

Back at the main base camp, you could hear drums beating all night and all day. We found out later that we were in the midst of witchcraft, and they were calling and drumming all night to bring down curses upon us. Those people didn't want Christianity, so they were trying to curse us. They were praying against the work of God.

One day a drunk person came to the main camp and tried to attack me. The pastor and his team quickly prayed against him and removed him from our camp. That same night, Lynda was attacked in her dreams by a demonic force, and she woke up with a bruise on her arm. She said that the voice that came through the drunk man was the same voice that attacked her during the night.

We headed back to Santa Fe rejoicing in all that the Lord had accomplished through us. Upon our arrival, the attacks on Lynda would continue. That spirit tried to break her neck and tried to silence her by pushing down on her throat. I called back home to my son-in-law and had him call the church group for prayers for us. The Lord had shown me a picture of a military campaign, and we were trapped on the frontlines of this conflict and warfare. We were inside in a bunker or a dug-out hole and were under extreme attack from the enemy.

The prayers that went up for us came down on our enemies. As result of the prayers, we were able to move from the frontline to a place of safety. But we still weren't out of trouble yet. Lynda was physically shaken by what had happened to her. At this point, Pastor and his wife prayed for Lynda, and we then headed back to Canada. The pastor showed concern for us as he drove us to the bus terminal. This was our introduction to spiritual warfare and our training ground for future ministry.

The Lord showed me again different levels of spiritual beings in high-ranking positions over various countries. I told the dream to Pastor, and he confirmed the various countries in South America that were heavily involved in witchcraft, voodoo, and mixing it with religion. They would often combine these forms of witchcraft with the local religions. That would explain why Pastor Daniel would stop on the roadside before heading up to Formosa to be among the Wichi Indians. He knew that we were in a spiritual battle and that prayer was one of the weapons we would need again and again. Paul instructs believers to *"Put on the whole armor of God ... For we do not wrestle against flesh and blood, but against principalities ..."* (Ephesians 6:11–12a).

Back in Canada, we rejoiced in the outreach among the Wichi Indians and how we were able to deliver their much-needed supplies. They also added an addition to their training centre for the equipping of the pastors. Whatever happened to Lynda during the ordeal in Argentina seemed to have settled down. But not for long.

We were in Mexico for vacation and were celebrating our wedding anniversary. One evening, Lynda began manifesting strange behaviour. She first said that she wanted to kill herself, and then she was thrown to the floor and began banging her head against the tile floor. With her long fingernails, she began strangling herself. Then a voice came out of her mouth, but it wasn't her voice. The demonic voice said, "You are not worthy to live." She began asking for drugs and saying, "I'm going insane. Take me to the hospital." Then she went to lie on the bed for what seemed a very long time. She began throwing herself back and forth like a rag doll, lifting her body into the air. Whatever had a hold of her was tossing her back and forth. It was crazy, and then for the next three days I was engaged in spiritual warfare. This bizarre behaviour turned into a full-blown suicidal attack.

I thought to myself, *Perhaps if we change hotels, that might ease the conflict.* So we packed up and moved to a much nicer place. But it just got worse, and now we were on the sixth floor of a newer hotel. This time she wanted to jump out the window. This battle went on for three days. I had to stand in front of the windows so she wouldn't jump out. I was totally exhausted and worn out by the battle. I told the devil, "Okay, I'll come back to Mexico and preach the gospel."

I called my sister in Canada and told her what was happening. I asked her to meet us at our home and bring her pastor. I knew he had knowledge of deliverance ministry. I changed our airline tickets and headed to the airport. On our way to the airport, Lynda tried to jump out of the car, and the driver was going fast. I held on to the door handle until we arrived at the airport. I was able to get us an upgrade to sit in business class, hoping and praying nothing more would happen to her.

On the plane she began to manifest again but not as severely as at the hotel. She was biting down on a hand towel and seemed very agitated. We arrived late from Cancun and went home. My sister and her pastors were waiting for us. I was totally exhausted and so was Lynda. This was now day four of these manifestations.

The pastor had a word of knowledge as he was praying for Lynda. He said, "I see what seems be like an octopus sitting with three long arms clinging to the top of your head." As the pastor shared this, Lynda began manifesting again. Her eyes rolled up and only the whites of her eyeballs were showing. She began throwing herself back and forth on the sofa. Pastor prayed, along with my brother-in-law and sister and myself. I'd never been in a battle like this before, nor have I since.

As the pastor was discerning these three arms over Lynda, we recognized them as fear, insanity, and death. Before Cancun was developed into a resort, it was known as a fishing village and a place where they brought the insane people. Now it's known for its dream: insanity and drugs! The spirit of fear and death. Lynda kept on saying, "I want drugs" and "I am going insane; take me to the hospital." Later she told me that the enemy was telling her, "I'm going to kidnap and murder your grandchildren if you say anything about the voice of fear." The enemy gained access to her mind because of the spirit of fear. Now that door was open, and these spirits that dominated this area of Cancun—the spirit of insanity and the spirit of drugs—had gained access.

Just before we left for the vacation, there'd been a plane crash involving Lynda's co-workers. Four people died in the accident, which weighed heavily on Lynda's mind. One of the men who died attended our church. On the day of the flight, he changed seats with his co-worker, and she survived. At one point, Lynda had taken on three roles in the organization as a result of the plane crash. So we'd headed to Cancun for a rest, but it turned into a nightmare. The battle would continue for another three weeks or more, but not as intense.

A month after that, Lynda was attending a conference in Banff, Alberta and was manifesting again. It was bizarre; she wanted to commit suicide. So we headed back to Winnipeg, and she attempted to open the car door to jump out. Back in Winnipeg, it was time to get medical help for her. I took her to the emergency room at Seven Oaks Hospital to see a psychiatrist. He diagnosed her with clinical depression; her body and mind could no longer handle the stress of the past three or four weeks. I was reluctant to leave her in the hospital, but I knew in my spirit she needed professional help. The doctor seemed like a nice man and wanted to help her. So she was admitted to the psychiatric ward, and I asked the doctor how long she'd be in the hospital. He didn't know.

"We're going to have to find the right medication for her."

I left the hospital not knowing how long she'd be in there. I hadn't eaten much that day, so on the way home I stopped at Subway and stood in the parking lot. I quoted the Word of God to myself, from Romans 8:28: "*And we know that all things work together for good to those who love God, to those who are the called according to His purpose.*" I said to the Lord, "I love you and trust you. When I don't see immediate results, I know you hear us and care for us! And nothing can separate us from your love." No matter what you're going through, you can trust His heart of love for you!

Lynda was hospitalized for one month in the psychiatric ward. Believe me, it was hard to leave her there! But the battle was taking a toll on both of us! We'd done everything possible—prayed, rebuked, and resisted the devil—and now we needed to take the next step and seek medical help. God gives medicine to help us. If you can defeat the enemy with common sense, then try common sense. The battle we went through has helped so many others to be set free from their captivity.

Before entering the hospital and before our Banff trip, people were calling our house for prayer. One lady who called was suicidal, and we prayed over the phone and she began to cry uncontrollably. God delivered her from the spirit of suicide. Another call came in from a backslidden believer calling for restoration. A friend who called was in a deep depression. As we prayed for him over the phone, he said, "There's an angel in my living room." It seemed like so many called with various prayer requests. They had no idea what we were going through at the time. Lynda had a dream, and the Lord showed her a picture of the church caught in a bunch of elastics. The church was struggling to get untangled. Then she saw a flaming sword slicing through the elastics and setting people free.

We carried that anointing around the world, setting the captive free. At the same time, the devil was using a group of people at church to divide and spilt our congregation. I wasn't surprised at some of the people who were involved. They were just baby Christians and wanted to be leaders but never were steady long enough. If they were unhappy and always complaining, they'd just take it with them wherever they went. Some of those who left saw their marriages fall apart and their children rebel. I wasn't surprised. Others went on in their ministry. I was happy for those who remained faithful. The first thing one needs to do is forgive people. The devil uses bitter people who slander others; they're just doing the devil's work. As my former lead pastor would say, they're just puppies nipping at your heel.

I spoke to our presbyter about the conflict, and he said that sometimes revival happens when people leave through the back door. They had no idea what we were going through at the time. The devil uses whoever is willing to partner with him. He never plays fair. If you're in a battle and still standing, he turns up the heat, just like he did to those three Hebrew men who were in the furnace, and the king told the people to turn up the heat seven times hotter. The heat was turned up hotter, but we are still standing! Over the years we've seen some of the people who attended the church. It was always good to see them living for the Lord.

Lynda was off work for a total of three months, so she didn't have to deal with the work, her situation, or the church split. What the devil meant for evil, God always turns into good. He always remains faithful!

"You will keep him in perfect peace, whose mind is stayed on You, because he trusts in You. Trust in the Lord forever. for in YAH, the Lord, is everlasting strength" (Isaiah 26:3–4).

Keep your mind steady in every conflict; renew your mind, as the apostle Paul says in Romans 12. With renewed minds, the result is perfect peace.

The Lord will always take you through the conflict. You may have to go through some unpleasant things, but at the end of it, He will be your portion and high tower.

> He who dwells in the. secret place of the Most High shall abide under the shadow of the Almighty. I will say of the Lord, "He is my refuge and my fortress; my God, in Him I will trust. Surely He shall deliver you from the snare of the fowler and from the perilous pestilence. He shall cover you with His feathers, and under His wings you shall take refuge; His truth shall be your shield and buckler. You shall not be afraid of the terror by night, nor of the arrow that flies by day, nor of the pestilence that walks in darkness, nor of the destruction that lays waste at noonday. A thousand may fall at your side, and ten thousand at your right hand; but it shall not come near you.

Only with your eyes shall you look, and see the reward of the wicked. Because you have made the Lord, who is my refuge, even the Most High, your dwelling place, no evil shall befall you, nor shall any plague come near your dwelling; for He shall give His angels charge over you, to keep you in all your ways. (Psalm 91:1–11)

You may go through the fire, but like the three Hebrew children, there is the fourth man in the fire. And He will bring you through no matter what you're going through. He will be with you! He promises never to leave us or forsake us.

Around this time, the pastor from Santa Fe, Argentina wanted to know if we were interested in going to a conference in Florida and to the Brownsville revival. It was past registration for the conference, but Willy knew Steve from his time in Argentina. He was able to get us into the conference, but before that he wanted to take us to see the man God was using to bring revival to Argentina's cities. Signs and miracles and deliverances were happening in his ministry.

I was eager to meet him because I'd always wanted to see revival, from my earliest days of conversion. Back in those days, God had me praying over nations for revival. So we went to meet him in the next city from where we were in staying. One of his assistants was taking the service that night. There were two tents set up behind the platform; one was white, and the other was yellow. The platform was huge; it was high enough so that people could actually stand up underneath the stage. As it turns out, that's where the prayer team prayed during the message for souls to be saved, and they were doing spiritual warfare. There must have been at least twenty-five to fifty people praying right under where the preacher was preaching.

After the preaching, the people were called forward for salvation, so they were lined up in front of the platform. During the altar call, people either manifested a demonic spirit or were baptized in the Holy Spirit. The altar workers went up two by two and stood next to people. When the manifesting took place, two workers either carried the person or escorted them to where the two tents were set up. As it was later explained to me, the people being delivered were put in the yellow tent, and the people receiving the baptism of the Holy Spirit were in the white tent. As we were walking by the deliverance tent, I looked in, and sure enough, there was a young man screaming and foaming at the mouth. He was being prayed for by a team of workers. This would be the beginning of our ministry into Argentina, where we would serve for over twenty-five years.

We made it to the Brownsville Revival for a pastors' conference that Pastor Willy knew about through his connections. So Lynda and I headed down to Florida to attend this life-changing event. Because we'd paid for the conference, we had first opportunity to enter the building, and seats were set aside for us. The lineup to get into the building was extremely long, and people had been waiting from the early morning. Someone told me they had been to the revival meeting several times.

There was this expectation in the air, but the crowd of pastors seemed somewhat quiet. Suddenly the room was filled with a loud noise. The revival crowd were inside the building, and now it would go to the next level of excitement. The worship and praise music came alive, and the crowd sounded like we were in a rock concert. Then the evangelist, Steve, came and preached. I wasn't impressed with his preaching, as I was raised under expository preaching. But he was going for souls, calling for repentance from the crowd. There was something definitely happening in the building, and the altar was full of people. In the afternoon we heard from the likes of Pastor Yonggi Cho.

During the break, I headed to the bookstore in the parking lot. There was quite a large crowd, and people were buying books and CDs. I'd had an interest in revival from the early eighties and had travelled to many Indigenous communities that had been in revival, so the singing and dancing weren't new to me. But God was doing something extraordinary. In the bookstore and on my way to the checkout, I asked the Lord why the people were coming. He answered, "Because they are thirsty."

In 1999, the Lord was speaking to me about the great commission and going into all the world to preach Christ. It was at this point that I let the church committee and our district know that I would be resigning my pastoral position and going into full-time work as an evangelist to the nations. The church plant was now under the district level and was considered a developing assembly. We had paid down the mortgage considerably on the building. We raised funds to replace the outdated furnace and put in air conditioning before we left. We managed to put in place a pastor's salary of 50 per cent for the next two and half years. I gave three months' notice and didn't know what lay before us. One Native evangelist told me, "If you're going to be an evangelist to the Native people, you'll have to sing and preach." I could preach, but I had no musical gift, nor could I sing. I already had two strikes against me, but God not only sent me to preach to First Nations people, He also sent me to the nations with the message of salvation. With my involvement with the NNLC, I had already made connections with many pastors throughout Canada and the USA.

Months went by, and no invitations came my way. I began to doubt whether I'd made the right decision. We had a mortgage payment and two car payments and one salary coming into the household. We had to sell one car in order to kept going forward. It seemed like a setback in my mind. To say I was discouraged is an understatement. It was more than I could bear. I lay in bed, not knowing where I was heading. It left me discouraged and doubting. Did I make the right decision?

Months seemed to have gone by, and then one day the phone rang. It was Pastor Roger Cree. He was pastoring in Taholah, Washington and wanted me to come and do revival meetings. It was the beginning of a relationship that lasted for many years. Pastor Alfred Brown heard I was doing meetings in the area and asked if I was available to do meetings with him in the Squamish, Washington area. We also developed a good relationship. These men were considered to be elders within the Native American Fellowship. I was starting out on the path of the vision God had given me to preach the gospel nationally and internationally.

The meetings in Washington were new to me, and I enjoyed working with brother Brown and, of course, brother Cree. Roger Cree not only had me busy with the church meetings, but we also visited jails and hospitals. He was such a good man, and we worked together very well. He then moved back to Wisconsin and invited me to come and preach in his community. We did prison ministry meetings together and then visited his oldest son. Brother Cree and brother Brown were visionaries and builders of the Kingdom of God. I respected them both and enjoyed the many meetings we had together.

Pastor Bruce Brown invited me to speak at Fruit Land Bible Camp in Washington state. It was a family camp, so we decided to take our grandchildren with us, Matthew and Caroline. They both were active at camp. Caroline was always helping in the kitchen. She'd get up early on her own and make a beeline to the kitchen. They both sang in the choir, and brother and sister Brown and others sat around Mathew at snack time and talked with him. He just loved all the attention.

Brother Brown wanted to take us out for a steak dinner, so we loaded up the van and off we went to the local restaurant, which just happened to be connected to a casino. Matthew and I were walking through the casino, and his eyes grew big. "Look, Grandpa, video games!" It was such a blessing to have our grandchildren come along, and during the day we'd take them swimming down at the local lake. There were teenagers playing on the dock near the deep water. I kept my eyes on him, but the teenagers stepped up and helped. It was reassuring that they were watching over them.

Pastor Roger Cree and Pastor Alfred Brown were men whom I respected and were good friends. They both have gone on to be with the Lord. I feel a sense of obligation to continue to come alongside younger men in ministry and be their friend and help in any way possible. Over the years, you accumulate skills, insight, and wisdom in ministry that is invaluable in order for you to pass it on to others. My goal in ministry has been always to come alongside other ministries to be a servant and help them. I have always wanted to be partners in ministry and never at any time to replace people in their ministry. There are too many in the mission field today who want to claim ministries they never planted or worked to obtain. They'll say, "I planted three hundred churches in Africa." No sir, you stole those churches by promising something you never delivered.

As time went on, I would eventually reach eighty-five Indigenous communities in North and South America. I had spoken to national leaders with The Native American Fellowship of the Assembly of God in many states in the USA and the National Native Leadership Council. When God opens a door, no one can close it. The Lord opened doors not only in the Indigenous communities but also among other groups.

We were invited to join our friends on a trip to South Korea in 2000. What a blessed time we had. Our daughter Jeanette paid for Lynda's airfare, so she joined me. The conference was sponsored by Yonngi Cho's brother, who had a church membership of 150,000—not as large as his brother's church in Seoul, whose membership was 700,000-plus. The conference was well attended, with delegates from around the world, and there was no charge. You only had to pay your own airfare. They were in a large building, like a hotel; we had our own room and all the food you could eat. There was a large delegation from the Philippines, Canada, the USA, and other countries. We heard testimonies of what God was doing among the nations. They had aggressive mission programs around the world.

On Friday night, we attended their prayer meeting, and the building was packed with people praying. Some of them came right after work to attend these evening prayer rallies. Then they took us on a tour of their prayer cell groups. Lynda and I were sent to have lunch with one group of ladies, and they were so kind and generous.

Before going to Korea, I was invited to speak with a group of Korean youth connected with Love Corps. The crowd was a large and excited group of fifty-plus youth, all the way from Korea. Pastor Brown had a partnership with the Korean people. He was the pastor of Vancouver Native Pentecostal Church, and they had established a long working partnership, spanning many decades. The Korean group had a burden to reach the Indigenous people of Canada and beyond. The youth were on fire for God. I was touched by their passion to reach souls for Jesus. That was twenty-four years ago; they're probably married with children, and who knows where they are today. But God knows! They could be missionaries and pastors serving somewhere in the world today. Thank God for His grace.

I met several Filipino pastors who were eager for me to come to the Philippines. I agreed to go, and that was the beginning of a long partnership with the Filipinos.

Lynda and I stayed on after the conference and had someone from the conference drive us to Seoul. It was about a two-and-a-half-hour drive from where we were staying. The man didn't charge us for the trip, and someone else from the conference booked us a room in Seoul at the Hilton Hotel. He knew a brother in the Lord who was in management. It was a five-star hotel and such a nice place—beyond what we expected. The cost of the room normally would be $500 US a night or more, but we got it for $150 a night, including breakfast.

It was a special moment when we visited Yonngi Cho's church. It was amazing to hear and see their vision. The service we attended had twenty thousand people in attendance. That was only one service; they have seven services a day. Their services are livestreamed to the many congregation members that make up the nearly 700,000-plus members. The Sunday school was held in a high-rise apartment block. It was at least twelve storeys high, if not taller.

They shared with us the history of their humble beginnings from the 1950s, when they used an old army tent left over from the Korean War. This would be the beginning of a ministry that would have a global impact.

They then took us up Prayer Mountain, and we sat and prayed for Canada and the nations of the world. Lynda and I prayed for revival for Canada, especially for First Nations people. Our dear friends Jack and Peggy were on the trip with us, and they were also involved in First Nations ministry. As we sat there on Prayer Mountain, many others gathered in different locations. Some of the people stayed longer, and I heard that there are prayer retreats throughout the year, and some come for many days and even weeks.

Well, it was time to travel back to Canada. Eventually we would be part of revival meetings in Canada and USA and other parts of the world. The year was 2000.

In that year, I followed up with the pastor from the Philippines. After a number of attempts to reach him, there was no communication. During the same time, Pastor H.H. Barber introduced me to Danny and Remy, who are Filipinos. Pastor Barber had been on a trip to the Philippines with them prior to us connecting with them. It was the beginning of an amazing outreach to the Philippines that would last for many years. We planned on having a crusade or evangelistic meetings and workshops with the local pastors.

The date was September 11, 2001, and we were in the Philippines, along with a team from Canada. Danny and Remy invited three friends, and Lynda and I had invited a young man named Tim Bath. I'd met Tim during revival meetings in Tyendinaga Mohawk Church. He was such a talented young musician and could play just about any instrument you put before him. The Lord used him in many different ways on the trip. He has gone on to be with the Lord now. We sure miss him. He was gone too soon, but never forgotten.

Our meetings went on in spite of what happened in the USA on September 11. It did have an impact on our crusade, and the numbers were far lower than the bishop had expected. It seemed like fear had gripped that nation, and few people were out and about. We still experienced a tremendous number of people who received Christ in their lives. Bishop Isagurrie was truly a man of God and believed in miracles. He was the spiritual father of Danny and Remy. He also owned and operated a large school and was the bishop over many churches in the Philippines. He was well respected among his peers and well-travelled in the Philippines. We worked with him for many years through the decade and saw firsthand thousands of souls won for Jesus. So many people were healed of various illnesses, from the blind seeing to the deaf hearing and a wheelchair-bound woman rising up and walking again.

In 2001, we held several meetings in the greater Manila area and then travelled to a placed called Tuguegarao City. Our mission team along with the bishop travelled by bus, and Lynda, Tim, and I flew up north by plane. On the way from Manila, the mission team experienced a delay in the mountain region. Apparently, a mudslide held them up, but they eventually made it to the city. That was only one of many obstacles we encountered on this trip: first 9-11, then a mudslide in the mountain and a downpour of rain in the Manila area.

When we were holding meetings in the Manila area before heading up north, we were at the venue and the crowd was really small. The rain must have hindered them from coming out. I had never seen such rain like that. It was pouring buckets of rain. One of the pastors who was part of the crusade committee stood up and prayed that the rain would stop. As soon as he finished praying, the rain stopped immediately. We had the breakthrough and breakout. The crowd rushed into the building; hundreds, if not thousands, of people came through those doors. Tim was leading the worship along with the local musicians. They worked very well together. Those Filipino men and women are so talented in so many ways, from the worship team to the dancers waving banners. I just love these people. They have such a gift of hospitality built within them.

Back in the building, the anointing fell on people, and now the outpouring of the Holy Spirit fell on the crowd. There was a great gathering of people responding to the message; hundreds rushed forward, some for salvation and others for healing. God was moving by His Spirit. The prayer team was in place, and the many pastors in attendance helped pray for those who came forward. The pastor who prayed for the rain to stop was one of the committee members involved in the planning session. He was a Baptist pastor working alongside the Pentecostal and charismatic members. The bishop told me later that he was always challenging the decisions of the committee and was very difficult to work with, until he fell and tripped and broke his ankle just before the meetings. The rest of the committee members prayed for him, and God healed his ankle instantly. From that point on, he was the biggest supporter of the meetings.

The bishop rented a mansion for us. It came with a swimming pool and restaurant attached. We had more than enough rooms for the team. Tim was out and about in the neighbourhood gathering coconuts. I'm not sure how he got them, but he did. Tim was one of the nicest young men you could ever meet. Such a talented man who gave his all for Jesus.

Back in Tuguegarao City, the team finally arrived at the hotel, and we were happy they all made it safely. The hotel was located right on the main street, and the traffic noise was loud. No mansion this time, and the air was so polluted we could smell the fumes in our room. We thought initially it might be bug spray, but as it turned out, we were breathing carbon monoxide in our bedroom from all the traffic below. Keep in mind that there were no emission controls, and there was a cloud of pollution in the air.

The bishop started organizing the crusade as soon as he arrived. He invited a deaf college group to come and do skits and drama. They were really good and had prepared themselves well for outreach. The worship team brought it all together, and the Word was preached.

We faced another obstacle in this area. This time it came from a religious group. The local priest was going door to door in the neighbourhood and threatening the people if they attended our meetings; he told them that they would not be buried in the church cemeteries. No doubt that brought fear into the hearts of many. But it didn't hinder the many who came; they were hungry for God and needed a miracle. The poor have very few options when it comes to medical care, especially with serious illnesses. They will come for prayer for healing. In most cases, God heals them.

In spite of the persecution, the people came by the hundreds. The deaf team had at least twelve members in the group. During the altar call, some of them came for prayer. The bishop brought them onto the platform, and God healed three of them from their deafness. They were speaking and hearing. Wow, what an awesome moment! There was so much joy among us in spite of the obstacles the enemy put before us.

Afterwards, Bishop wanted to take us to a special restaurant. We loaded ourselves into a four-seater Jeep, and thirteen Filipinos jumped in for a ride. There were seventeen of us in a four-seater Jeep. The food at the restaurant was awesome. There was a fish pond connected to the restaurant. I have eaten food from all around the world, from a seven-star hotel in Dubai to eating with my hands in a refugee camp. But that night in Tuguegarao was more than special. Despite breathing in fumes for three nights, the food had such special flavour to it. It was like heaven prepared the food; it was sweet like a honeycomb. This would be one of many times like this while visiting the Philippines.

Because of 9-11, the security was over the top at the airport. We went through five security checks before getting to our gate. The Philippines is one of the poorest countries in the world. I was somewhat taken aback by how many armed security guards were protecting businesses. There were armed guards guarding MacDonalds and Jollibee, and anyone who carried cash had security. They have a high crime rate and many kidnappings and low-level drug pushers. Prostitution runs rampant throughout the cities.

We visited a woman's prison to share the gospel. When we arrived, to our surprise, we saw children inside the prison with their mothers. It was set up like dormitory, and the room was filled with women. We heard that many were serving a life sentence for drug trafficking. They were from the underprivileged and poorest segments of society. It was sad to see the conditions they were living in, especially their children. I'm not sure how long the children remain with their mothers. In any case, it was sad to witness.

The bishop had arranged for us to stay at a mission house somewhere in the Manila area. Metro Manila has a population close to 15 million people. Poverty in the Philippines has been linked to bad governance, corruption, and a political system dominated by political families. The country's poorest provinces are ruled by political dynasties. Natural disasters have exacerbated poverty in the Philippines.

While we were staying at the mission house, the coordinator at the house wanted to know if anyone needed a massage. A local pastor was available to give massages at a low rate. This pastor turned to out to be a former prisoner and was hiding from a criminal element. He had quite a testimony that he shared with me. It was one of those conversations you never forget. He told me that he'd been in the military at one time, and the leadership was corrupt. One of the top leaders ordered him to kill someone, and he refused his command. As a result of disobeying him, his life was now in danger. The officer he'd disobeyed was reaching for his gun, but he pulled his out faster. He shot him first, but the general didn't die. As a result, he was sentenced to prison but now was on the hit list of the corrupt military leader. Now his story gets even more bizarre and crazy. His military training skills were his means of survival in prison. His only source of money came by having human matches, like cock fights. Two men would be tied together by a leather strap on their wrist and had knives for combat. It was a fight until death. I asked how many fights he'd been involved in, and he said five. He'd earned 30,000 pesos or $700.00 Canadian.

His story got even more bizarre. He told me that the guards allowed criminals out at night to rob and steal. They'd return later and share the stolen property with the guards. He was telling me these stories as he gave me a massage. He was able to escape from prison. In his mind, he never got fair trial. The general recovered from his wound, but now the man was on the run and hiding from this group of thugs and murderers. By the way, he gave his heart to Christ and is born again. I gave him some extra pesos and a pair of sunglasses to help disguise himself.

Tim was up for his massage. I said, "Tim, make sure you show him respect and give a good tip." I don't think I'd ever had a five-time murderer give me a massage before or since. His hands were very strong and powerful, but thanks be to God, he's now a new creation in Christ Jesus. He told me about the attempts on his life, how his house was torched and set on fire. He tries to see his family but is always aware that he's on the hit list. Amazing heart-wrenching story.

Many things happened aside from the crusade events. If I could interview the thousands of people who'd been touched by Jesus since 1996, could you imagine the stories of souls that were saved, lives changed forever, relationships restored, bodies healed, depression lifted, demon possessed set free? I'm in total awe of what God has done through His people, and I had a small part in it. The people from our home church, Calvary Temple, helped us with so many of our outreaches to the Philippines, as did the friends and family members who had a burden to reach souls for Jesus. With the little resources we had, God performed so many miracles.

We travelled to Danny's hometown, a place called Vigan City, in 2002. This would be one of many trips to Vigan City and the surrounding area. The team from Canada and the local leadership had planned a major outreach to predominantly a Roman Catholic area. The pastor had booked us in a renovated mansion in the middle of town. A Filipino brother would be instructing the local leadership on godly governance. He was such a nice man to work with and was well-known in the Filipino community.

Danny and Remy brought their teenage children with them on this outreach. This would be their first trip to the Philippines with their parents. It was an exciting time for them, but it was a culture shock as well. They'd been raised in Canada and had lived there all their lives.

The bishop had rented a stadium in Vigan City and had at least twelve local pastors, if not more, working with him. He had sent funds to bring people to the crusade stadium. They came by truckloads from the surrounding area. Hundreds gathered for an amazing outreach.

The first night of the meetings, approximately 1,500 to 2,000 people showed up. The praise and worship team and the Word were powerful. The altar call was given, and around 1,500 people came forward for prayer. The team prayed for everyone that night, and that was only the first night. Back at the hotel, the brother who'd come to help with the governance workshop said to the bishop, "You got yourself a strong evangelist to pray for that amount of people on the first night." I wasn't aware that at the crusades in the past, they prayed for people on the last night. Thank God He had given us the breakthrough anointing to start the crusades, and it would be that way in every service afterwards.

I always prayed and believed that God would be with us at the beginning. I had been in settings where preachers would wait till the end of their meetings to give an altar call. Jesus said to His disciples in John 4:35, *"Do you not say, 'There are still four months then comes the harvest'? Behold, I say to you, lift up your eyes and look at the fields, for they are already white for harvest!"*

I believe God wants to give us an accelerated harvest! (John 4:35)

He wants to give us accelerated opportunities. (Revelations 3:8)

He wants to give to give us accelerated power. (Luke 4:18)

He gives us the task and the anointing. (Acts 10:38)

The rest of the crusade events went like that nightly. It was truly remarkable, with an amazing presence of God. Keep in mind that this area is 99 per cent Roman Catholic, and they can place a strong emphasis on works in salvation.

> But God, who is rich in mercy, because of His great love with which He loved us, even when we were dead in trespasses, made us alive together with Christ (by grace you have been saved), and raised us up together, and made us sit together in the heavenly places in Christ Jesus, that in the ages to come He might show the exceeding riches of His grace in His kindness toward us in Christ Jesus. For by grace you have been saved through faith, and that not of yourselves; it is the gift of God, not of works, lest anyone should boast. (Ephesians 2:4–9)

A number of people were baptized in water after crusade; at least twenty people made that decision. With brother Danny's help, we went down to the local swimming pool, and the people who'd received Christ were baptized openly and unashamed of their new faith in Jesus Christ. They were baptized in the name of the Father and the Son and the Holy Ghost.

This partnership with Bishop and his group went on for many years. I admired and respected the bishop. He was a spiritual father to many under his leadership. His brother was such an anointed translator for most of our crusades. He had a good command of English and preached with power. He was the bishop's right-hand man, someone he could trust. The bishop no doubt had many challenges and obstacles in his path, but he just kept his hand to the plow.

At one planned crusade, and to my surprise, the attendance was down considerably. I was disappointed and shared my concerns with the bishop. We had provided more than enough funds to make the event possible. The bishop shared that half of the local leadership of pastors had pulled out their support. He didn't tell me why, but I could speculate that some of these men wanted more money or say in the event. This seemed to happen more than once working with these local pastors. One time we were organizing a crusade, and the people working to make it happen demanded more money. I called the bishop, who knew these men, and he was upset with them. Working in these third-world countries, it was no surprise to me that some, but not all, were corrupted by their poverty. Unfortunately, this mindset enters the churches and leadership.

My personal experience working in these countries is that it can be a drain on your energy and time. There are organization that help third-world countries facing horrible times of famine and drought. Is it enough? Absolutely not!

There are three types of leadership I have experienced working with.

1. Those who are what I call professional beggars.
2. Those who have the ability to organize an event but have no financial resources.
3. Those who have the means to provide for a keynote speaker and bring him or her from abroad.

Pastor James Okot from the African church was heading to Uganda for an outreach and workshop in a place called Lira. His wife, Grace, asked if I could go with him. She knew he couldn't carry the event himself. I'm not sure how he found himself without another speaker, and I was already making plans to head over to do a conference in the Philippines. Lynda was going to join me there, but she'd be travelling by herself. I booked my around-the-world airfare ticket and was heading to Uganda, East Africa to join my friend James Okot in Lira. It was an amazing conference and a blessing to speak to the leadership in Lira and preach the gospel. It was a lot of travelling in short period of time. I went around the world in thirty days, passing through Amsterdam, Uganda, Kenya, Dubai, the Philippines, and the USA in thirty days. That's not including travelling by cars, buses, and taxies. I must have travelled at least sixty hours by cars.

My son Patrick helped me in Uganda, and Simon Peter drove me to Entebbe airport. It's so important to have reliable people to work with when you travel to these countries. Patrick has grown so much into a man of God, and I'm so proud of him. Simon Peter has been leading his fellowship and no doubt has planted eight thousand to ten thousand churches in East Africa.

When I left East Africa, Lynda headed to the Philippines to meet me in Manila. We had coordinated our travelling time precisely to arrive at the same time in Manila.

That was an amazing connection, and we headed to the hotel. I had no idea how we were going to the place in the mountains. The bishop called me at the hotel and said we'd be leaving that night and would have a six-hour bus ride to a town, and then we'd head up the mountains with another all-terrain vehicle.

Bishop said, "I'm sorry to say that the conditions are very rough. I ask that you don't bring sister Lynda with you to the mountain people." He explained that these people had a history of being head hunters. I thought I heard him say it stopped in the 1960s. So sister Lynda stayed behind in Manila.

The driver showed up and we headed up to a place in the mountains. I had no idea where we were going, and it seemed that way for most of our trips to the Philippines. But God knew. We spent many hours travelling into the mountains on gravel roads with no guard rails and a several-thousand-feet drop below us. I was sitting up front with the driver and could see the very long drop below. The driver was so excited to see the bishop, he kept looking back and talking to him. They were, of course, speaking in their language and laughing. I told the bishop to please tell the driver to keep his eyes on the road. There were no guard rails and a certain death if you plunge over the mountain.

We arrived at our destination, and it was not what I'd imagined. It seemed like the place was on the side of the mountain. The young pastor greeted us and was so grateful we'd made it for the Fire Conference. His church building had three walls and a tin roof to cover the area. He escorted us to our sleeping area, which was made out lumber and had a few bedrooms. It was like roughing it big time. The kitchen was just outside our sleeping area, and it opened at four in the morning. You could hear the cook chopping away at vegetables and chicken at 4:00 a.m. I fell asleep at 1:00 a.m. There were outhouse toilets and a barrel of water connected to an outdoor shower. It seemed like the roosters and cooks were competing over who could make the loudest noise.

Sister Lynda was back in Manila waiting for our return. She had no idea where I was, but she trusted in the Lord for our safe return. The Fire Conference moved forward and the people began arriving on their Jeepneys. They came from all over the mountain areas hungry for God. This would be a major outreach and catalyst for our next crusade the following year. At least two hundred people gathered under the hot tin roof. There was so much joy and overwhelming gratitude expressed to us for coming and holding the conference. The presence of the Lord was so tangible. Some people didn't want to leave the conference, some stayed in the area, and others loaded up their Jeepneys and headed back to their side of the mountain.

In spite of the rough conditions I had to endure, it was worth it. There was an amazing sense of joy unspeakable and full of glory. They were glad that an international evangelist would come all the way from Canada to minister to them. I was the first Canadian evangelist to come to the mountains. Keep in mind, I'd just arrived from East Africa from another conference with Pastor Okot, and now I was on the side of the mountain preaching among former head hunters (not this group, but their ancestors). By that time I was tired from travelling and preaching, and I needed a rest. The conference was a success, and I was so impressed with the young pastor building a church on the side of the mountain. He'd put this conference together and hosted us with joy and a deep sense of gratitude.

It was time to head back to Manila, so we made our way down the mountain. I believe we headed down to place called Bam Bang to catch a bus to Manila. I was beyond exhausted and needed a hot shower and change from my dirty and dusty clothes. Brother Danny and I travelled by bus to Manila. He was going to help me get to my hotel, but I told him I could make it by myself. The bishop had told me, "When you get a taxi, let him know you'll give him some extra pesos and he'll get you to the hotel quick." So I did that and off we went.

It turned out to be the ride of my life. The driver was crazy and speeding down the streets of Manila. Now Manila must be the densest area, with 15 million people, and everyone is in a hurry. It turned into a white-knuckle ride, and I held on for my life. He was speeding and nearly missing cars, Jeepneys, and people on the way. We came upon a car accident, and the police and people were standing around the vehicles. The taxi driver honked his horn at the police and told them to move out of the way. He missed his turn, and rather than go around the block, he put his car in reverse and headed toward the hotel. I figured the bishop was right when he said he would get me to the hotel the quickest way possible. But he was still half a block away, so I said I'd walk the rest of the way. I wasn't sure if he was going to speed off with my luggage in the back seat, so I reached over and opened the back door to retrieve my belongings. I paid him the pesos and was grateful to live to see another day.

In the meantime, sister Lynda was waiting back the at the hotel. She'd been out shopping and was enjoying catching up on her rest. And definitely praying for our meetings. I was covered in dust and extremely exhausted from my journey up the mountain. After a very long, hot shower, a good meal, and plenty of rest, I started to feel somewhat normal. I shared my experience with Lynda. Now I knew why the bishop hadn't wanted her to come on the trip. I'm sure she would have survived and enjoyed the trip, although it was one of the most challenging experiences in the Philippines so far.

Bishop told me that he and his brother had gone to the mountain people thirty-five years ago to reach the former head hunters. At the same time, the Communist party was also trying to recruit these people for their cause. So he said he had to lay low for a couple of years before trying to reach the people with the gospel. The Communist party sent threatening letters to him, telling him to stay away from the mountain people. I enjoyed working with men who had a never-give-up attitude. Some men will quit at the slightest problems. Not the bishop. He demonstrated courage in the midst of the battle. Bishop told me that he and his brother would travel up to the mountains, and on the way down they'd sit on logs from the logging truck. Whatever it takes to reach the lost for Christ.

> After the death of Moses the servant of the Lord, it came to pass that the Lord spoke to Joshua the son of Nun, Moses' assistant, saying: "Moses My servant is dead. Now therefore, arise, go over this Jordan, you and all this people, to the land which I am giving to them—the children of Israel. Every place that the sole of your foot will tread upon I have given you, as I said to Moses ... Be strong and of good courage, for to this people you shall divide as an inheritance the land which I swore to their fathers to give them. Only be strong and very courageous, that you may observe to do according to all the law which Moses My servant commanded you; do not turn from it to the right hand or to the left, that you may prosper wherever you go. This Book of the Law shall not depart from your mouth, but you shall meditate on it day and night, that you may observe to do according to all that is written in it. For then you will make your way prosperous, and then you will have good success." (Joshua 1:1–3, 6–8)

A LEADER'S TRAITS

A leader's courage develops as the fruit of encouragement. Moses revealed this leadership role while shaping Joshuas to be the young leader. He encouraged him in leading God's people into the Promised Land, emphasizing the seriousness of his task. Then the Lord Himself encouraged Joshua after Moses died, telling him not to fear but to be strong and courageous. The officers of Israel's army also encouraged Joshua, promising their loyalty and urging him to take the leadership. Those who would shape leaders, encourage them. Those who follow should do the same.

Our Joshua-Jesus would take us into the land of promise. There are eight thousand promises in the Bible. The Old Testament saints had five books and we have sixty-six books from which to receive the revelation of God's inspired Word.

Joshua led them into the Promise Land.

Jesus, our Joshua, leads us into the Land of Promises.

God said to Joshua that every place the sole of his foot tread upon would be given to him, as He'd said to Moses. From the wilderness of this Lebanon as far as the great river, the River of Euphrates, all the land of the Hittites, and to the Great Sea toward the going down of the sun would be his territory.

Our Jesus said that wherever we put our Amen, meaning coming into agreement with God's Word and promises, will be ours.

These meetings would lead to an even bigger event the following year. This time we'd be holding a major crusade in the town of Bam Bang. The mountain people would be joining us in town, along with many others in the surrounding areas. Bishop had gathered sixty pastors to join us for a major outreach. What an amazing time we had in the four nights of meetings. They were coming by the bus loads and in Jeepneys; thousand were gathering. In all, ten thousand people came for the crusade.

We had plenty of dancers and worship teams. The place exploded with worship and singing and dancing. They were dancing with their cultural expression of their faith in Christ. The stadium was packed, and nobody wanted to leave. It was joy unspeakable and full of glory. The celebration fell from one person to the next, and soon there was a huge circle of people moving around and around. It seemed to go on forever, and the people didn't want to stop. The bishop and his wife had been waiting for this moment for over three decades. I had never been in such a celebration setting like that in the Philippines.

We had another gathering the following year with our Canadian team: Pastor Johnny and Tony from Quebec, and our Filipino friends, Danny and Remy. Lynda and I were thrilled to have our Indigenous Cree friends from Quebec join us. These men would also join us in Argentina for a major outreach. It was always my desire to see Indigenous people be involved in missions. They'd supported mission work by giving and praying, and now it was hands on in another country. They were both thrilled to be involved in the work. Johnny and the church he pastored were such a great encouragement in helping to reach the lost for Christ.

Two Indigenous ladies from North Carolina joined Lynda and I on a crusade in Vigan City, Philippines. They were both anointed, one in worship and the other in teaching, and they carried a prophetic gift. Susan Oxendine and Cheryl Bullard were from Hope Mills, North Carolina. They were both such a blessing as part of the team. I should also mention Julie Cooper, a Cree lady from northern Quebec who also joined us in Argentina. Our goal was to bring as many Indigenous people with us to the mission field as we could. We are still hoping to bring even more if the Lord should tarry. Gordon Iserhoff will be joining us for our East Africa trip in 2024 in the country of Uganda for two major conferences. Gordon also joined us in Argentina thirteen years ago.

Back in Canada, I was travelling across the country and speaking at churches and holding camp meetings. I was invited to northern Quebec to a community called Ojibougamu. The Cree community was just settling in the land of their ancestors. I'm not sure of all the history, but these people had been displaced. Now they have land and huge financial settlements from the government. They were still living in makeshift houses, and in some case in tents. The local pastor put up a tent in the centre of the new location and would be holding a tent revival meeting. I have been back many times since the relocation. The community has developed with paved roads, a school, a community centre with swimming pool, and a rich history of the Cree people.

I have held camp meetings among the Cree people since 1989 and have enjoyed the many years of fruitful meetings. I have a deep love for the elders and the trailblazers who have taken the gospel message to their communities. I have met men and women of God over the many years, such as Billy D. and Johnny W., Matthew C., Alfred C., Harry M., Johnny D., Wille G., Matthew G., George. G., Malcom T., George H., Allan E., and so many other gifted speakers and singers. The leadership in these Cree communities have brought blessings and prosperity. Our earlier years of doing camp meetings and leadership training have proven fruitful. Most of the communities had a passion for missions, sending men and women to the mission fields of West Africa, the Philippines, Argentina, Russia, and many more places that I'm not aware of. But I believe they heard about missionaries such as myself and wanted to do something more for God.

I think back on one of the mission trips to Uganda, when we met a Native American lady from Wisconsin in a shopping mall in Kampala. I said to Lynda, "That lady looks like she's Native American." We introduced ourselves to her and asked her what had brought her to East Africa. She was married with children and grandchildren back in the USA. She told us that when she was a child attending Sunday school and hearing about the people of Africa, the Lord gave her a burden to reach them with the gospel message. Now that she and her husband were both retired, they had committed themselves to go to Gulu to look after an orphanage for at least one year. She said her children thought they were a bit crazy, considering they had grandchildren. But the Lord placed that in her to reach the African people.

We were certainly moved by her testimony and encouraged by her faith. I mentioned to her that I had been to Gulu a few times and I left it at that. I had been there when I witnessed children leaving the surrounding villages to come and sleep on the streets of Gulu. They left the village because of the killing, kidnapping, and rape there. Crime runs rampant in that part of the world. A group of rebels had formed what they called The Lord's Resistance Army. They would kidnap the children, male and female, and make them part of the army. The boys were child soldiers, and the girls were made sex slaves. The city was in a horrible mess, with garbage dumped in the centre of it. Last year I was back in Gulu, and the city looked to be in a better condition, considering Uganda is one the poorest countries in the world. I still have that image in my memory of the children and adults gathering in Gulu to sleep on the sidewalk. Things like that touch you deeply.

In 2001, I received a call from Pastor Larry from Kitimat, British Columbia. I first became aware of Larry from our National Native Leadership Conference in 1988 in Saskatoon. I saw this crazy guy in the sound booth running and jumping up and down during the worship and praise time. Larry was part of the delegation from B.C. attending the NNLC. Back then, the B.C. delegations carried the vision across Canada under the leadership of Pastor James Kallappa and his group from the B.C. district. I'm sure if you heard Larry's testimony, you too would be jumping and praising God.

He called me from B.C. and wanted me to come and do revival meetings. He said we could go for ten days. When I arrived, the board decided they could only do seven days due to budget limitations. It was evident revival had come, and we were committed to it. The revival meetings lasted six weeks, and I preached every night for forty-two days straight. Larry and his beautiful wife had been praying for revival for a number of years.

Larry not only pastored the church, but he also had a cleaning contract with a local grocery store and other places. He worked all night, and the evening services were dedicated to the revival service. During the course of the revival, Larry's wife was hospitalized for serious health issues. In spite of her condition, she told Larry that they had prayed and waited too long for revival, and he should continue with the meetings. There were many conversions, and eighty-five people were baptized in water. The Lord brought healing and deliverance to many over the six weeks.

Pastor Larry brought in Danny Martin from Vancouver to help Richard with the worship and praise. There were others on the worship team from the town of Kitimat who came to help. Danny not only came to help, but he also took on the role of youth pastor and eventually would become the lead pastor. His revival commitment lasted almost twenty years from the day he received the call from Larry. My brothers in the Lord, Larry and Danny, have gone on to be with the Lord. I thank God for these faithful servants of the Lord. They have gone to receive the rewards and will hear the Master say, "Well done, my faithful servants; take up thine inheritance."

The revival was moving forward, and Pastor Larry told his board that they needed to bring Lynda for the revival. That was great. I hadn't seen her for three weeks, and we were only halfway through. Lynda was still working full-time, so she came and was part of the history-making event. She gave up most of her holiday time to come to revival meetings.

Most of the new converts were wanting to be baptized in water, but the church building didn't have a baptismal tank. It was winter time, so the water outside was too cold. We had a meeting of the minds, and Art L. had the idea of renting a hot tub from town and bringing it to the village of Kitimat. I said, "Please anoint it and bring it into the local gym." We were holding the revival meetings inside the gym because there wasn't enough room in the church building. The crowds on the weekend were much larger, so our revival meetings were held in the gym.

The hot tub arrived in the village, but we couldn't bring it into the gym because the floor was made of wood. The hot tub must have weighed a few thousand pounds and would have definitely crushed and ruined the floor. So they decided to do it outside of the building. It was the first baptismal service held outside in the winter. It was cold, but the first group of twenty-nine really didn't care. God had touched them and they fell in love with Jesus.

There would be more healings and deliverances throughout the six weeks. Some nights the church building was filled to capacity, somewhere over two hundred people. On the weekends, we were back at the school gym with more people coming. News spread throughout the village and into the town. One night a group of around twenty teenagers came to the gym to heckle us. So openly and publicly I rebuked them and told them to be quiet. They settled down, and at the end of the service, I called people forward for prayer. Those youth came forward. I spoke about suicide and depression that night, and God was wanting to set people free. They came and fell to their knees and some on their backs. The heckling crowd was saved and set free. Pastor Larry told me later that when I rebuked them, he thought we had lost them from the service.

The services afterwards moved forward with power and the anointing. The crowds were witnessing for the first time a genuine revival, and we were making history. The local girls' basketball team was heading to a tournament and were trying raising support for their travel. I said to Pastor Larry, "This is an opportunity to bless them for their tournament." So we took up a love offering to help them reach their goal. They were overwhelmed with the gift. In return, they sent us money to help us in the revival.

The revival was beginning to touch the village. One of the men in the village was saved in the revival meetings. He was the local bootlegger, and his house was the party house. But Jesus saved him and set him free. He went home and poured all his booze down the drain. His partying and bootlegging days were over. There must have been hundreds, if not thousands, of dollars of booze poured down the drain.

Simon brought his sister to the revival meetings and she was saved as well. They both came every night and sat in the front row and never missed a service. Simon's sister worked as cook in the restaurant of the local care home. At times she sat in the church building in the front row with flour still on her clothes. Some nights she never made it home but came right to the revival services. Simon was also a giver and tither. One time he had his fishing permit and was heading out to the ocean. Before he even left the channel, a larger vessel pulled alongside of him, and the vessel's caption said they had more than enough fish to fill their quota. Simon said they gave him enough fish to fill his quota, so he turned his boat around and headed back to the village. He said he saved a huge amount of money in fuel alone. He recognized it was the hand of the Lord that blessed him.

Another man came from Terrace, B.C. He was at most of the services and was a big giver toward the revival meetings. There were so many good things happening during the revival. Keep in mind that during revival, however, there are three spirits working at the same time: the Holy Spirit, the human spirit, and the evil spirit. This has been true in most, if not all, revival meetings.

I had now been living in one room in a hotel in town for almost six weeks. The powers of darkness were not happy with what was happening in the village. The battles were sometimes furious in the invisible realm. I was often attacked in my dreams by the local evil spirits. One ruling spirit had been there since time immemorial. This spirit would come and put his chiseled face made of wood or stone next to my nose. These ruling spirits came to harass, torment, and intimidate me. Prayer, praise, and the Word kept me throughout the revival. I would keep my worship music playing 24/7 and spend a great deal of time in prayer.

I met with the pastor one time in my hotel room, and we sat before the Lord in the stillness of the moment. The pastor never told me anything about what was happening in the church. I learned that the less communication with the pastor, the less I knew, the better. This would give me freedom to speak and preach and be led by the Holy Spirit. I have often asked pastors not to give me any information about issues in the church. In some situations, the pastor sometimes just wants to unload their burdens. But my preference has also been the less I know, the more freedom in the Spirit I have.

I believe Pastor Larry was being accused of telling the evangelist the issues in the church. It was never the case, and only once did he come and check on me. I mentioned to the pastor that with all the new converts, he might want to consider a discipleship class for them. But how was that going to happen? We were meeting nightly. We had a challenge before us, and we were now into six weeks of meetings. I met with the pastor and informed him that it was time for me to go home. He was sad yet understanding at the same time.

Three men drove me to the airport, and it was very sad moment for them. They had been touched by God, and I was the one God was using for the revival. I was greatly blessed to have been part of the move of God. It's one thing to have revival, but time is needed for discipleship. The leadership wanted to continue in revival, and they did for some time. I'm not sure how long they continued, but it eventually came to a complete stop. Their hearts were sincere, but it was time to make a shift.

There are many lessons to learn during revival, and holding things together and discerning is crucial. Many things happen at the same time: the Holy Spirit, the human spirit, and an evil spirit. Was it the human spirit wanting the revival to continue and the evil spirits bringing havoc? In spite of it all, Jesus received all the glory and praise. Many of the saints who helped in so many ways have gone on to be with the Lord. It's never about one person but the body of Christ cooperating together to see God move in supernatural power. Sometimes in the revival egos can get in the way. Some want to be the centre of attention, and others complain about the smallest things. But the Word of God says we are overcomers in Christ Jesus. He that overcomes will inherit all things: *"To him who overcomes I will grant to sit with Me on My throne, as I also overcame and sat down with My Father on His throne"* (Revelations 3:21).

The revival fire would take me around the world to many places and countries. In some places we had nine weeks of revival. In some situations, pastors and congregations weren't interested in revival. In the midst of chaos, some things happened, and it could get messy. I tend to focus on the positive and believe that revival will happen no matter what door opens or closes. I have always been hungry for revival, from my early encounters with God in the private places, praying and believing God to move by His Spirit.

The body of Christ needs to be encouraged and equipped for the work of God. That equipping comes through the ministries listed in Ephesians 4:11–13:

> And He Himself gave some to be apostles, some prophets, some evangelists, and some pastors and teachers, for the equipping of the saints for the work of ministry, for the edifying of the body of Christ, till we all come to unity of the faith and of the knowledge of the Son of God, to a perfect man, the measure of the stature of the fullness of Christ.

The call to empower people requires mentoring, training, imparting, and discipling—all aimed at preparing the body for stability and increase.

The Greek word for equipping implies:

1. Recovered wholeness, as when a broken limb is set and mends;
2. A discovered function, as one of the physical members is not properly operating.

The work of ministry is the enterprise of each member of the body of Christ and not the exclusive charge of select leaders. Taken together, verses 11 and 12 reveal that the task of the gifted leader is to cultivate the individual and cooperate ministries of those under the leader's cares and influence.

Equipping, or *katartismos*, means making fit, preparing, training, perfecting, making fully qualified for service. In classical language the word is used for setting a bone during surgery. The Great Physician is now making all the necessary adjustments so the church will not be "out of joint."

The revival in Kitimat will always have a special place in my heart. Pastor Larry was such an easygoing man of God. He carried a prophetic anointing upon him to carry the revival and vision forward. It takes courage and strength from God to move in that direction for revival. He was bold for Jesus and had a passion for lost souls.

I was back in my home city of Winnipeg, and the revival fire was still alive and burning in my heart. George Gunner invited me to attended NNLC in Val-D'or, Quebec. It was such a blessing to be around friends I had met from across Canada. The services were awesome, and the place was full of Indigenous leaders. My dear friends Mavis and Noreen were there from Kanesatake, as well as many Cree friends and co-labourers in Christ. I have preached among the Mohawk communities of Tyendinaga, Kahnawake, Akwesasne, and Kanesatake.

I had been invited to preach at camp meeting with Art Brant, the pastor at Akwesasne. He has now gone on to be with the Lord. He was a man full of joy and loved the Lord. He shared that he knew he was called by God to full-time ministry but waited forty-plus year for that to become a reality. The last time I saw Art Brant was in Robson, North Carolina, where Lynda and I were being recognized for forty-one years of ministry among Indigenous people of North and South America. Art was remarried to another good friend of ours, Lillian, who was an accomplished gospel singer.

Art also invited a church group from an American church, and they brought a sense of joy and wanting to do something for the Lord. The tent was put up outside the church grounds, and the team gathered to preach for souls. It wasn't an easy task. That little church had been under attack many times from within and without. One night someone came into the tent around midnight with a fire and a feather in his hands, and he was moving up and down. This was reported by the young people who'd come from the church down south. I asked them what they did, and they said they prayed once they realized it was an evil spirit. The pastor told me later that a group of medicine men had gathered against us and wanted to hinder our efforts to reach souls for Jesus. Christianity is frowned upon in Mohawk communities, as it's looked upon as a White man's religion.

Lynda and I were just recently in Tyendinaga for the celebration of our friend John's life and ministry. He also has gone to be with the Lord. The celebration was in honour of a man who loved God and his people. John was instrumental in taking the Native American Fellowship across the USA, holding workshops and revival meetings in the evening services. It was an honour and pleasure working alongside him in many of the gathering of NAF around the USA. He loved the preached Word, loved his family, and, most of all, loved Jesus. I'm sure he could have written a book on his earlier days with the American Indian Movement and helping with the crisis in Oka.

There was another community called Kahnawake, where I worked alongside my friend Pastor Joy. These meetings were often supported by people from other Mohawk territories. After many attempts to reach the community, a decision was made to hold our meetings on neutral ground rather than in the church building. It turned out that we had two weeks of revival meetings in a Mohawk territory, perhaps for the first time in the community's history. It was heavy lifting and certainly wasn't easy. Pastor Joy would eventually move to Uganda and become Missions Director. All the training ground in Kahnawake would be helpful for her accomplishments on the mission field. She has a no-give-up attitude and was determined to fulfill the call of God in her life.

Joy also attended conferences with the NAF across the USA and has done work in East and West Africa. I was glad to have helped her with the call of God upon her life. You never know when you'll be used as catalyst for someone's breakthrough and breakout. Believe God has a place for you to service Him no matter what obstacles are put in your way.

After the revival in Kitimat, B.C., it seemed I was on the road and living out of my suitcase in motels, or perhaps someone's basement or in a Sunday school classroom at a church if the camp couldn't afford to put me up in a motel. In some places God would supply my needs, and other places didn't have much to give. But I never had any demands on finances. I trusted God would supply my needs. Most places gave me an honorarium or a love gift. In some cases, there wasn't a whole lot of love. I would try to make it easier for smaller congregations to team up with local churches and spread the burden to fly me to their communities.

Looking back at the time Lynda and I were at Prayer Mountain in Seoul, Korea, and at the revival in Kitimat, B.C., I realize that these were the catalysts to move forward with the message to the nations. In 2003, I travelled to East Africa twice in one year, eight weeks in Uganda alone, and once in Russia and various place in Canada and the USA, including twice in North Carolina. I spent a lot of time in British Columbia: Kitimat, Prince Rupert, Port Simpson, Bella Bella, as well as in Quebec, Prince George, Toronto, Arizona, and many more places.

Russia alone was a special place to travel to, considering I'd never been there. But to make it more special, I was travelling with my former lead pastor, H.H. Barber. I was saved under his ministry and served as a deacon on his board at Calvary Temple and was eventually on staff with him and served our Indigenous community. He was the man who would help establish Calvary Temple Native Fellowship Church. He helped raise the funds to make it happen, and we would become a developing assembly with our own building. Pastor Barber helped with his own funds. He cashed in an investment of $95,000 to help with bridge mortgaging. With a handshake and trust, he would be paid back his funds. We were on our way to move to our new location on College Avenue.

In 2003, I went with him to Tambov, Russia, along with Rick and Sharon Bowering and another two men from Saskatchewan. It was quite the experience preaching in Russia. We were met at the airport and taken to our accommodations in an older apartment block somewhere in Moscow. We stayed the night, and the next day headed to Tambov. We all had our assignments as three preachers: H.H. Barber, myself, and Lorne. A young man would be doing children's ministry. We had one translator for three preachers. That would prove a challenge in and of itself. The ride to Tambov was interesting. H.H. Barber was giving updates on the roads that had seen major repairs since his first visit to Russia. We stopped at a local grocery store that looked well stocked with items. There was a security guard outside the store holding an AK-47. Pastor Barber made reference to his previous trips when people were lined up outside stores hoping to get something, but there was a whole lot of nothing.

We arrived at the church in Tambov and were escorted upstairs to our rooms. Within twenty-four hours of our arrival, Pastor Barber had already preached three times. The people just loved him and were grateful for the many years of his support. Pastor had some of his books translated into the Russian language. The books were quickly picked up by the church people.

The lead pastor of this growing church was Ukrainian. He came to Canada to study in Swan Lake, Manitoba. Then he came to Winnipeg and connected with Pastor Barber, and they remained close friends. When we walked into their building, we saw that they had built an exact replica of the pulpit Calvary Temple had on their platform. A good number of Ukrainian pastors from Kiev attended the conference. There were men from Siberia who had travelled five days on a train to attend the conference.

That meant ten days on a train to come to all the way to Tambov and return. One of the pastors shared that they were under a great deal of persecution and people had burnt down their meeting place. His funds were very low to supply for his own family. He had to make a choice to travel to Tambov or feed his family. His wife encouraged him to go to Tambov, so he purchased a ticket and headed for a ten-day round trip by train.

As I have travelled around the world preaching the gospel, I've met many men and women who are making huge sacrifices to spread the gospel of Jesus Christ. My flight delays and lost luggage are nothing to compared to these men and women of faith, sleeping on floors and being away from home for months at a time. Another pastor from the USA attended the conference. He had worked with the Tambov church before and was also a guest speaker.

I was surprised with the food they served us, as it was like food we eat here in Canada. There were several hundred men and women attending the conference. I was wondering where they were eating, so I went downstairs to the basement and found them eating cabbage soup. Some of these leaders had been subjected to persecution and even put in Gulag camps for their faith in Christ. The young ladies wore head coverings and dresses down to their ankles, and they were very respectful to their leadership.

One of the guest speakers made what seemed to be a funny and light-hearted joke about himself. Some of those serious leaders who did hard time in the Gulags didn't think it was funny. Their sense of humour didn't coordinate with our Canadian culture. The next day, they went into his workshop and pulled their young people out of his class. I sensed some of the people had a very serious approach to the Word of God. As well as wearing a head covering, the women wore no jewellery. Wearing a tie, in their minds, was worldly. When it was my time to preach the Word, I wondered if I should wear a tie and take off my gold wedding ring.

Plans were being made for us to travel to Kiev, Ukraine and hold more meetings. That meant a twenty-hour bus ride with Ukrainian leaders. Before that would happen, we all needed visas to get into Ukraine. We surrendered our passports to get our visas. They have an underground black-market system in place. My guess is that's the way business gets done more quickly. Within three days we had our visas to get into Ukraine, and, of course, it cost money. I think we paid $200 each to get it done.

We had three speakers and only one translator willing to travel the twenty hour bus ride. Pastor Barber and I decided to come back to Canada and allow Pastor Trapper to head to Kiev with the busload of Ukrainians. He was ready to get on the bus, but something happened. This might have been the same group that pulled the youth from his workshop. He didn't go and came back upstairs with suitcase in hand.

By this time, Pastor Barber and I had made arrangements to head to Moscow. With the conference behind us, our train was leaving around midnight. We had a taxi driver to take us to the train station, and we were running behind schedule. So we quickly made it to the train station and started looking for our train. We were under the impression that our host had taken care of the fee for the taxi driver. Pastor Barber and I were in full stride at a fast pace looking for our train. The taxi driver was now in full pursuit behind us, wanting to get paid. We finally got the issue sorted out and boarded the train. We had to share a coach with two other men who were eating and drinking beer. I thought to myself, *Hopefully these guys don't drink all the way to Moscow.* They were respectful and took the top bunks, and Pastor and I had the bottom bunks.

Wouldn't you know it, I had to use the bathroom in the middle of the night. Well, I couldn't find the latch to open the door. I was trying to be quiet and not wake anyone up. I eventually found my flashlight and the latch and made it just in time to the bathroom.

Upon arriving at the Moscow train station, I was amazed at the number of trains coming and going. It seemed like we'd walked quite a distance to find a taxi. We headed to the apartment where we'd stay for the night. The apartment was old and rundown looking. It was what the Communists built to house their people. A couple of elderly people were sitting outside. The man was drunk, and the lady was trying to get him inside. The apartment was very small and was sectioned off with a small living area. Our host could speak English, which was good.

Pastor Barber asked if I wanted to see Red Square, so the host and I headed to Red Square. It was much farther than expected. We headed down at least three storeys below ground to the subway system. The place was packed with people. Every person for themselves, pushing and shoving to get on and off the train. I made sure I kept my eyes on our host. I had no idea how to get back to the apartment if I lost sight of her and we got separated. I took my passport and airline ticket and money with me. I thought if we got separated, I could at least make my way to the airport the next day. I kept my eyes on her and at times stood on my toes making sure we didn't get separated.

We finally made it to Red Square and made our way to Lenin's Mausoleum. That day they had him inside and not on display. We visited a local church with the Golden Dome, the Cathedral of Christ the Saviour. The inside was awesome with the hand-painting on the walls of the last supper of Christ and His disciples. It was within walking distance of the Kremlin.

Soon it was time for coffee and our ride back to the Soviet apartment block. The shopping mall near the coffee shop was definitely for the rich, and I saw all the latest fashions that money could buy. I found out later that the Russia Mafia runs everything in town, from ordering a taxi to buying goods and service. They all dress in black. Wouldn't you know it, that day I was dressed in black and walking with a blonde Russian woman down the shopping mall. I wonder what they were thinking. Back at the apartment, our host made dinner and then we were up early to catch a flight back to Canada. It was an amazing journey and a rich experience to travel and minister alongside my friend Pastor Barber.

My friend Willy from Argentina was in Winnipeg and stayed with us for a few days. Willy was the pastor we worked with in 1996 on our first trip to Argentina. He'd invited Lynda and me to come and hold revival meetings in the city of Santa Fe, about a six-hour bus ride from Buenos Aires. This would be one of many returns back to Argentina to work alongside Willy and his wife, Nelda. We had tremendous moves of God in those revival meetings, some that lasted as long as five weeks. I encouraged Willy to move outside the church building and go into the neighbourhoods. So he put up his yellow and white tent and we moved to different areas and saw tremendous miracles, healings, and salvations. One tent meeting lasted three weeks in Santa Fe. We held meetings every night.

Different cults were working in the area with witch doctors. Pastor Willy told me about an incident that happened during our revival meetings. He received a call from a local witch doctor, who told Willy, "I have three hundred people under my authority, but my marriage is in trouble." Pastor prayed for him, and there were many more unusual events. Scores of people were delivered from demon possession. You could hear people screaming as they were being set free from demonic powers.

A young lady in the tent meetings was suffering from an eating disorder. She looked horribly underweight. She came for prayer one night and could barely stand to her feet. She was just skin and bones. She had anorexia and was wasting away. She started coming every night, and every night was at the altar for prayer. By the time the three weeks of revival meetings were over, she was able to walk on her own strength and no longer had her hoodie on her head. Her countenance had changed and now she was wearing makeup and had gained some weight. We witnessed a transformation right before our eyes. Nothing is impossible with God, and all things are possible for them that believe.

One night a very big man staggered into the tent. He came forward for prayer, and God instantly touched him. He later shared that he was going to commit suicide that night but had heard and seen the tent meeting. He came in, found Christ, and was delivered from the spirit of suicide. The chains were broken off that night. A pastor's wife came forward for prayer, and the Lord touched her. She hit the pavement and took off running for blocks. God did amazing things in those tent meetings in Santa Fe.

Pastor Willy was trying to establish a church plant in a different area of the city. He had scheduled me to preach in this tough neighbourhood. It was dangerous. Pastor actually had four security men watch his car in case it was stolen or vandalized. We entered the building, and it was full of people. Part of the building had no roof, just walls. We finished our worship then moved into the closed area that actually had walls and a roof. I preached and then we had an altar call. One of the men came forward for prayer. I prayed for him, and he fell to the ground at least ten times; each time he sprung back to his feet without using his hands. I looked out of the corner of my eye and saw the men from the church peeking around the corner and watching what was happening with this man. I found out later that he was really violent and had punched one of the deacons in the church. It seemed everyone was afraid of him because he was so violent. He finally stopped jumping to his feet and was glued to the floor. The Holy Ghost pinned him down, and we had the victory that night. The church people were jumping for joy, and the bully was finally put in his place.

Around the same time, we had put up the tent in a local park, and the crowds started filling it. One night a lady was getting robbed next to the tent standing by the bus stop. We had an off-duty police officer on security that night. He pulled out his gun and ran after the thief. I'm not sure if he caught the thief.

There is a long history of prostitution in the area, some going back to the third or fourth generations. There is corruption, poverty, and street crime, and corrupt government officials run rampant. The people seemed to protest daily. Often you'd see them on the streets, in some cases burning tires and stopping traffic. Pastor Willy told me he was in the area holding meetings, and prostitution was running rampant. They were now getting saved and delivered from their bondage, but the local crime bosses were losing their women and money. Willy said that gangsters showed up at the tent and began shooting toward the platform. I asked Willy what he did, and he said, "I stayed on my feet and kept preaching while the bullets were flying in every direction."

We were in Buenos Aires holding a meeting with the General Superintendent of the Assemblies of God of Argentina. The church is located in a dangerous neighbourhood, so we flagged down a taxi near our hotel. Pastor Willy told the driver where we wanted to go. The taxi driver told us get out of the cab; he refused take us to the church. Then we tried another taxi; this time the driver looked like a seasoned veteran and said to us, "This is your lucky day, boys." And then he told us why it was our lucky day.

The church we were heading to was located in a dangerous part of the city. The crime rate was very high; apparently the criminals would break into your vehicle while you were sitting at a stoplight and would take anything valuable, even your life. The driver said, "I know a safer way to get you men to the church." That's what he meant when he said it was our lucky day. I thought he might have been exaggerating, so after the service I talked with some local young people who could speak English. Sure enough, the driver was right.

The pastor took us out for dinner after the service. We had a great time of fellowship and enjoyed the Argentinian meal. The pastor and his wife could both speak English. He shared his burden to reach the people with the gospel of Jesus Christ. He said they had ten thousand trained Bible school graduates who were not active in ministry. He didn't say why they weren't involved. My guess is that they would have to plant a church. That seems to be the major issue of church government. You plant and it's yours to grow and nurture.

I encouraged Willy to take a mission team from his church and go up north to minister to the Indigenous people. They had never done anything like that before, so they were challenged to move from their comfort zone. Yes, we had taken his people to cities close by for meetings, but never twelve hours away in the Province of Chaco.

Pastor had a connection with a couple who once headed up his Sunday school program. They had moved to a place called Saenz Pena. This is where I would meet Pastor Ken Johansson and his wife, Alba. They had a work going with the Indigenous people. This would be the beginning of a long and fruitful ministry with these precious saints of God. Pastor Alba has gone on to be with her Lord Jesus. She was an Indigenous person, and we had an immediate connection. They had a ministry with the Toba Indians who lived in the Saenz Pena area. There could be at least five thousand or more Toba Indians living in the Saenz Pena area. Their living conditions could be described as third-world and all the problems that come with that.

Ken is now remarried to a Toba Indian lady named Veronica. They still carry on with their ministry to the Toba Indians. I really have lost track of how many times I went to Saenz Pena. On one of the first trips into this area, we were invited to speak at Ken's son's church. The evening service started late, and it was dark outside with no street lights. The building seemed to be in the middle of nowhere. The young people from Willy's church were with us on this trip. All this was new for them; some had taken time off work, and others were students. But they were willing to do whatever they could to help.

We arrived at Pablo's church and climbed up a two-storey stairway and arrived in a dark room. They escorted us to the front seats. I had a sermon prepared, but the Holy Spirit changed the direction. I ended up sharing about our first and second mission trips among the Wichi Indians in the Formosa area. Willy is an excellent translator, and the Word was powerful. At the end of the service, they turned on the lights in the building, and the place was packed with mostly Wichi and Toba Indians. What a powerful encounter with the Holy Ghost that night. The young people who'd come with us from Santa Fe helped in the prayer time. It was a totally awesome experience. There was so much freedom and power in the Holy Ghost. The glory of God fell that night and would remain with these people. Willy and I had now seven churches to work with in the Seanz Pena area and beyond. That was good considering that when we first arrived, we were helping Pastor Daniel with his church plant.

Pastor Johnny Dixon was with us on one of those trips to Saenz Pena. We had to get him to the airport at three o'clock in the morning to go to Resistencia to catch his flight to Buenos Aires. After that, Willy and I were off to Santa Fe for another eight-hour drive. We were exhausted by the time we arrived back in Santa Fe. Johnny had also brought Tony, Gordon, and Julia from northern Quebec to Santa Fe, and Julia preached. Gordon had meetings with the youth of the church in Santa Fe, and Johnny led in worship.

One night Johnny went off by himself to an ATM machine to get some cash. He was followed by a thief who tried to rob him. Johnny thought at first it might have been Tony or Gordon playing a trick on him, so he grabbed the person's wrist as he tried to put his hand into his pocket. Johnny turned around, and there in front of him was a thief. The man pushed Johnny to the ground, and the money went flying in the air. I asked Johnny what happened next, and he said the thief tried to reach for the money that fell to ground, so Johnny kicked him in the head. Johnny was so traumatized that he didn't join us for supper; he stayed in his room. Like good Indigenous friends, Tony, Gordon, Lynda, and I had a wonderful time laughing at Johnny's dilemma. We asked questions like, "I wonder where Johnny is tonight." Someone said, "Well, he may be out fighting crime or changing into his Superman cape." All in good humour, of course!

While I'm on the subject of thieves, we were in Jamaica holding special tent meetings on the island. We were in the downtown marketplace, and someone tried to pickpocket me. The place was packed out with people, and I was keeping my eyes on the youth who were with us. One of the young people was our granddaughter, Caroline, so I was on alert for them. In the meantime, the thief opened my pocket. As he did, the ladies in the market started yelling and pointing in my direction. I turned quickly, and sure enough, the person was starting to run away with my money in his hand. He rubbed up against me, and the money fell to the ground. I think he must have gotten away with $15.

I was almost robbed of my passport on the border of Uganda and Kenya, this time by two border guards with AK-47s strapped to their shoulders. They were searching through my luggage as we were entering back into Uganda. We were heading across the border with our luggage on the back of our bicycles. One of the guards took my passport, and I could see out of the corner of my eye that he was putting my passport into his pocket. He tried to distract us before going through my luggage. I went right up to him and spoke with authority, telling him to give me back my passport now! He reached into his pocket and pulled it out and handed it back to me. As we were crossing the border on bicycles, the guard shouted out, "Be careful, there are thieves over there." In the meantime, he was trying to steal my passport. Apparently, there is a market for stolen passports. One always has to be careful and alert.

In Argentina, we ran a conference in an older established Russian church in Saenz Pena. The pastor had been touched by revival and wanted to see his church move in Pentecost. I preached in his main service and at the conference. It was a blessing to be in a church that had been established by the Europeans from the old country. During the evening revival meetings, God moved powerfully and touched everybody in the building. That evening scores of young people were touched by the Holy Ghost and were jumping and shouting like they were at a football game. The pastor of this church had been touched by revival and had tears in his eyes and a burden for the church. It was an I-shall-not-be-moved church. Tradition was taking the spiritual life from the people.

Pastor Daniel made arrangements for my hotel stay. It was an old building located in downtown Saenz Pena. During the night, it was also filled with young people drag racing and partying on the streets. I don't think I fell asleep until early morning. The next day I moved out and found another hotel.

The first local pastor we worked with had such an old car, it had no heat, no wiper blades, and holes on the floor. He used rubbing alcohol to wipe the morning frost off his windshield, but he had joy in his heart. He'd tried living in Sweden at one time, the birthplace of his father, but moved back to Argentina and married a local girl and had two children. They tried planting a church in Saenz Pena, but it didn't happen. Their business was broken into and robbed of everything. There was so much crime and robbery. One night as I was walking back to my hotel, two guard dogs were running after me. Just as they were about to attack me, their owner called them back. As I got near to my hotel, I saw a robbery in progress. These men were stealing something that looked like a hot tub, or maybe a swimming pool. They were loading it onto the truck. I was walking nearby, so I picked up the pace, hoping to make it back to the hotel before they spotted me. I pretended to be on my cell phone. I made it back to the hotel safe and sound.

Pastor Ken had arranged an outdoor meeting in the neighbourhood where the Toba Indians lived. Many hundreds gathered that night, and I could see young teenagers standing in the back of the crowd. When I gave the altar call to receive Christ, they made their way forward and gave their lives to Christ. They now had been touched by revival and went home saved and filled with the Holy Ghost.

The following year I was back in Saenz Pena, and Pastor Ken had me scheduled to do two services on Friday night. The first church service lasted longer that expected, and I was concerned for the second service. The young Toba Indian youth were waiting for me to come and speak. This was the group that got saved during our crusade meetings we'd had outdoors the year before. They were waiting, and it now was around ten in the evening, but they remained in prayer. What a presence of the Holy Ghost was in those meetings! These young people had been touched by God.

After one of the services, Ken had I walked through the area where the Tobas were living. There were young people drunk and some taking drugs. Some of the young people were passed out and leaning up against cars. Some knew Ken and showed respect and shook his hand. Ken has given his life to reach the Toba Indians. He was originally from Sweden and met his wife in Buenos Aires while they were both working in a bakery. Now they had a ministry with the Tobas, and when his first wife died, the whole Toba community was in mourning for the loss of their beloved spiritual mother. Alba was a spiritual mother to many of the Toba Indians. I was blessed to have known her, and she always hugged me like I was her son. We shared many meals together as we partnered to share the gospel message with her people. Alba will forever be remembered for her love and kindness; it was a sad day for everybody when she died. She left a legacy and made a difference to so many people. Never forgotten and always remembered for her love and compassion.

When the young people from Santa Fe came to help us, they handed out invitations in the local parks in Saenz Pena. They were special young people, filled with the Holy Ghost and power. They are now young adults and married with children. Some of them moved to other countries: Israel, Italy, and Spain. We've maintained contact with them through social media. They continue following us and the countries we have visited. They will always have a special place in our hearts. Abigail, who is now married and living in Italy, graduated from law school. Jessica worked for a Jewish school in the nearby city of Parana and is now married with children and living in Israel. She was one of the worship leaders in Santa Fe.

My translator, Franco, is married and has one child. He moved to Spain. Franco had helped me in Seanz Pena and in Santa Fe. As matter of fact, I was the first English speaker he translated for in Santa Fe. He did an excellent job in those services. He would later come and drive eight hours to be with me in Saenz Pena and help me with translating.

Back in Santa Tomas, I had dinner with him and his mother and brother. What a nice family and lovely dinner. For me it's always been about establishing relationship with people on the mission fields of the world. During many altar times, I prayed with him and his wife. At that time they had no children, and the Lord spoke through me a word of knowledge. The Lord said his wife would be pregnant on January 1, and the baby would be boy. On the exact date of the word of knowledge, she took a pregnancy test and was pregnant. Later she had an ultrasound, and sure enough, it was a baby boy! The boy actually came with us on one of our visits to Saenz Pena.

The work in the Province of Chaco began to expand not only to the Toba Indians but also to national Argentina. Pablo set up four churches for me to go to in the Province of Chaco: Villa Angela, J.J. Castelli, and two others. J.J. Castelli was the place where Pastor Daniel had to get welding done on his truck on our first visit in 1996.

In J.J. Castelli, I worked with a new pastor and his wife. They were both involved with the church and also had a private Christian school. I was uncertain where I was at first. I called Lynda on a daily basis, no matter where I was in the world. I told her I was in a place called J.J. Castelli. She said, "Don't you remember? We were there when Pastor Daniel's truck needed fixing." I had forgotten the place, but I remembered the truck needing repair. So there I was, some twenty plus years later, ministering the Word to a church group.

The translator was a young teacher. She knew English but had limitations in translating. The pastor's wife had a little more command of English, so she helped with the Word. The pastor also invited some other pastors to join us. I eventually returned twice to this church group.

We had some powerful services. The evening service started at 8:00 p.m., and I was able to share with the school during the day. I walked from my hotel one evening, and when I arrived at the church service, I was surprised to find the door locked. I could see people in the room setting up for the service. A man was trying to get into the building, but the door was locked. I motioned for him to follow me to the back door. He followed me, and we entered the building. He went right to the back row and sat down.

The pastor's wife translated for me that evening, and at the end of the service, people came forward for prayer. The man who'd been locked out of the building came last for prayer. He had a piece of paper in his hand. He spoke about his situation. He'd been ordered by a local judge to go church or go to jail: "Go to church and have this paper signed by the pastor, and if you don't, you will have to go to jail." So here he was at the altar with his paper in hand. He had tears in his eyes, as the Lord was dealing with him. He told me that his brother was a pastor in Formosa, which is near the Paraguay border. We were there on our first visit to Argentina. I led him in prayer to receive Christ in his heart. I told him that the judge might have ordered him to come to church, but it was his brother's prayers that brought him to the service and to Christ. As it turned out, he was known as the most violent man in J.J. Castelli. But that night the chains fell off him and he was set free by the power of the Holy Ghost. He went home with a new and clean heart.

The next day, Pastor asked me if I could share with the students during the day, and I agreed. The next morning, I shared first with the younger group, and later I shared my testimony with the older group. Over the years, I hadn't shared much of my personal testimony. I wanted to preach the living Word, where Christ was lifted up. I said I would do it if the students were very attentive to my testimony.

The younger group was a bit restless but they listened. Then the older group came and heard my testimony. I said, "Before I start, I want you to know that before you born, I was in J.J. Castelli, about twenty years ago." I had their attention now! They were listening very carefully to every word. I told them that God had a plan for their lives, and I quoted from Jeremiah 1:4: *"Then the word of the Lord came to me, saying: "Before I formed you in womb I knew you; before you were born I sanctified you; I ordained you a prophet to the nations."*

In Hebrew, the word for "knew" means, I recognized you, I designed you, I appointed you. You already have a divine appointment in the mind of God, from the foundation of the world. You are not an accident. You weren't created just to fill up the world; the world was created so that you would have a place to fulfill your destiny.

The Lord also said that before you were born, He sanctified you. The Hebrew word for "sanctified" is *gadash*. It means, "I set you apart for a special reason and purpose, and I dedicated you; I chose and secluded you."

Suddenly revival was breaking out. The teachers went up on the platform, picked up their instruments, and began to worship God! The Holy Ghost began to take over the service, and twelve young people stood and received Christ into their hearts. I said, "Okay, turn around and face your fellow students and repeat after me." They publicly confessed Jesus Christ in front of the whole student body of the senior high school. When the teachers picked up the instruments and played worship music, nobody wanted to leave the room. There was such an anointing that fell in the place.

There was an older student in attendance, and the pastor's wife asked if I would pray for him. The young man was actually around twenty or twenty-one and hadn't graduated from high school. The pastor said he was always falling asleep in the classroom. So we took him into a private room, and he was slumped over the table. The pastor didn't have time to translate the prayer. I told him there was no need for translation. The demon knew who I represented: King Jesus. I laid hands on him and could literally feel the power of the Holy Ghost flow down from my arms and onto this young man. It was like a bolt of electricity that touched him. He was set free from the spirit of slumber, and the chains fell off him. It was like that electric current I had experienced when playing under the bridge at the age of six. But this didn't hurt me or the boy; he was set free.

The next day, the parents called the school to ask what had happened. One parent said, "My son came home, and he was different, changed." Thank you, Lord, for bringing revival to this church and school. Over the following days, students would drive by me on their motorbikes and yell, "Hey, Alfred," and wave their arms in the air.

One of the teachers and translators invited me to her parents' place for a barbecue the next day. I know never to turn down an Argentina barbecue. They picked me up the next day, and we had a wonderful time of fellowship and food. Her parents were both teachers at a local public school, and her father the principal. After a wonderful meal, the principal invited me to come and speak and introduce myself to his staff.

Before entering the building, we were greeted by at least twelve Toba Indian children on the playground. We finally made it into the school building, and the staff were waiting for us. To my surprise, half the staff were Toba Indians. They began to ask questions about Indigenous history in Canada. I tried to answer their questions, and they had a ton of them, but our time was limited and classes were starting soon. I showed them my Canadian Status Card of my Indigenous identity. One of the men wanted to take a photocopy of my card.

There are years and years behind trying to obtain land settlements and status as Indigenous people of the land. There is a long history of the Toba and Wichi Indians that hasn't been told. They're trying to obtain their rights as Indigenous people. The principal showed me their living conditions. It reminded me of what I had seen among the Wichi Indians and the third-world poverty. The principal told me that many of the children drop out of school without any direction in life. The drug cartels are using them as drug mules to transport drugs into Argentina and beyond. The drugs are cheap and highly addictive, and the Toba Indians are bound up in poverty and drug abuse. They walk through the jungles for the cartel and bring it into Argentina for distribution. I mentioned to the principal that it would be great to come into the school and share my testimony. He said that would be great, but it being a public school, it would be more of a challenge.

After seeing firsthand the village and public school system, it definitely speaks volumes about the social problems facing these people. The contrast between the private Christian school and the public is quite evident. The private school has Christian leadership overseeing the daily programs, and part of their funding comes from the government, which I am told is a miracle in and of itself. But they have top ratings for students graduating from their school.

It was a fruitful time with Pastor's Lujan and his staff. They treated me with so much kindness, and to visit J.J. Castelli after twenty years was awesome. Some breakdowns in life are all part of God's eternal purpose and plan. Never count yourself out of God's purpose for your life: *"And we know that all things work together for good to those who love God, to those who are called according to His purpose"* (Romans 8:28).

Purpose: The word suggests a deliberate plan, a proposition, an advance plan, an intention, a design.

That day we broke down and had to turn around and head toward J. J. Castelli for repairs, God was working out His eternal purpose, not only in my life, but in the lives of those people and the most violent man in town. The grace of God is so much bigger and grander and deeper and wider! God is working and putting His plans and purposes together. Who knows what could possibly happen in the lives of these young people?

"For I know the thoughts that I think toward you, says the Lord, thoughts of peace and not of evil, to give you a future and a hope" (Jeremiah 29:11).

The other place Pastor Paul had me go to was Villa Angela. The lead pastor had recently died and left the church for his wife to oversee. The whole family was grieving, including the church family. He was well liked and a visionary for the church. In spite of their loss, the church family was still moving forward. The lead pastor was carrying a heavy load, as it had been a family-run church.

I arrived to do special meetings, but their translator was only available for one night. I didn't speak Spanish, and they didn't speak English. Some of them attempted to speak English, but only one word at time. So I suggested that the group meet me early in the afternoon and I would go over my sermon with them. They arrived, with four of them able to help translate my message from English into Spanish. I broke it down into four parts, knowing none of them were able to translate the whole message. They came eagerly to help with the sermon.

The worship was their strength in the church. They had worship leaders and dancers waving flags. When it was time to preach the Word, my four assistants and I, with the help of the Holy Spirit, got through the message, and the whole church group came forward for prayer. The pastor's wife who had taken on the responsibility of leading the church was having extreme headaches, and the burden of the church was on her shoulders. The grief of losing her husband was too much, and she now was at the breaking point. I prayed with her during the altar call. The heavy load she was carrying was broken off, and the chains came off her. She was experiencing freedom for the first time since her husband had died. That night tears were shed and joy was coming in the morning.

The next day there was a total shift in the church body, from grief and mourning to joy unspeakable and full of glory. One young man helping me during the series of meetings was on fire for God. Although he had once attended the church and was dating the pastor's daughter at the time, he had left the church, but I'm not sure of all the reasons. He wanted to reconnect with his former girlfriend, but trust had to be built up again. So the former lead pastor's daughter was not only grieving the loss of her father, but now her former boyfriend was trying to make amends. I could sense he was sincere and knew he had made a mistake.

The following year I returned to speak at their conference. There were two other pastors involved in the conference who were from Brazil. These young men had been touched by revival and were blessings to the body of Christ. This time I brought my translator, Franco, from Santa Fe. The young man who had invited me, along with the former pastor's son, first met in Saenz Pena. They were all hungry for more of God in their lives and were meeting an international evangelist from Canada to be their speaker. They were thrilled to have me come, these young men on fire for God. They said they wanted to learn as much as possible from me, so they followed me around and stuck by my side throughout the meetings.

Pastor Carlos Inguez eventually married his sweetheart and they now have a child. It looks like he's filling the role as lead pastor. They are a dynamic couple filled with the Holy Ghost and fire. God knew that His people needed help to climb the mountain before them. I was there at the right time. God's timing is perfect, and He is always on time.

> Have you not known? Have you not heard? The everlasting God, the Lord, the Creator of the ends of the earth, neither faints nor is weary. His understanding is unsearchable. He gives power to the weak, and to those who have no might He increases strength. Even the youths shall faint and be weary, and the young men shall utterly fall, but those who wait on the Lord shall renew their strength; they shall mount up with wings like eagles, they shall run and not be weary, they shall walk and not faint. (Isaiah 40:28–31)

Pastor Ken and his fellowship invited me to be a keynote speaker for their National Indigenous work. This is their largest gathering of representation of Indigenous people from the surrounding countries and parts of Argentina. They've had up to five thousand people gather for this outdoor meeting, and it would be held in Seanz Pena. It was such a powerful gathering, and they had so many different bands playing music. At least two thousand people gathered that night. It was awesome to be their keynote speaker. Then they made me an honorary citizen of Seanz Pena and gave me gifts. I received a large bottle of honey and a handmade bow and arrow set. I was thrilled to see many Indigenous people from different parts of the country.

The local newspaper and media people came and interviewed me at the hotel. They wanted to know why I was in Seanz Pena. When God opens doors, no man can close it. I did the interview, and then Willy and I headed back to Santa Fe. On the way, Willy must have dozed off while driving. We hit a speed bump, and the tire went flat. It was very hot and windy out. By the time we finished changing the tire, it was time to head to Santa Fe.

We pulled up to the hotel. My clothes were greasy from changing the tire, and my hair looked like I'd just woken up; I had bedhead. I walked into the lobby holding my bottle of honey in one hand and the bow and arrow in the other. By now I had come to know the hotel staff very well. I offered them some honey to taste. They showed up with their glasses to get a shot of honey, and I decided to give them the whole bottle of honey; they were so happy. I found out later from Willy that there was a drought and honey was in short supply. I just gave them perhaps a few hundred dollars with of honey. But the victory was sweet.

The young lady who worked as the receptionist at the hotel spoke English, so she became my friend and helped in so many ways over the many years of travelling to Santa Fe. One day I was walking through the lobby and turned to her and said, "One day you will own this hotel." She thought it was funny, but the Holy Spirit was speaking through me.

On another visit to Santa Fe, I noticed that the name of the hotel had changed from Holiday Inn to InterTower Hotel. It might have been the best hotel in town. It was about twelve storeys high and had a nice restaurant and rooftop pool. The name change came with new ownership. The receptionist was now married and working from home. Apparently, her father had bought the hotel. That means she now could be part owner of the hotel. From receptionist to working at home, married, and having children. I remember her bringing her baby to the hotel.

They all knew why I was in Santa Fe. I had a problem. How was I going to bring this bow and arrow home? It didn't fit in my suitcase. So I headed to the outdoor mall on St. Martins Boulevard. After looking for something and coming up empty, the shop owner suggested buying a guitar case, one of those flexible ones. It worked.

Soon I was back in Canada after another fruitful time in Argentina. It amazes me over the many years of travelling to Argentina and speaking no Spanish how God provided and watched over me. Buenos Aires has a population of ten million people. I sat and watched people coming and going and asked myself, "Who will go and speak the gospel of Christ to these people?

How then shall they call on Him in whom they have not believed? And how shall they believe in Him of whom they have not heard? And how shall they hear without a preacher. And how shall they preach unless they are sent? As it is written: "How beautiful are the feet of those who preach the gospel of peace, who bring glad tidings of good things!" (Romans 10:14–16)

Our ministry to Argentina extended over twenty years and has proven fruitful and such a blessing. Pastor Willy arranged many different places for me to preach throughout Argentina. We were heading up to Resistencia one time, and Willy had made arrangements to stop in Cordoba on our way back. He set up a meeting in the local Bible school, run by an America missionary. There were at least thirty students in chapel service that morning. Some were single men and women, and there were married couples. The teacher greeted us and welcomed us to the chapel service. He mentioned we had forty-five minutes for the chapel service.

We'd just come out of revival meetings up in northern Argentina for at least two weeks. That morning in chapel, the Holy Ghost came down and settled among us. I was attentive to our time restriction, but the professor overseeing the chapel service whispered in my ear, "Don't be concerned about time; besides, they're all in my next class." Breakthrough and breakout were about to happen.

The students came forward for prayer, and many were touched by the Holy Ghost and were on their knees weeping and crying out to God. They slowly got up and moved quietly out of the chapel—except for one young lady. We approached her and asked how we could pray for her. With tears running down her cheeks, she said everyone in college had been baptized in the Holy Spirit except her. We laid our hands on her and prayed for her to receive the Holy Ghost with evidence of speaking in tongues. Within moments, the Holy Ghost touched her and she began speaking in tongues as the Spirit gave the utterance. She headed to the next class, and a few of her friends were waiting for her outside of the chapel. I could see them hugging and embracing her. The joy of the Lord fell upon those students. Never count yourself out. He promised to pour out of His Spirit on all flesh, upon your sons and daughters.

Back in Santa Fe, Pastor Willy arranged for us to visit a men's prison. Pastor Johnny, Tony, and Gordon were with us as we went to see these men. As we approached the prison and were going to enter, the guards asked us to wait a few minutes, as there was an issue with some of the prisoners. In went the guards with their guard dog. A few minutes later, they came back out and said it was okay to go in.

As we approached the area of the prison where we were going to speak, you could hear them worshipping and praising God. The atmosphere was charged, and you could sense God was going to do something supernatural. The prisoners were respectful and thanked us for coming. There is a tea drink called mate, a herbal drink, served in a hollow gourd and drunk through a metal straw called a bombilla. The prisoners have this drink, and the custom is that everyone drinks from the same straw. At least fifty prisoners were passing this drink around to everyone in the room. It was our turn to drink, and I thought to myself no way was I going to drink from that straw. Who knew what disease could be passed on.

When the service was over and it was time to leave, Pastor Johnny ended with a song, "I Feel Like Travelling On." Standing behind me, one of the prisoners whispered in my ear and said, "I feel the same way." I found out later that he was a pastor's son who was doing five years in prison.

On the way out as we were leaving, we could hear Tony's voice saying, "Help!" The guard had mistaken him for a prisoner and had closed the iron door. We had a good laugh and told the guard he belonged with our group. Before I exited the building, the prisoners asked if I could speak on their Internet ministry. They said it reaches within Argentina and other countries in South America. What a witness these men were within the jail cell and surrounding area. The joy of the Lord filled that section of the jail that day—joy unspeakable and full of glory! Their combined voices of worship and praise filled the place. They had heavenly voices that rang out.

In 2002, Pastor James Okot invited me and David Rose to East Africa to preach the gospel. This would bring life-changing moments for me personally. I knew many years ago that I would one day be travelling to Uganda. The year before, Pastor James had invited me to come and join him for his next East Africa trip. I just happened to run across him at the Winnipeg airport. I was leaving for a preaching assignment, and he was just coming back from Uganda; that was in 2001.

Brother David Rose was eager for me to meet Pastor Okot, and we met that year and were praying for our next trip. David and Norma were visiting us, and I told David he was coming with us. Norma turned to David and said, "You need to go with them." This would be one of many trips we would take together to Uganda.

Pastor James was originally from Sudan, and at that time there was civil war in the country and it wasn't safe to travel there. Pastor had us visit a refugee camp approximately three hours outside of Kampala. At that time there were at least 25,000 displaced people living in the refugee camp. We stayed in the camp and slept in a mud hut with a grass roof. Our meals were served outdoors, and if you got a fork, you were blessed. We arranged to speak in the marketplace outside the local brew house. It was there that the locals would gather and consume alcohol. It was in the heart of the marketplace.

The speakers and sound system were set up and it was time to preach the Word. The people had gathered to hear the good news, and people were now coming and accepting Christ as their personal Saviour. The next day we were back at the base camp. During the day, I noticed this three-foot-long, black and yellow reptile going into our hut. This is the same hut we would be sleeping in for the night. You had to bend really low to get into the doorway. Four of us were sleeping in the hut. No light, just your flashlights and your single bed with a mosquito net.

The local missionary introduced us to his guard dog before we went into our hut. He said the dog had been trained to watch over the property, and any strangers who hadn't been approved by him or passed the sniff test would face the consequences. His name was Packey, and his introduction to us was to sniff us so that he knew we were welcomed at the camp. Wouldn't you know it, David and I had to go outside in the middle of the night to use the bathroom. There were no bathrooms, but close by was a vehicle tire. Well, guess who showed up—Packey! He did the sniff test and, thank the Lord, we passed. This dog was raised to hunt lions; he was a razor-backed Tanzania dog. That was only one of many tests we would have to pass. By the way, the hut is made out of mud and cow dung. Yup, cow dug! Pastor Okot told me he slept in a hut and the cow dung wasn't quite dry!

Our inconveniences certainly didn't compare with the hardships these people were living in. There was close to 25,000 or more refugees from Sudan living in the camp. Those numbers would grow considerably over the years. The unrest in Sudan would go on for decades. By the time the civil conflict ended, nearly 2.5 million people had died as result of the civil war. These people had lost everything imaginable, from their homes to sons and daughters and careers. Their dignity was taken away and so much more. They were suffering while living in a foreign country and in the middle of nowhere. Their very lives depended on the United Nations for food and education. It was heartbreaking to live among the people and witness firsthand the tremendous suffering. They all were living in these mud huts with straw roofs.

Pastor James knew many people in the camp. He had fled from South Sudan himself. He was separated from his family for years and would eventually be reunited with his wife, Grace, who was now living in Winnipeg. That story is a remarkable miracle in and of itself when all hope was lost. But Jesus opened the door of his captivity, and the chains were broken off. He is an amazing man who loves God in spite of all hope being lost. He remained faithful to God, and we would travel back and forth to Uganda for many years. No matter where we went, he was always concerned for our safety and comfort. He opened the door for us to travel to East Africa and beyond. Pastor Okot has struggled with his health over the years but always had a burden for his people.

We visited several of James's friends he knew from Juba, Sudan who were living in the camp. Some of the huts were untidy and it looked like garbage had been thrown around. Then I noticed a tall man standing upright, and his property was well maintained. I asked Pastor James if he knew the person, and he did. He was a former general in the military, now exiled and living in this refugee camp. There were actually many professionals, from business owners to teachers and other professional people, in the camp. Some of the children were born in the camp.

Although our conditions were uncomfortable, we had little to complain about. The food was unpleasant at times. I ate some foods but avoided others. We had an outdoor shower made for us. The ladies in the camp do all the hard labour. They set up a makeshift shower with a folding straw door to cover us while we showered. That was our introduction to Ugandan ministry.

I met a travelling evangelist visiting the camp. He was on his way to a village to preach the gospel. He said it would take him two days to walk to the village. He told me he could speak five or more languages. I asked him how that works with so many dialects. He told me they would sit in a circle and the conversation would be translated by various tribal groups. I was impressed by his heart to reach these groups and walk for two days. I met another pastor from Busia, Kenya. I will tell more of that trip later.

Back in Kampala, we also had a meeting with one of the local key leaders of Uganda. He was well-known and respected among most of the top leadership in Uganda. He set up meetings for us and showed us the schools he was running and the care he was providing for orphans. Everywhere you looked, all you could see was suffering, poverty, and injustice.

Pastor Alex, our crusade co-ordinator, set up meetings within Kampala and outside the city. Many souls were saved, and we all were extremely blessed. The hosting pastor would invite me to his church and fellowship to preach every time I came back to Uganda. That same year I met two struggling pastors, Patrick and Richard. These two men would become my sons in Uganda. Both had been to Bible college in Turkey and were now back in Uganda to begin their ministry. Over the many years of going to Uganda, Patrick would become my right-hand man as I navigated my way through the culture and understanding of their dreams and visions. Those early years I watched and listened to the hearts of the people. People who come and do all the talking don't learn much or progress in their ministry. Patrick would travel with me throughout Uganda, preaching and teaching. One time we ministered for one full month. We moved eleven times from village to village to hotel to hotel. He came with me to South Sudan, Kenya, Tanzania, and throughout Uganda.

There were more invitations than I could possibly respond to. Instead of me going, I would give funds to Patrick and he would go to several East Africa countries. I met one leader who was bishop to over seven hundred churches in East Africa. The church he pastored had over ten thousand members. He told me I could go to any of his churches. That alone opened a door to many opportunities. Throughout the years, invitations would come from Sudan, Tanzania, Congo, Rwanda, Kenya, Nigeria, and Cameroon, West Africa. Lynda would eventually come and join me in East Africa near the end of my travels. We stayed at a mission house run by Roman Catholics. It had been our home since first arriving in Kampala.

We arrived past midnight on our first trip to Uganda, and the staff at the mission house were nowhere to be found. There was security guard with his dog, and he carried around a rifle with him. I was grateful for the security, but that dog barked most of the night. The guard found us keys and off to the room we went. We were all jet-lagged after travelling over twenty hours and not sleeping since leaving Canada. The room was nothing fancy, but it had a bed and they kept it clean.

The first night I bunked with brother Rose, I don't think I slept much. He was so tired and snored so loud. It was like a freight train coming through the room. The next day, I demanded my own room. We were up and ready to meet our host and begin our ministry. Our first meeting was held at the Imperial Hotel; the food was decent, and I ate there many times. The mission house's food was not good at all. Over the years, the food has improved.

There was a coffee shop and an Internet place next to the Imperial. The server was really slow, but it served the purpose. Over the years, shopping malls began to pop up and more restaurants would open. The now have a Champs Chicken. It might be the first Western franchise in Uganda. The cell service has improved, and calls can be made just about anywhere.

Pastor James warned us about pickpockets, and to be mindful all the time. They grab and run. One day I was walking back to the mission house, and I was being followed by young boy with running shoes on. I knew he was a grab-and-run kid. I turned around and told him, "Don't you dare try to steal my phone." I knew from the beginning I had to navigate around Kampala for myself. Sometimes Pastor James would be gone for a few hours or even two days meeting his friends. I'd take a bus packed with locals to the downtown area by myself and get a feel for my surroundings. I would either walk back to the mission house or take a taxi. They have Ubers available, but you need to use caution and wisdom. There are plenty of scammers and con men trying to get something for free. Pastor Okot advised Lynda not to wear her jewellery in public places. The thieves grab and run.

During our first trip to Uganda, brother Rose met a young couple from Kabale staying at the mission house. He engaged in conversation with them and found out they were pastors visiting Kampala. David has the gift to engage with people and strike up a conversation. He told them he was travelling with an evangelist who could pray for them. David asked me to pray for the couple, so I went and prayed for Pastor Kizza and his wife, Margaret. This would be the beginning of a relationship that has been in place ever since. Today Apostle Kizza has been holding a World-Wide Revival Conference in the town called Kabale, a six-to-seven-hour ride from Kampala. In 2024, he'll be holding the twenty-five-year anniversary of World Wide Revival Conference. This is the same amount of time I've been travelling full-time as an international Evangelist.

After our first meeting at Kampala Kolping Mission house, I was back in Canada and received a call from Pastor Kizza, inviting me to go to Kabale as a guest speaker. Keep in mind that this was only two months since I'd first met him. I said yes to the invitation.

I arrived back in Uganda and was off to Kabale. Back then the roads were really bad, with huge potholes everywhere. It should have taken six hours rather than eight. Kabale is near the Rwandan border and contains high hills; it's much cooler than Kampala. I took Patrick and Richard with me for our first meeting in Kabale. This would have been their fourth World Wide Revival Conference. And for the next twenty-two years, Kabale would be part of my ministry to Uganda. During COVID I spoke over Zoom. So I never missed a conference in the last twenty-two years.

They rented a tent and put it up in the stadium in the centre of town, which was something new in the town. The tent was quite old and looked like it was patched together. During one of our meetings, it was raining so hard that the tent began to burst and break open.

Over the years, the ministry has grown so much that the crowds are into the thousands. They have a radio program, Bible college, and church plants. They bring in international speakers from East African countries, the United Kingdom, the USA, West Africa, Canada, and many more. Over the twenty-two years, we have reached tens of thousands of people with the gospel message. It's been amazing journey travelling back and forth from Canada and participating as a guest speaker. I've met many gifted and talented speakers from around the world.

I have so many stories of salvation and deliverances over the years. One time I was preaching, and at the end of the message I gave an invitation for people to come and receive Christ. The people in attendance came running to the altar, like they do in most services. This particular session, a very large women came to the altar. She looked like she'd been in a street fight. Her face was scratched and bruised. It was like facing Mike Tyson and Hulk Hogan. The workers tried to keep her off the stage, but she pushed them aside and was heading for me. The Holy Spirit said, "Whisper the name of Jesus." I did, and as I said "Jesus," she hit the ground and began to foam at the mouth and move her body like a snake. Keep in mind there was music playing and prayers going up, and it was just very loud. I believe the local people were learning a lesson, including myself. It's not how loud you preach or how loud you pray but just the mention of His name! She was the most violent person in town and was banned from Kabale. But Jesus and the Holy Ghost had other plans that day. Whom the Son sets free is free indeed. The level of faith reached another dimension for all of us. The people who responded were set free from demonic oppression and depression. Over the years, multiple people have been set free by the power of the Holy Ghost.

Back at the refugee camp there was a pastor attending the conference. He was from Busia, Kenya, a border town of Uganda. He invited me to come and speak at a pastors' conference in Busia. He promised that there would be two thousand pastors attending. So I made arrangements to attend the conference the following year, 2003. Patrick would join me on this trip, so we made arrangements to be dropped off at the border town of Busia. It's a border crossing and very busy with long-haul trucking.

The pastor greeted us as we went through immigration and then took us our hotel. The hotel looked and felt like a jail house. It had a huge iron gate with barbed wire and broken glass on the walls. They had a security guard outside the complex, and the door was locked at night. The room were very small. I had single bed and small shower in my room. I must admit, it was creepy. At night I heard this banging sound underneath my bed. No way was I going to get up and see what was making the noise.

The next day Patrick checked on me. He looked underneath the bed and, sure enough, there was this huge bug the size of my palm. He took it outside and threw it away. That was the beginning of our introduction to Busia. The quality of food was terrible. I ate rice and boiled eggs most of the time.

To get to the conference, we hired bicycles, which is the main mode of transportation in that area of Kenya. If you were lucky, you had a strong man to carry the extra weight, which included my briefcase. Well, the driver didn't have the strength to get over the hill, and we fell off the bike. It was amazing I had no broken bones. I landed with my right arm and hand extended. I got off the ground and back on the bicycle. On our way to the church, we had to travel through a huge pile of garbage. As we got closer to the church, we saw children playing nearby in an open field. They were shouting "Mzungu," meaning "White man." They ran to get closer.

We walked into the church building and saw eight people sitting in the front row. I asked the pastor where the two thousand pastors were. He had lied to me. There were just four adults and four children. I spoke with the pastor privately and confronted him about lying to me. He had no answer and didn't know how to apologize. Besides this meeting, he had also set up meetings in another town. I told him he had broken trust, and there would be no other meetings in the next town. I told him I'd forgive him, and since we'd travelled that far, we'd hold the three-day meetings as scheduled. But we wouldn't be going to the next town. He would have to explain himself to the next group.

The service began with the eight people. He had a rented sound system, so the village people knew we were there and ready to have services. It was tough going at the beginning, and I was discouraged by the lying and the small crowd. The Holy Spirit whispered, "Preach Jesus." So with all I could give, I preached Jesus. The crowd started to increase, and I noticed people standing outside and not coming into the building. By the third night, more people were coming in; the third night was to be our last night of preaching. Instead, the Holy Spirit was nudging us to move forward with more meetings. I informed the pastor and the people that we'd have another service the next day. By the time we had finished speaking, seven nights had passed. There was a sense of the presence of Holy Ghost because we were going night by night.

The people in village only knew we were there by the sound machine and the two lightbulbs hanging from the ceiling. We were using the power from the next house over from the church building. On Friday night, the power went out in the village, and that included our source of power. The pastor began to put candles in the windowsill and looked for matches to light them. I told him to let the people know the services were still on. I sensed the Holy Spirit saying to assemble the people to pray. I instructed the pastor to gather the children playing near the building and lead them in worship.

We began praying and worshipping God for the next thirty minutes. Then I noticed our lightbulbs flashing and coming on. Then the sound system started up, and we had power again. But that was only the beginning. I looked outside into the village, and the village had no lights on except ours. We had lights and the power was flowing. It's not unusual for power to go out in Uganda, and it could stay off for days or longer. It was a supernatural act of God. There was no other light visible in the village. That was the breakthrough and breakout service we needed.

The people who'd been on the outside standing on the path started coming into the building. Now the building was full of people. Revival had broken out in that little village church. One lady came up to me and spoke in good English and told me the history of the church. She said the last pastor had used witchcraft and Christianity mixed together. The church had fallen seven times in a similar manner before our arrival. She told me that when we started the meetings, the people were afraid to come into the service. But the more they heard the name of Jesus, the less fearful they became. She thanked me for coming and helping to get the church back on its feet.

Not only were souls saved during the meetings, but someone said a woman with AIDS was healed. The Busia Revival was a challenge with many obstacles, but in the end, we got the victory and Jesus got the glory. It was now time to head back to Kampala and join Pastor James and David for another pastors' leadership conference.

We travelled, preached, and held crusades in many East African countries: South Sudan, Uganda, Tanzania, and Kenya. I sent Patrick to Rwanda and Burundi. In Uganda, I've been to Gulu, Lira, Mbale, Kampala, Mbarrara, Kabale, Jinja, and Adjumani.

Gulu was a challenging place in many ways. Pastor James gave $1,000 to one pastor from Gulu to make arrangements for our crusade. When we arrived, he was nowhere to be found, and neither was the thousand dollars. The local pastor who was part of our crusade committee was approached by a political party who were holding a rally in town and needed a pulpit. In exchange for the use of the pulpit, they would allow us to use their platform and sound system for our crusade. What they had was beyond our expectations, and the pastor agreed to their terms. So we held an outdoor crusade with their sound equipment and platform. The cost to rent this type of platform and sound equipment would be more then $1,000. That night many souls were added to the Kingdom of God. My guess is the people who had come to the political rally stayed and heard the gospel.

It was heart-wrenching to see the village people come and sleep on the sidewalks of Gulu. They'd leave their village before nightfall because of the thieves and thugs that roamed the countryside. The next day, Patrick and I took a bus back to Kampala. It was leaving at 7:00 a.m. and, to our surprise, the bus was leaving on time. There are usually delays because they won't leave until the bus is full of paying customers. Our bus was full, and we were heading to Kampala. I said something to the effect of "Thank you, Jesus" out loud. The ticket agent was a Muslim man and got angry at the statement. He said, "You cannot say that." I didn't respond to him, but a big man behind me stood up and said that I could say anything I wanted. Then he said if I couldn't say it, they'd all get off the bus. The ticket agent backed down and didn't say another word. I called that man who stood up for me my Black angel. On many occasions, God protected me from potential harm.

The bus ride to Kampala took six hours. The bus was old and had hard plastic seats, and the drivers were under pressure to get to their next stop. So they drove way too fast for my comfort level.

Upon our arrival in Kampala, Patrick warned me that there were many thieves at the bus terminal. When we arrived, it seemed like there were thousands of people coming and going. Patrick went looking for our luggage, so I found place to stand against so no thief could steal my belongings. Our luggage was secure and we headed to Kampala Kolping House.

The hotel in Gulu was something else. I woke up and made my way to the bathroom to brush my teeth. To my surprise, the sink was full of ants. The toothpaste from the night before had ended up in the sink, and I guess ants like toothpaste. On the subject of ants, I was in the Philippines in a place called Bam Bang, and that hotel had an ant problem as well. This time the ants were crawling in my bed and under the covers and on me.

In the hotel in Gulu, a young person who worked in the restaurant told me her story and her work situation. She said they treated her like a slave. She started work at 6:00 a.m. and worked until 11:00 p.m. She hadn't had a day off in three months. They paid her $50 a month, or $1.66 a day. We tried to give these servers extra tips. Stories like that are not unusual. The young person working the restaurant in Busia told me she applied for a job at Disney World and got an interview. She spoke five languages and had a good chance of getting the job. But her dad got sick and needed medicine. She emptied her savings for her daddy and missed her opportunity for the job, which would have lifted her out of poverty. Some of the many languages she spoke were Japanese, English, and Swahili.

Back in Gulu, Pastor James had a friend he considered to be his mom. She helped him in his education and to escape from human trafficking. His uncle had treated him like a slave and tried to blind him by blowing smoke in his eyes. It was quite a remarkable testimony of deliverance for Pastor James. We went to visit his mom, and she put on quite a feast. I was eating food I had never eaten before. The food was great and so was the fellowship.

We held meetings in northern Uganada in place called Adjumani, which is located close to the Sudan border. The civil was war was still going on in Sudan, and people were fleeing to Uganda. We were going to hold a crusade in Adjumani and the surrounding areas. Adjumini's hotel was a terrible place. It was like we were in jail; the rooms were very basic. They had iron doors and iron bars on the windows. There must had been at least thirty people staying in the same hotel. There was one bathroom and a place to shower. It was extremely hot out, and we had no fan and definitely no air conditioning. At night they locked the main iron gate, and a guard was stationed inside. The food wasn't that good, and there was no cold water to drink.

The electric power in town only came on for four hours a day. After that, there was no power until twenty-four hours later. David and I were having lunch, and the hotel was trying really hard to give us the best service possible. The server came and asked us what we wanted for dinner. We both said we wanted chicken. By the time we finished lunch, the server walked in with a live chicken under his arm. The chicken looked at us as he passed by the dining room. David and I couldn't help but laugh, and then we heard the chicken give his last word.

We had one translator to work with for our meetings. He was a young, fiery evangelist living in Adjumani. That was twenty-three years ago. We had to get permission from a local official to speak in the surrounding refugee camps. He cautioned us not to go among the Muslim group in case we started a riot. He assigned us a security guard to watch over us; keep in mind, many people were still fleeing from Sudan, so he was concerned for our safety. The person he assigned to watched over us came with us as we went from village to village preaching the gospel. We were preaching from the back of a half-ton truck and had a portable sound system set up. I still have that image of that older man standing right front of a speaker with tears rolling down his face.

Back in town, our host, Evangelist Cosmos, set up a platform made out of wood right in the centre of town. It was quite high off the ground, and he had a good sound system that could be heard from a good distance away. Although we weren't in the Muslim neighbourhood, I'm sure they heard the messages. David was busy handing out gospel tracts and being mobbed by the children. He was actually running away from the mob. This location was an ideal place to hold our meetings. It still wasn't safe for us to travel into South Sudan and Juba. But we would eventually enter into Juba once the civil war came to an end.

There were many amazing testimonies to share from our outreach in Adjumani. A witch doctor was saved and then showed up with potions and other items he used to bring curses. He was giving up his livelihood and burned all those items. I still remember the eighty-nine people who got saved and baptized in water during our meetings. The local pastors were involved in the water baptisms. I'm glad they got involved, as it was big task to baptize that many people. Besides, the water looked murky, and who knows what was in the river? I wasn't going to find out!

We used this area in Adjumani in the middle of town again and again for our crusades. I was preaching when the sun was going down, and next to the grounds were several trees where bats lived. They would start flying around, and swarms of them would take to flight. One of them decided he didn't like the message I was preaching, and he pooped on me. It landed on my head and glasses. I just kept on preaching and wiped the poop off my head and glasses. That night God moved in a powerful way; souls were saved and the Kingdom of God was extended. Keep in mind these people had suffered and been displaced and lived in the worst poverty possible. Any of our hardships were nothing compared to their suffering.

After the meetings, we'd head back to our hotel and sit in the courtyard. We always had pastors come by and want to talk to us. We often fed them and heard their stories. One man from Juba thanked us for coming and then said it was a great encouragement to know they hadn't been forgotten. That statement has always been a reminder to me not to forget these people. I am still committed to going to northern

Uganda. My heart is always for these people. I must preach Christ and make His name known!

Adjumani has a local radio station that broadcasts into several countries, such as South Sudan, Congo, Uganda, and Kenya. We've been on the station many times and preached the gospel. The local pastor said it reaches millions of people. It could be the only communication they have from the outside world.

We had done several meetings in Lira, and God did amazing things in these meetings. Pastor David Rose worked tirelessly raising support for books and bicycles for these pastors. He was full of zeal and found a place where he could preach the gospel. The meetings in Lira area were held outdoors. The weather was not favourable. The clouds were gathering, and it looked like our meetings would be cancelled. Someone prayed, "Lord, please hold back the rain." And He did! I looked up into the sky, and the clouds took on the form of a horseshoe. They parted, and the sun shone through long enough for us to finish the message.

At the same meeting a man shared his testimony. He told us that at one time he was a right-hand man to the leader of the Lord's Resistance Army. He said, "I might have caused the death of your loved ones. I am sorry for my actions, and I understand you may want to take revenge and murder me. I am willing to lay my life down for Jesus now." It was a powerful testimony of a life that was transformed by the power of the Holy Ghost. He got off the platform and walked through the crowd, and nobody harmed him.

There were pastors who walked and rode bicycles to the leadership conference. I spoke with one pastor who had come five days by his bicycle. There is a hunger for God and to receive instruction. We might be the only group providing leadership instruction. The leaders not only came during the day, but they were also part of the crusades to reach souls. Many didn't have the means to bring this type of ministry to their churches because of their poverty. But they gave their time and effort to help us reach people for Christ.

That particular time the hosting pastor was so desperate to reach souls that he took us to the very spot where the local people throw away their garbage. We preached from a half-ton truck and souls were saved.

Over twenty-three years of ministry in East Africa, neither of us were harmed or got sick. Although, post-COVID, Lynda and I arrived in Uganda and made our way to the mission house, and it turned out we were both infected with the virus. Lynda's case was much more mild. I had a severe case. I had no energy, and my head was hurting badly. We laid up in our hotel room for eight days and then found the strength to head to Kabale and Adjumani. I travelled through four airports to Uganda so I could get somewhere in our travels.

One time Pastor Okot and I were losing our voices in Lira. The local pastor asked if we were drinking any type of juice. We said yes, back at the hotel. He said they mix that juice with the local water, and the local water was causing us to lose our voices to preach. Once we heard this, we stopped drinking the juice, and our voices returned.

There were plenty of opportunities to instruct these men and women. They came from villages and were provided a mat to sleep on the floor of the church building. During the day, food and drinks were provided for them. One pastor told me a story of a lady who carried her dead child to another village. The lady knew people were praying in that village, so she strapped her child to her back and headed in the direction of the village. As soon as she laid the child down of the ground of the village, the dead child came alive again!

> And these signs will follow those who believe: In My name they will cast out demons; they will speak with new tongues; they will take up serpents; and if they drink anything deadly, it will by no means hurt them; they will lay hands on the sick, and they will recover. (Mark 16:17)

Back in Juba, I had booked into the same hotel I'd stayed at with the rest of our Canadian mission team. This time part of the structure had burned down. It was next to the place we had stayed before, so they gave me a single type building to stay in, with air conditioning and running water. However, this time there was a rat in my room. It was a big one looking straight at me from the washroom, so I got up and slammed the door. Patrick dropped by to check on me, and I told him there was a rat in my room. He checked it out and found nothing in the bathroom. I decided to go see the hotel staff and tell them there was a rat in my room. They said they could move me to another room. I asked them why the cats and dogs around the complex didn't scare the rats away. She explained that they were afraid of the rats. I though to myself, *Okay, let me move to the next room.* I sensed there were rats in the new room, so I called around and found another hotel, The Juba Grand Inn.

The room in the new hotel was totally closed up. The only way a rat could get in would be by the toilet, so I closed the lid and settled into my new room. The next day in the courtyard, a chimpanzee was walking around. He was looking for food, but the waiter chased him away. But he came back, opened the refrigerator door, and ran away. So I went from rats to a chimpanzee all in one day.

The food at the hotel was much better than from where I'd just come, and I thanked the Lord for that. Pastor James showed up and we planned our meetings in Juba. We held meetings in the marketplace, and as we began our meetings, I could see dark clouds coming in our direction. I preached with urgency, but the people couldn't see what I was seeing from a distance. I finished preaching, the crowd responded, we prayed, and moved out quickly.

Lynda would come and join me sometimes just for few days and then head back to Canada. On one of our trips, we stopped in Dubai for a few days. I had the telephone number of a local pastor living there. Our friend back in Canada had given me the number, so I called the pastor. He said they were meeting at a local hotel and invited us to join them for Friday morning service. The pastor and his wife were from India.

We arrived for the service, and there in the front row was an East Indian couple. We took our seats and the service began. A fair-skinned man said to the congregation, "We have a couple from Canada joining us today." The pastor invited me to share where we were from and where we'd been. I told them we were from Winnipeg, Canada. The East Indian lady began to cry. After the service, she came up to me and said she thought that they had a guest from Canada who would be from Toronto not Winnipeg. As she wiped the tears away, her makeup smeared under her eyes because she'd been crying so much.

She told me her son was living in Winnipeg. He had been working in Saudi Arabia and left his wife, and his marriage ended in divorce. She gave me her son's name and telephone number and pleaded with me to call and visit him. I told her I would make contact with him when I got back to Canada.

I called him when I arrived in Winnipeg, and he invited us over to his house. He knew I had been in contact with his parents, so Lynda and I visited him and his girlfriend. They both were new to Canada, and she had just given birth to their child, but the baby had health problems. He was open to receiving prayer. We ended the night and prayed for their baby.

A few years later, I was preaching the Christmas morning service for our West Indies Fellowship. To my surprise, who walks up to me after the service but the young man with his girlfriend. The baby had been healed and they had more children, and they were all in church. The prayer request came from a hurting East Indian couple working and living in Dubai with their prodigal son living in Winnipeg. God is amazing!

Back in Dubai, the pastor and his wife picked us up the following day and took us out for dinner. He was a successful businessman from India; his fairness came from his grandfather, who was from Ireland. Apparently, the English had been offering land in exchange for help subduing the uprisings in India. So his grandfather married an East Indian woman; he called himself a half breed. I hadn't heard that term in a long time. That was a slang word back in the day. Today we call them the Metis Nation.

The pastor and his wife took us shopping for gold, as our sister from Winnipeg had given Lynda money to buy gold for her. The pastor then told me that there was a church spilt in Dubai, and they'd moved to the hotel to conduct their service. Dubai allows churches to have services, in spite of the fact that it's a Muslim country. The couple's son in Winnipeg told me later that his parents visited Winnipeg after they left Dubai and are now back in India, retired. They were school teachers in Dubai and were old enough to retire with a decent pension.

A lady from Winnipeg gave me the phone number of a relative living in Dubai. I called and asked for the person, and someone came on the phone who had an East Indian accent. I told him that Susan had given me his number. He offered to pick me up, so I gave him the name of our hotel. The dinner was good, and we stayed with him for few hours, then he dropped us back at our hotel. As he was leaving, he turned to me and said, "Could you please pray for me and my son? Our relationship is strained." So I laid my hands on him in the lobby of the hotel and he began to cry.

When we arrived back in Canada, I told our friend that I'd spoken with her cousin George in Dubai. She said, "I don't have a cousin named George in Dubai." I'd dialed the wrong number and talked to George, but it was a God moment. God doesn't make mistakes, and this man had a divine encounter with Jesus. We must be obedient and willing to encounter whomever God puts in our path. I have spoken to strangers in airports and have had a word of knowledge for them.

God may drop a word about their occupations, which opens the door for further conversation, like the young man who sat next to me on a flight out of Uganda. He was from the United Kingdom and was on spring break. Not sure where to go, he'd decided to come to Uganda. He said he met up with a group of young people and went on a party for the next week. He travelled from town to town partying. He looked extremely hung over from drinking booze all week. I could smell the alcohol still on his breath; he was fortunate nobody harmed him or took advantage of him in Uganda. The subculture of partying and drugs exists within Uganda.

He then asked me what I did for a living. We were thirty thousand feet in the air, and I had a captivate audience for the next five hours to Dubai. He didn't last five hours awake, but he heard about a man called Jesus. You can't run far from God! He will find you, whether you're running to Winnipeg from Saudi Arabia or trying to find something to fill the void inside your life, like the young man from United Kingdom.

A taxi driver in Dubai, who was from Uganda, told me his story of trying to find his way back to Uganda. His wife and children were living in Kampala, but he lived with his girlfriend in Dubai, and they liked to party. He claimed to be a Christian, and I told him to get right with God. "Your problem is easy to solve. Break up with your girlfriend and stop your partying. You'll save money and get back to your family."

Many people in Dubai come from a variety of countries, and English is spoken within the hotel settings. Many Filipinos work in that part of the world. Often they have to work two years before their employer will pay for their airfare back home. Many of them have a family back home: a husband, children, and parents. So many of these jobs have no future, but these people have resilience and a no-give-up attitude. We've been to the Philippines and seen firsthand the poverty of the people. In most cases, it's a struggle just to get by in that environment. We don't just view ministry in an open, public manner; it's a lifestyle. We see people for whom Jesus died and who need Him. In our travels, we've encountered many hurting people who need a word of encouragement.

Paul wrote in Colossians 4:6, *"Let your speech always be with grace, seasoned with salt, that may know how you ought to answer each one."* The person sitting next to you in Starbucks, or in your office, needs to hear good news. We have a message of good news, whether we're preaching in the poorest countries of the world or the richest countries. I have preached to people who literally own just the clothes on their back, as well as to people who have so much money, they'll have enough for generations to come. Some of the rich people have their own set of problems. Money can't buy them peace, comfort, or joy. Their lives are empty, and they have no purpose or direction. Their idea of retirement is hitting a little white ball around on green grass. In some cases, they have as many problems as the poor, such as disobedient children, health problems, and financial worries.

But we are called to be witnesses. In Acts 1:8, Jesus tells His disciples, *"But you shall receive power when the Holy Spirit has come upon you; and you shall be witnesses to Me in Jerusalem, and in all Judea and Samaria, and to the end of the earth."*

Distinctive features of the early church:

1. The early church witnessed to all men. First of all, they had source of "supernatural power." This power was needed to make them effective witnesses.

Their first assignment was to be witnesses, and this was the basic program in spreading the gospel throughout the earth. Christians were to be witnesses. A witness is not necessarily a preacher. A preacher expounds general truth, but a witness speaks from personal experience of something that actually happened to them. Not all Christians are called to be preachers, but I believe all Christians are to be witnesses.

The apostles were witnesses! One historical event was the resurrection of Jesus: *"And with great power the apostles gave witness to the resurrection of the Lord Jesus. And great grace was upon them all"* (Acts 4:33). The apostles were eyewitnesses of the resurrection! Notice that the apostles' first witness was their personal experiences with God raising Jesus from the dead.

What was true of the first twelve apostles was true of the apostle Paul. Paul was on trial for His faith in Christ:

> Therefore, having obtained help from God, to this day I stand, witnessing both to small and great, saying no other things than those which the prophets and Moses said would come—that the Christ would suffer, that He would be the first to rise from the dead, and would proclaim light to the Jewish people and to the Gentiles. (Acts 26:22–23)

Witnessing: Giving evidence, attesting, confirming, confessing, bear record, speak well of, giving a good report, testifying, affirming that one has seen, heard, or experienced something,

Paul's first responsibility was to be a witness to everybody, small and great.

2. The pattern of the early church was supernatural; everything about the early church was supernatural.

The four main supernatural areas were: their praying, their preaching, the way they directed their ministry, and the fact that their message was attested.

Acts1:8 Sent out with supernatural power!

Acts 1:14 Supernatural prayer

Acts 2:1–4 The outcome of their prayers! Heaven opened and the Holy Ghost was pouring out, with supernatural power and speaking in tongues and praying in tongues: *"And when they had prayed, the place where they were assembled together was shaken; and they were all filled with the Holy Spirit, and they spoke the word of God with boldness"* (Acts 4:31).

> To them it was revealed that, not to themselves, but to us they were ministering the things which now have been reported to you through those who have preached the gospel to you by the Holy Spirit, sent from heaven—things which angels desire to look into. (1 Peter 1:12).

They preached by the Holy Spirit, who came down from heaven with supernatural power: power sent down from heaven by the Holy Spirit!

Paul describes his preaching in 1 Corinthians 2:4: *"And my speech and my preaching were not with persuasive words of human wisdom, but in demonstration of the Spirit and of power."* He relied on the Holy Spirit! Paul wanted those believers' faith to be founded not on the wisdom of men but on the power of God, the supernatural power of God.

> For I will not dare to speak of any of those things which Christ has not accomplished through me, in word and deed, to make the Gentiles obedient— in mighty signs and wonders, by the power of the Spirit of God, so that from

Jerusalem and round about to Illyricum I have fully preached the gospel of Christ. (Romans 15:18–19)

In their prayers, in their preaching, in the way they were led! *"For as many as are led by the Spirit of God, these are the sons of God"* (Romans 8:14). They did not merely depend on human planning but on the supernatural power of God.

The Lord will lead you to people who are seeking Him.

We headed to South Sudan, the home of Pastor James Okot. The civil war between the north and south was coming to a close. At least that was their goal. It had been going on for the last twenty-plus years, and 2.5 million people had died as a result of the conflict. We didn't know what to expect as we made our way to Juba. We flew from Entebbe into South Sudan. The first time we flew into this area, it was heartbreaking to see firsthand the conflict and the consequences and aftermath of war.

As we entered the airport, one guy travelling with us pulled out his camera and wanted to take pictures. A lady in front of us who recommended not to take pictures. She was a Mzungu lady and obviously knew the region. Close by the airport was a mine sweeper, looking for mines. We headed to the mission house operated by the Norwegians. It had at least five bedrooms, and we had two of them. The others were occupied by strangers.

We held meetings during the day at a local church building. Pastor James knew the pastor here, and this would be our place for daytime workshops, and then we'd make our way to a local area that was used for sporting events. It was extremely hot outside; it must have been at least fifty degrees Celsius. It drained your energy, especially while preaching and teaching with a translator. The buildings around the church had been bombed out. The streets were full of people walking and going nowhere. The roads were uneven, and you would see blind people trying to walk. There were drunks lying in ditches. The poverty was horrible, and the stench of death seem to linger in the air. I can't imagine the sufferings and hardships of these people.

Back at the mission house that night, I was attacked in my dreams by what I could only describe as horrible looking creatures. There were two of them with what seemed to be three feet of razor-sharp teeth coming out of their mouths. It was a horrible presence of evil; the only explanation I received later was that these were demons of war. My heart was beating fast and fear was coming upon me. Then suddenly a person stepped between me and these demonic creatures. The voice spoke with authority, and He said, "You cannot have him. I have redeemed him with my blood." I woke up and it seemed like my heart was beating out of my chest. Whatever that creature was, it was pure evil, no doubt the demons of war. How else can you explain 2.5 million dying?

There's a memorial sign on the highway leading to Juba regarding the tragic outcome of war. We had travelled this road before. It was paved but it was no picnic. There were burnt-out tanks on the roadside, and along the road were warning signs telling you not to go beyond a certain point. There were land mines along the road and in the fields that still hadn't been removed, perhaps thousands of them. You had to be careful not to cross the line. That would only be the beginning of the horrible effects of war.

I was back in Kampala from one of many trips into South Sudan. I met Lynda there and tried to explain to her what I'd just witnessed in Juba. As I was telling her about it, I felt these terrible emotions coming over my body and mind. For a brief moment, I felt what they call PTSD, or post-traumatic stress disorder. And I had only been in Juba for a week, witnessing firsthand the consequences of war. What about the people who lived through it? Like my friend Pastor James, who lost his family and was separated for years from them. He had a thriving business before the war machine took over his livelihood.

Back at the Norwegian mission house in Juba, I thought I'd get ahead of the guys and have a shower, but to my surprise, the water tank was empty. Trevor came into my room and checked on me. I was tired and exhausted from the heat and there was no water. Trevor noticed a building within walking distance of the mission house. He said he was going to check the place to see if they had any rooms available. He came back twenty minutes later and told us there was a hotel down the road called the Juba Beijing Hotel. He'd spoken to the staff, and they told Trevor that the hotel wasn't open yet and they were going through trial runs with the staff. But they didn't turn Trevor away; they told him that they were wiling to give us a reduced rate to move into the hotel.

We took that opportunity to move over to Beijing. They offered us our own room, air conditioning, and cold showers. They provided a lower rate than normal, and we were in a pickle and needed to move, considering we had no water at the mission house. The hotel was fairly basic. It was structured like a trailer home with attached plastic floors and walls, but it had air conditioning. We moved in and settled down, feeling grateful for the opportunity to be there.

A number of Chinese people were visiting the hotel, and we gathered that they were the investors in this project. They were very generous and kind to us and offered all the food we could eat. Of course, this was Chinese food. But it was definitely a break from the food we'd been eating. By this time we were all running out of the health bars we'd packed away in our suitcases. There were definitely days when that was all I would eat.

The Chinese investors had a party to celebrate their pre-opening. Soon after their party started the alcohol began to flow. Most of them were intoxicated by this time. There was karaoke machine, and everyone became a singer.

Soon it was time to hit the bed, and believe me, the mattress was only one inch thick, and it was hard. There was a soft pillow, but we weren't there for luxury. We were there because we were hungry, tired, and exhausted from the long days of ministry.

Soon we were back to our workshops ministering to the leadership in Juba. A group of singers came from Khartoum to minister among the Sudanese. They drove all the way from northern Sudan to the south to reach the people with the gospel. They were a blessing to us, and now we had a number of people helping our meetings. Those ladies from Khartoum had a singing and dancing ministry, and it was a big hit among the Sudanese. One of their songs resulted in them rolling on the ground and getting back on their feet. They wore white shirts and black skirts. After they finished their skit, they stood to their feet and were covered with dust.

At the closing of the service, we preached the Word and invited people to receive Christ into their lives. There was a tremendous response to the message that God so loved the world that he gave his only begotten Son, and whoever believes in Him should not perish but have everlasting life. Sometimes help comes in different ways. God knew we needed the Beijing Hotel to regain our strength and have a good night's sleep. He knew we needed help from the ladies from Khartoum. Without their presence, our meetings may not have turned out the way they did. We were grateful for their contribution to the advancement of the Kingdom of God in Juba.

> Now concerning spiritual gifts, brethren, I do not want you to be ignorant; you know that you were Gentiles, carried away to these dumb idols, however you were led. Therefore I make known to you that no one speaking by the Spirit of God calls Jesus accursed, and no one can say that Jesus is Lord except by the Holy Spirit. There are diversities of gifts, but the same Spirit. There are differences of ministries, but the same Lord. And there are diversities of activities, but it is the same God who works all and all. But the manifestation of the Spirit is given to each one for the profit of all: for to one is given the word of wisdom through the Spirit, to another the word of knowledge through the same Spirit, to another faith by the same Spirit, to another gifts of healing by the same Spirit, to another the working of miracles, to another prophecy, to another discerning of spirits, to another different kinds of tongues, to another the interpretation of tongues. But one and the same

Spirit works all these things, distributing to each one individually as He wills. (1Corinthians 12:1–11)

On an earlier trip into Juba, my passport went missing for a few days. I finally got it back from the pastor who took it and said that I needed another government stamp. It turns out I'd paid for that service, and the immigration military said I didn't have an official stamp, and they wouldn't let me board the plane. I had no idea where the embassy was located and had no telephone number to reach Pastor James. The military squeezed almost $200 US out me before allowing me to board the plane. In most situations, I would never allow anyone to shake me down for money. The military was in charge, and they ran the place. They were basically the goon squad going around shaking money out of people.

Several military generals with their own small army camped right inside Juba. In every corner of the street, military men stood guard with AK-47s strapped over their soliders. The place was so tense, any small thing could trigger a riot. As a matter of fact, there was a riot close by the church where we were holding workshops. I believe it was a tribal issue in the marketplace between warring factions. The military had to be called in to settle the dispute. The war between the North and South may have ceased, but there was still those who wanted power within the government. With the discovery of oil in the region, everyone wanted something. There is ongoing corruption within the country and plenty of poverty and sick people everywhere you turn. The suffering of humanity at its worst stems from years of war and conflict. The church was dealing with the conflict of tribal wars and the influence of Muslims among the people.

We were holding gospel meetings in the marketplace in Juba. Across the road were rows and rows of shack-like buildings housing what turned out to be brothels. The crowd that gathered was large. The people were pushing and shoving one another to hear what we had to say. They had security guards with four feet of rubber hoses, hitting people who wouldn't listen to them. We were preaching the love of God, and the security guards were hitting the people with these rubber hoses. One man was hit on the forehead and got a huge lump. I went over and put a cold bottle of water on his forehead. The security guard seemed to have it in for him, so I brought the man closer to where we were sitting. They have what's called mob justice, meaning people take the matter into their own hands. Depending on the severity of the crime, it can end in death.

A man on his motorbike was trying to manoeuvre through the crowd. It wasn't a smart move on his part. He accidentally hit someone in the crowd, and they turned on him and beat him. That's their form of instant justice! No police. No court system. You take the law into your own hands. Lawlessness prevails, and whoever has a bigger gun or clan wins, hands down. I met a lady from China hired to be a police advisor to the Juba government. She was a tall lady and spoke English very well. I found out she was living in Juba and was hired to train police officers. She had a one-year commitment and a family back in China.

In 2007, I conducted services in Barrow, Alaska and in Anchorage. We had revival meetings in Barrow that lasted six weeks, and the services continued nightly. It was such a powerful move of God. We were making history in one of the most remote places in the world. This place has the coldest days and no sunshine for at least six weeks of the year. I'd told Jesus many years and that I would go to the ends of the world. The year prior I was in the same place and had meetings that lasted three weeks with another pastor. The following year, I was invited back by the new pastor to hold revival meetings. But there was something different about these meetings. The worship was more focused on Christ and the work of the Holy Spirit. The year previous there'd been some tension and the atmosphere seemed more chaotic and undisciplined. People were carrying their old hurts with them.

Some of the leadership had burned bridges with other members of the body of Christ, and there was no sign of repentance. They only wanted to feel good about themselves. You can't carry around old hurts, unforgiveness, and an unrepentant heart and expect God to show up and bless you.

The following year, the new pastor arrived and invited me to come and hold revival meetings. The atmosphere was much different, and there was a hunger for God. Besides that, the people were teachable and wanted to see God do something in their lives. These people had gone through years of poor leadership in their community churches. There were church splits, and one particular leader was creating this negative atmosphere. I decided to visit the church that caused the split and listened to one of his sermons. He was preaching at a funeral service, and rather than comfort the people, he scolded them and threatened hell if they didn't get their lives in order. His order rather than God's will. This man had been in the community too long. He was isolated from the outside world and his fellowship. A call to his presbyter would have helped him, and he could have gone on a sabbatical. That's one of many problems working in these isolated communities, especially in Alaska. Everyone had a "pull up your bootstraps" attitude, which will turn into legalism. Do my will because I know better. These leaders just pass down their bitterness. These wounded sheep needed the Word preached in love and comfort in the Holy Spirit.

The meetings began with Pastor David leading us into the presence of God, and we worshipped in spirit and truth. At the end of the service, I called people to come forward for prayer, and many responded. I asked for a man to help me with the altar call. There was a heavy-set man sitting close, so I called him to help me. The first person who came forward for prayer fell to the ground, and the man helped to catch the person. He caught the first person and laid him down. Then we went down the line and prayed for at least twelve more people. He caught each one of them and laid them down. Why do you need someone to catch people? Mainly so that people don't get hurt. Some people fall down under peer pressure rather than allowing the Holy Spirit to touch them. In order for people not to hurt themselves, we have helpers in place.

I didn't know that this man was scheduled for shoulder surgery the next day in Anchorage. He had his airline ticket and had booked time off work. That very morning when he helped lay down the first person, he was instantly healed of his shoulder and back issues. Now we had our first healing miracle, and that sparked a six-week move of God. Revival came to that little church in Barrow, Alaska at the top of the world. For the next six weeks, we held services nightly, and people were healed and touched by God.

The man who'd been healed had access to the local swimming pool at the school. We baptized 125 people in that pool. It was amazing to see so many people filled with joy unspeakable and full of glory! The Holy Ghost fell on some of those ladies as they tried to make their way back into the change room. They fell under the power of the Holy Spirit and down they went. They must have lay there for at least fifteen minutes, laughing uncontrollably.

My friend Big Bob was always somewhere in the crowd cheering us on. He was a big Inupiaq man. Apparently, he'd carried six people and won the Eskimo games. Big Bob had a real transformation in his life because of Christ. He liked to party and would get into hotel brawls with whomever. I'm not sure who would want to fight a five-hundred-pound man who was all muscle. Big Bob would often help in the nursery and act as door watcher. One time a drunk came into the church and wanted to interrupt the service. Big Bob just sat on him until he quieted down. Once the man realized he had no chance to overcome Big Bob, he surrendered.

Then there was Big Paul, another big man but not as heavy as Big Bob. If an evangelist ever needed protection, these men were there to help. Big Bob was a storyteller. He had many stories of his culture and way of life in that harsh environment. They still practised whaling. Whaling captains would lead a group of whalers to hunt down the whales. Big Bob related a story about when he was training under these captains. You had to be really quiet on the ocean in the hunt for whales. The captains were strict, and rules had to be followed; if you were unable to follow the rules, you wouldn't be invited on the team.

A young lady told us about being out on the ocean with her dad. They were moving in and around floating ice, and her dad told her to get out of the boat. She thought they had reached land. It wasn't land but the back of a sleeping whale. She walked on the back of the whale. Oh my! I once tasted muktuk, which is whale blubber with skin. I chewed and chewed, but it wouldn't break down, so I just swallowed it. In the meantime, the locals were dipping it in a variety of sauces.

Big Bob's remedy for any colds or aches and pains was seal oil. The weather was extremely cold on top of the world, and there was no sun for weeks. It was a harsh environment to live in. I once saw a group of teenagers walking around in shorts when it was minus thirty-five degrees outside. I made reference to how cold it was, and they said, "We're Eskimos." Many times either before or after services I would soak in a tub of the hot water. There were also polar bears that roamed the town looking for food. I think someone told me that after I had walked back to my hotel several times. One of the men in the church circled the town with a loaded rifle on polar bear watch.

Who would think that the top of the world—Barrow, Alaska—would have tourists. Apparently, they come from all over the world. I met one lady who'd been to the bottom of the world and had come to the top of the world. I'd been in Buenos Aires, Argentina—not quite the bottom of the world but close enough. And believe me, that's a very long way. I know because I did it, with stopovers in Toronto, Winnipeg, Minneapolis, Anchorage, and into Barrow. I stopped in Winnipeg to change clothes and see Lynda. I get tired just thinking about it.

The Inupiaq value respect, spirituality, compassion, humility, sharing, avoidance of conflict, and cooperation. For many Inupiaq, their identity is closely linked to the land, which influences what happens to the land. It helps create their vision of themselves. The Inupiaq strive to live in harmony with their surroundings and consider themselves a vital part of the wilderness. They're the same people as the Inuit of Canada and Greenland and speak the same language but with different dialects. My Indigenous heritage shares the same values.

Bob mentioned in one of his many stories that the Cree people would travel from Canada to trade with his people. They've had their struggles with their tradition and modern values. They have their social problems, like many of the villages I visited in Alaska and throughout these small communities. Sometimes they seem to be forgotten by the outside world. In some places, alcohol, drugs, and suicide have affected many people. Our revival meetings touched many people within a short period of time. They began playing my sermons on the local radio show, which was aired in the nearby villages. Big Paul drove his snow machine across the tundra in one hour to come to the meetings.

During the revival there were many deliverances, salvations, healings, marriages restored, baptisms, and many more miracles. People who were living together got married. One lady had an open sore on her foot that wouldn't heal. She was a teacher at another church and living with someone. I told her that she needed to repent and let the man know that he needed to find another place to live. She went back and told him that they either needed to get married or he'd have to move on. She came back during one of the services, and God healed her open wound. Some people want a touch from God but they don't want to be obedient to His Word. That lady obeyed and God touched her and healed her.

As the meetings progressed, Lynda joined me for a few days and then headed back to Canada. The day before she arrived, a major snowstorm had passed through Barrow. It's not uncommon for flights to be cancelled or delayed. I prayed, "Lord, please stop the storm." Wouldn't you know it, but the next day the storm had stopped and the sun was shining again.

Our meeting place after the evening service was Sam's restaurant. I think that during our revival meetings, Mama Lee made a lot of money. Besides, she served the best food in town.

A Korean man would come and sit at the back of the church building. He drove a taxi in town and had a gambling and drinking problem. In one service, God touched him in a supernatural way. One night he invited us to a barbecue in the middle of a Barrow winter. When we arrived, he was cooking in his garage, and I tell you, that Korean barbecue in minus thirty-five degrees tasted absolutely delicious.

Walter often had us over to his place, and sometimes twenty or more people showed up. He always had a pot roast cooking all day long. It was a real treat. The price of food in the far north is extremely expensive. I wouldn't be surprised if that roast cost him a few hundred dollars. Brother Walter had a Bostonian accent, so when he said, "Let's have a party," it sounded like "Let's have potty!" And we did exactly that; we partied in the presence of the King of kings and Lord of lords.

Some of these people had good paying jobs, but the cost of living was really high. A few ladies got together and made me a beautiful Inupiaq parka. It had wolf trimming around the hood, with a mink collar and wolverine trim on the bottom. The ladies are known for their sewing and have their own style and signature. They put it together within three days. I know you shouldn't ask the price of a gift, but I found out it could have easily been sold for $2,500 US. That's only one of many gifts these people gave me. I should mention that the church people paid for Lynda's ticket to join me, although it would be another three weeks before I would see her again in Anchorage.

Life in that environment isn't easy to cope with, especially when there's no sun for six weeks. It seemed like depression hung over the people because of the lack of sunshine. Their cultural expression is important to them, and sometimes the whole village and surrounding villages came together for a week of celebrations. They had dancers, music, and drums and their unique clothing. There were some tense moments when we wondered if we should continue with our revival meetings or not. I had no attachment to their cultural expression. I knew we had a move of God that was making an impact. The water baptisms down at the pool were more thrilling to me than watching someone dance to an unknown deity.

In my dream, a mask would come into the room and circle me. I wasn't sure of the purpose of it, but I mentioned it to Big Bob, and he had a name for it. It was used in various ceremonies, and the shaman used it in his practice. Big Bob said they would say their prayers for me.

We moved forward with the meetings in spite of the pressure to stop. I know when revival comes, it can change the destiny of individuals, a church, a village, and a nation. Some of the people from other villages who were attending the cultural celebration came to the revival meetings. We kept on hearing about a revival that would come from the north. The year before, I'd been in Barrow holding revival meetings with Pastor Mike Curtis. The meetings were making news down south, and they sent up a TV crew to record the services.

There was a local TV program out of Anchorage that would be airing messages on their program from the year before, 2006. At that time we had three weeks of revival with Pastor Mike at New Beginnings Church. I believe it was *Heartbeat Alaska Film* with Jeanie Green.[3] I knew they'd sent a camera crew the year before to tape our meetings in Barrow.

A year later, Pastor David and Tina Matthews were lead pastors in Barrow. What a blessing to work alongside them. Since then, they have taken the ministry to another level. God is using them not only in Barrow but throughout Alaska. They have also travelled internationally, doing ministry in South America. I knew it was a big adjustment for them to move to Barrow. They have six children and are now grandparents. The year before, we had seen a powerful three weeks of meetings, but now we were in a position for another history-making event that would last six weeks in Barrow and three more weeks in the Anchorage Native Assembly. These meetings were conducted right after our Native America Fellowship in Anchorage. I spoke at the conference and gave them the update on the revival in Barrow. I had one night off in nine-and-a-half weeks before leaving Alaska. Lynda had now come twice to be with me in these revival meetings.

My preaching schedule was full throughout 2010 and into 2020. I had now been to several places in Alaska: Nome, Kotzebue, Kivalina, Noatak, Barrow, Red Dog, Anchorage, and in another village outside of Fairbanks. I flew into Fairbanks and the

---

[3] Jeannie Green, Alaska Film Collection, Sequoyah National Research Center, University of Arkansas.

next day flew to a small Native community. It was my first time in this community. I arrived at the local airport for my flight into the village and was the only one in the small terminal. Outside the terminal was a nineteen-seat prop plane. I said to myself, "That's great, a nineteen-seater, and I have the whole plane to myself."

When they called for us to board, I went outside and walked by the nineteen-seater sitting in the hanger. We headed toward a four-seater mail plane, just me and the pilot and a cargo full of mail. My luggage just fit into the back of the plane. The pilot looked like he'd just graduated from high school. I asked him how long he'd been flying, and he answered "Four months." After a long pause, he said that he'd flown ten years in Seattle, Washington.

I slipped on my Bose headset and climbed into the cockpit with the pilot. He looked at me and asked if I was a pilot. I said no and explained that I was wearing my noise cancellation headphones. That little plane made it into the air and off we flew. He made several stops before we reached our destination. He had mail for each small community we landed in. After several stops, we finally made it to the community where I'd be preaching for the next several days.

They took me to a building that looked like a band office. We headed upstairs to the room where I'd be staying for the few days. Sometime around 2:00 a.m., I heard voices and banging going on below me. I made sure my door was firmly locked and put my suitcase against it. I was in a strange community and knew no one. And they didn't know me, other than I led revivals in Alaska. As it turns out, the local gym was below my bedroom. The young people work out in the middle of the morning. I had no problem once I knew what was happening. No one gave me a heads up about the gym.

The next day the services started, and to my amazement, I discovered that the building was constructed of logs. A local Methodist minister was working with the Pentecostal group in the village. He told me that he'd had it with his denomination when they started ordaining people into the ministry who were living sinful lifestyles. He disagreed with this direction, so he embraced the Pentecostal people, and they embraced him as spiritual leader.

I was impressed with the log construction; it was beyond what I expected. The Methodist minister told me that a group of men had come from Norway to build it. He said it was worth over half a million US dollars. But he was concerned that they hadn't insured it yet. The people gave me gifts and made me honorary chief; they gave me a beautiful beaded necklace.

When the meetings were over it was time to catch the mail plane back to Fairbanks. I arrived at the hotel in Fairbanks for the night and was not impressed with the condition of the room. The rug was dirty and just not up to my standards.

I had a connection in Fairbanks named Jay, who was a friend I'd met in Puerto Vallarta, Mexico. I called him up, and He invited me to come and stay with him. I was more than happy to get out of that dirty hotel room. My friend took me out for dinner in one of the nicest restaurants in Fairbanks. He gave me a tour of his business; he was in partnership with his brother. Back in the 1950s or early 1960s, he and his brother bought as much heavy equipment as they could. They had the foresight to do that because Alaska would become a boom of projects. And now they had the equipment to lease out. They owned two planes, one a private jet worth eight to ten million dollars, and a prop plane worth another four million dollars. He also owned a car rental company in Fairbanks. He was a wealthy person but a very humble man.

I met him in Nuevo Vallarta at Paradise Church when I was the overseeing pastor for a few months. The lady opening the service mentioned that I had been in Barrow, Alaska. Jay had been there in the 1950s, at the beginning of his business. He came up to me later and introduced himself, and we then made several connections in Mexico. He bought himself a beautiful penthouse condo overlooking Bahia de Banderas Bay.

Back in Fairbanks, he showed me a shopping strip mall that he'd sold for $1,000,000 US. He said that was how he bought his condo in Nuevo Vallarta. He always treated Lynda and I with a meal or would take us out on his boat to see whales. He was one of three people who donated $15,000 toward a water well in Africa. I made the connection and Pastor Okot got the money for his orphanage to dig for water. The effects of the Barrow revival reached into Mexico and then East Africa. Today the children are drinking clean water. From that revival God took me around the world several times, preaching the good news of the gospel. You never know where your obedience will take you. Sitting outside that steel mill in the 1980s, I spoke a word of faith to myself. I actually had no understanding of how that was going to work. One step of obedience! One step of faith! One day at a time! God has ways to weave His purposes through His people.

Lynda and I had been to Mexico many times over the years. We have friends who were trying to help establish an outreach to children of the dump in Puerto Vallarta. They managed to connect with mutual friends who owned Paradise Village. They provided a platform for the mission to raise financial support for the children within the resort. They also provided a time for nondenominational services to be held onsite. After that Cancun incident with Lynda, I told the enemy that I would be back in Mexico and would preach the gospel. Over the years of travelling to Mexico, I have spoken to thousands of people from across Canada and the USA. I have met so many people during this time. In some cases, the people have enormous wealth. The kid from the hood speaking to multimillionaires for Jesus!

I remember speaking to a crowd of a few hundred people; it was in an outdoor setting because all the salons were in use. This older couple came up to me after the service with tears rolling down their cheeks. The gentleman said, "We've gone to church all of our lives, some fifty-plus years, and for the first time we understood the gospel." Thank you, Jesus, for you saving your power. That mission for children grew over the years and now is a mission for the whole family. The owner of the resort built this multimillion-dollar housing project. It's quite the facility that matches any resort in that area of Mexico.

When I first started helping with the preaching aspect of this mission in the early nineties, I also said to the people involved that they needed local pastors to give oversight to the mission. After at least ten failed attempts to find the right Spanish-speaking pastor, they finally found Pastor Javier and his wife, Miriam, to oversee the mission and the church service. They are the right people; they have a love for God and for the people. This past winter, 2024, I came alongside him and helped with the preaching. It was twenty-nine years ago that the enemy tried to stop us from going back into Mexico. But by God's grace, He made away! Never give up on your dream! Never allow your circumstance to stand in the way of reaching your destiny!

"*If God is for us, who can be against us?*" (Romans 8:31b); "*Yet in all these things we are more than conquerors through Him who loved us*" (Romans 8:37).

Our Philippines trips were awesome. We worked alongside men like Pastor Victor De Vera. Hey was the youth pastor who'd helped in one of our many crusades. He was also one of the worship leaders. He's from Santo Tomas, Batangas and is now lead pastor of Living Epistle in Santo Tomas. He put together a youth conference for us that was held in Santo Tomas. The mother church in Manila sent their worship leaders to help with this outreach. They brought high intensity music with lights and a fog machine. Other pastors joined us as well.

I remember one pastor with came with youth and drove four hours to attend the conference. He got up to share the story behind some of the youth he'd brought with him. He said some youths were outside his church building, singing and dancing and rapping. He invited them into the church and told them that they could come in and dance for Jesus. They came into the church and started dancing to Jesus music. They were also doing gymnastics, and the pastor said they were good at it. It was over the top, and the youth looked like they'd rehearsed for that opportunity. The performances included some dangerous feats. The floor was made of cement, and there was no room for error. It could have ended with someone getting seriously hurt. As I watched them, I thought they were as talented as any professional gymnast. It brought an intensity and huge impact to the local churches. The bishop from Manila came on one of those nights to participate and check how things were going.

Each night, the altars were filled with young people giving their lives to Christ. Revival broke out, and they ran around the conference hall, waving flags with joy unspeakable. What a night of celebration! I applaud the pastor who brought these street kids to the conference.

Pastor De Vera brought great leadership to the conference. I've known him for twenty-three years, and it has always been a blessing to work with him. This conference was held in 2014. The year before we were in Bam Bang for another amazing conference, as well as in Quezon City.

It just so happened that it was Lynda's birthday when we were in Quezon City. The church members gave her a dozen beautiful red roses. They were always supportive of our ministry in the Philippines. Without Bishop James Isaguirre's help to reach souls for Jesus, our impact might not have been as effective. The bishop and his wife have now gone to be with their Lord and Saviour, Jesus Christ. He had a daughter living in California who was well-established and wanted her parents to come to America. Bishop's response was, "Why would I go live there when all my friends are here in the Philippines?" He knew his mission field was in his own country. He remained focused, and his heart was for his people. He made a tremendous impact on the many children who went through his private Christian school. When we were in Manila, he had hundreds of students in his school. I believe his son has now taken over the ministry in Quezon City. I hope and pray that the Word of God will take deep root in the lives of these people who are now mostly adults.

Lynda reminded me of the conference we had in Baguio City. We were invited to the university campus to hold a one-day seminar. The young people were thrilled that we'd come to their campus to speak. The place broke out in revival, and the students were running around the room waving flags and dancing for Jesus.

Pastor Victor invited us back to the Philippines for another outreach in 2016. The crusade would be held in a place called Calauan. They built these tiny houses lined up beside each other, and multiple families lived inside these tiny houses. It was certainly third-world living conditions, and the poverty was overwhelming. There was no hotel in the area, but the pastor found one close to Calauan. It was being used as a brothel, so we stayed in Santo Tomas and found a hotel where we'd stayed before. It was just a one-hour drive to the event.

At this time, Rick Bowering would be joining me to help with the music. Rick had arrived before me and gone to another part of the Philippines to check on a person who *Faith to Live By* had been supporting for some time. We connected in Manila and drove to Santa Tomas together. Rick helped me get support for my next pastors' conference in Bam Bang, but he wasn't able to come with me.

Back in Calauan, the crusade event was like nothing I'd experienced before or since. It was held on a basketball court with a stage set up for the event. Out of nowhere, these huge black bugs began flying in the midst of us. It was like a plague of black bugs. When I arrived back at my hotel and took off my shirt, I found these bugs clinging to me.

We also had a pastors' conference happening at the same time. There was much poverty among these pastors, so it was poorly attended. However, souls were saved during the crusade.

On Sunday, Rick and I went to different places to speak. I was heading back to Calauan to speak, and Rick was staying in Santo Tomas. I ended up speaking at the pastor's home, and the little house was packed with local people. Keep in mind that those people were former squatters living in government housing. Perhaps thousands of them lived in third-world conditions. My driver was confused as to where we were going and ended up taking ninety minutes to reach the pastor's home. We actually had to ask around for directions.

The bishop arrived on Saturday to see how things were going, and he needed money for our pastors' conference in Bam Bang. I had no funds on me at the time, as they were back in the safe at my hotel. It was heavy lifting right from the beginning until we left. I had a few days to reach Bam Bang, and Rick was heading back to Canada. I still had another conference to do, which would take eight hours or more to drive to. I tried to hire a driver to take me to Bam Bang. Nothing is free in the Philippines, and they'll try to get as much money from you as possible. I had a few days to reach Bam Bang, so the negotiations began without much success.

A typhoon was heading toward the Philippines, right to the area where the pastors' conference was to be held. I was on the phone waiting for the bishop to tell me whether we would go ahead with the conference. As well, I was still trying to find a driver to take me to Bam Bang. The bishop finally decided to cancel the event. It was a good decision because of that typhoon. Facing a typhoon and bugs was a lot to deal with.

I made plans to head back to Canada. When I arrived, I sent the funds back to *Faith to Live By*, as they had sponsored the conference in Bam Bang. It was a good thing I still had the money in my hands or it could have gone missing in Bam Bang. Who knows what could have happened had the meetings not been cancelled? I would have been heading right into the storm.

It has been almost eight years since I've been back to the Philippines. I still remain in touch with Pastor Victor, and he has had his share of storms. His beautiful wife has gone on to be with the Lord. We sent him funds to help with her treatment, but her treatment was unsuccessful.

"*'For My thoughts are not your thoughts, nor are your ways My ways,' says the Lord. "For as the heavens are higher than the earth, so are My ways higher that your ways, and My thoughts than your thoughts'*" (Isaiah 55:8–9).

Kingdom dynamic is thinking "beyond." There's more power in one drop of the shed blood of the Lord Jesus to cleanse men's hearts from the stain of sin than there is in the accumulated filth of men's sin since Adam and Eve.

The years 2010–2024 flew by quicker that expected. Over the years, I'd share stories about my travels, and people would say that I had to write a book. Over the past decades, I have travelled across Canada many times. I remember travelling for two months and coming home in between assignments for twelve hours. Some people think that it must be glamorous to travel around the world. Not really. Only when you meet special people with whom you remain connected. We have developed long and loving relationships with a long list of people.

Just on Air Canada alone, I've travelled nearly 500,000 miles. I have easily travelled more than one million miles by air alone, not including ground transportation. Without the help and prayers of so many people over the years, these mission trips would not be possible. I truly believe that the best days are still ahead of us. The harvest is ready, and the Word has been spread throughout the nations. Daniel, the prophet, wrote, "*But you, Daniel, shut up the words, and seal the book until the time of the end; many shall run to and fro, and knowledge shall increase*" (Daniel 12:4). There is a global movement moving faster and faster, going to and fro, and a thirst for knowledge has steadily increased. The Church of Jesus Christ's best days are ahead of us. Global media is expanding at a fast pace and growing in leaps and bounds.

Christ has secured the victory for us—the Church's victory. What a beautiful promise we have in the Word of God: "*He who has an ear, let him hear what the Spirit say to the churches. To him who overcomes I will give to eat from the tree of life, which is in the midst of the Paradise of God*" (Revelation 2:7). God has made it possible for us to overcome. He expects us to overcome. "*He who overcomes shall inherit all things, and I will be his God and he shall be My son*" (Revelation 21:7). The overcomer gets everything, and the one who doesn't, gets nothing. It's one way or the other. No one has a monopoly on overcoming. We have faith in scripture and in Jesus. The death and resurrection of Jesus has brought final and irresistible defeat to Satan—a total defeat.

> And you, being dead in your trespasses and the uncircumcision of your flesh, He has made us alive together with Him, having forgiven you all trespasses, having wiped out the handwriting of requirements that was against

us, which was contrary to us. And He has taken it out of the way, having nailed it to the cross. Having disarmed principalities and powers, He made a public spectacle of them, triumphing over them in it. (Colossians 2:13–15)

Conflict and the Kingdom, Jesus Christ's triumph over sin and evil powers. These were accomplished on the cross. Other texts relating to this are: Ephesians 2:13–16; Galatians 3:13–14; 2 Corinthians 5:14–17; Romans 5:6–15; and Revelation 12:10–11.

In the Roman culture, if a general was successful in war, the Roman Senate would vote on this triumph. The general was placed in a chariot drawn by a white horse, and he was led through the streets of Rome, which were lined with people applauding him. And behind him was all the evidence of his victories: rulers, commanders in chains, Roman prisoners celebrating the victory that had already been won. Paul is saying that by His death and resurrection, Jesus was placed in the triumphant chariot and led through the unseen world, and behind Him were all the forces of Satan, led in chains. That is the totality of victory.

To obtain this victory, Jesus did two things for us. Satan's greatest weapon against us is guilt. As long as he can keep us guilty, we're no match against him. In this victory, Jesus has dealt with this problem of guilt. He has made it possible for us to be forgiven of all our previous sins: *"Having forgiven you all trespasses"* (Colossians 2:13). We have to believe that we're forgiven of all our previous sins. Secondly, Jesus abolished the Law of Moses, the means of being righteous with God. This doesn't mean abolishing part of the Word of God, or the lessons and history of Israel, but it abolishes the Law as a means of achieving righteousness with God. When Jesus died on the cross, He put an end to the Law by nailing it to the cross.

Jesus told Peter that he would deny Him three times, but Jesus had prayed for him, that his faith should not fail (Luke 22:31–34). Keep believing that your faith will see you through; never get moved away from your faith. Let no failures or accusations move you from your faith. Jesus died in your place, bore your sins, was made sin for you, and has offered the garment of His spotless righteousness. In the court of heaven, you are not guilty.

The battleground is the mind. We've been given weapons of victory to pull down Satan's strongholds and roadblocks. Satan builds up fortresses in the minds of men and women, first by preventing them from receiving the truth of the gospel. God has given us weapons of prayer, preaching, and praise to break down the strongholds. We have the weapons to bring every thought into obedience to Christ. People's minds can be released from false captivity and be brought into that obedience.

The first step of a young believer in Christ is to spend time in praise and prayer and reading the Word, being freed from the years of torment of the enemy who was living in their mind, rent free. The day I received Christ in my heart was the day the enemy got his eviction notice, but it took me time to figure it out!

> For though we walk in the flesh we do not war according to the flesh. For the weapons of our warfare are not carnal, but mighty in God for pulling down strongholds, casting down arguments and every high thing that exalts itself against the knowledge of God, bringing every thought into captivity to the obedience of Christ. (2 Corinthians 10:3–5)

Strongholds are first established in the mind; that's why we are to take every thought captive. Behind a stronghold is also a lie, a place of personal bondage where God's Word has been subjugated to any unscriptural idea or a confused belief that is held to be true. Behind every lie is fear, and behind every fear is an idol. Idols are established wherever there exists a failure to trust in the provisions of God that are ours through Jesus Christ. Some of the weapons that pull down strongholds are God's Word (Hebrew 4:12–13), the blood of the cross (Revelation 12:11), and the name of Jesus. Strongholds are pulled down, and confronting bondage breaks it, as these bondages are spiritual weapons. There are weapons at my disposal. Our praise goes to God. It doesn't make Him more powerful, as He is already powerful, perfect, and faithful and will equip you to be more than a conqueror. Paul said he could do all things through Christ who strengthened him.

In 2 Corinthians 10:5, Paul speaks of obedience (*hupakoe - hoop-ak-ch-ay*). The word signifies attentive hearing, to listen with compliant submission, assent, and agreement. It's issued for obedience in general and for obedience to God's command.

> My son, give attention to my words; incline your ear to my sayings. Do not let them depart from your eyes; keep them in the midst of your heart; for they are life to those who find them, and help to all their flesh. Keep your heart with all diligence, for out of it spring the issues of life. (Proverbs 4:20–23)

"*The entrance of Your words gives light; It gives understanding to the simple*" (Psalm 119:130).

"*Every kingdom divided against itself is brought to desolation, and every city or house divided against itself will not stand*" (Matthew 12:25).

Satan's primary attack against the Church is to divide us. Resist division.

"*And this gospel of the kingdom will be preached to all the world as a witness to all nations, and then the end will come*" (Matthew 24:14).

Prepare the way of the Lord, focus on the positive side, and proclaim the whole counsel of God.

"*But know this, that in the last days perilous times will come*" (2 Timothy 3:1). Perilous (*chalepos – Khal-ep-oss*) signifies harsh, savage, difficult, dangerous, painful, fierce, grievous, hard to deal with. The word describes a society that is barren of virtue but abounding with vices.

The great enemy is selfishness. The mark of the Church is unselfishness, a commitment to God to be servants.

"*All Scripture is given by inspiration of God, and is profitable for doctrine, for reproof, for correction, for instruction in righteousness*" (2 Timothy 3:16).

"*I charge you, therefore before God and the Lord Jesus Christ, who will judge the living and the dead at His appearing and His kingdom*" (2 Timothy 4:1).

Preach the word! Be ready in season and out of season. Convince, rebuke, exhort, with all longsuffering and teaching. For the time will come when they will not endure sound doctrine, but according to their own desires, because they have itching ears, they will heap up for themselves teachers; and they will turn their ears away from the truth, and be turned aside to fables. But you be watchful in all things, endure afflictions, do the work of an evangelist, fulfill your ministry. (2 Timothy 4:2–5)

Hold fast to scriptures. They are being attacked and undermined.

"*For I have not shunned to declare to you the whole counsel of God*" (Acts 20:27).

If you want to be popular, do not declare the whole counsel of God. Remember, we are answerable to God. Paul stated that their blood was not on his hands. We are watchmen!

Likewise you younger people, submit yourselves to your elders. Yes, all of you be submissive to one another, and be clothed with humility, for "God resists the proud, but gives grace to the humble." Therefore humble yourselves under the mighty hand of God, that He may exalt you in due time. (1 Peter 5:5–6)

"*For the kingdom of God is not in word but in power*" (1 Corinthians 4:20).

It's not a matter of theology, although theology has its place. It's also not a matter of intellectual pride. We need a demonstration of the supernatural. Someone said we do church so well, we don't need the Holy Spirit.

And I, brethren, when I came to you, did not come with excellence of speech or wisdom declaring to you the testimony of God. For I determined not to know anything among you except Jesus Christ and Him crucified. I was with you in weakness, in fear, and in much trembling. And my speech and my preaching were not persuasive words of human wisdom, but in demonstration of the Spirit and of power, that your faith should not be the wisdom of men but in the power of God. (1 Corinthians 2:1–5)

Why did the Holy Spirit testify to Paul's ministry? Because he focused on Jesus and Him crucified.

We need the word of wisdom and the word of knowledge. The word of wisdom shows us how to counter Satan's action and defeat him. The discerning of spirits shows us when we are face to face against demonic power.

"For thus says the Lord: 'Sing with gladness for Jacob, and shout among the chief of the nations; proclaim, give praise, and say, "O Lord, save Your people ...""" (Jeremiah 31:7).

Praying is discovering God's revealed purpose in scripture. Pray for the outworking of that purpose.

"Now to Him who is able to do exceedingly abundantly all that we ask or think, according to the power that works in us" (Ephesians 3:20).

We should align ourselves to His purpose, praying in faith.

"This will be written for the generation to come, that a people yet to be created may praise the Lord" (Psalm 102:18).

"Out of the mouths of babes and nursing infants you have ordained strength" (Psalm 8:2a).

What is the ordained strength of God's people? It is perfected praise. It silences the avenger. Why do we have to silence Satan? Because he is accusing us. Why doesn't God stop Satan from accusing us? Because God has given us the means to stop Satan. If you learn to praise Him the way He wants to be praised, it will silence Satan. The whole atmosphere will change, and people's hearts will be opened. The dark powers will be shaken and driven out.

There was a time when I was under the extreme attack of the enemy when some Christians poured out their evil bitterness against me. This horrible accusation was like a weight on my shoulders day and night for two full years. We went to Manhattan Beach Family Camp, and the morning speaker was sharing an ordeal he'd gone through. It sounded like the same thing I was experiencing.

> For in the time of trouble He shall hide me in His pavilion; in the secret place of His tabernacle He shall hide me; He shall set me high upon a rock. And now shall my head be lifted up above my enemies all around me; Therefore I will offer sacrifices of joy in His tabernacle; I will sing, yes, I will sing praises to the Lord. (Psalm 27:5–6)

I rose from my knees that day, and at the moment the heaviness was broken off of me. During those two years, the enemy was trying his best to silence me. The temptation was to give in to bitterness, but I refused. Just at my breaking point, God stepped in and said "Enough!"

This past week, I was at my dentist's office to have surgery; he had to pull a cracked tooth. Believe me, it was painful for several days. He told me to be careful, as there was a chance of infection. The pain was overwhelming. Just like that evil tongue that lashed out at me, it was painful, and the enemy's objective was to fill me with bitterness and unforgiveness. I refused to let that happen. Yes, I could have justified my bitterness, and the enemy would be happy with that. But I refused to live in defeat and allow those accusations to infect me. I praised my way out of it and obeyed the Word of God. In His time, He stepped in and lifted me up.

"For thus says the Lord: 'Sing with gladness for Jacob, and shout among the chief of the nations. Proclaim, give praise, and say, "O Lord, save your people ..."'" (Jeremiah 31:7).

In the New Testament, the word "herald" is used for preacher.

> Your sandals shall be iron and bronze; as your days, so shall your strength be. There is no one like the God of Jeshurun, who rides the heavens to help you, and in His excellency on the clouds. The eternal God is your refuge, and underneath are the everlasting arms; He will thrust out the enemy before you, and will say, "Destroy!" (Deuteronomy 33:25–27)

"And God is able to make all grace abound toward you, that you, always having all sufficiency in all things, may have an abundance for every good work" (2 Corinthians 9:8).

This is the victory of the Church!

"And they overcame him by the blood of the Lamb and by the word of their testimony, and they did not love their lives to the death" (Revelation 12:11)

It's more important to do the will of God than stay alive. That is commitment. They who are willing and committed are the overcomers.

John 3 tells the story of a man named Nicodemus, a Pharisee and member of the Jewish Sanhedrin (the ruling council). Nicodemus came to talk to Jesus at night. It may be that he was intimidated by his peers, the religious Pharisees who hated Jesus, and Nicodemus didn't want to be seen speaking with Jesus. Or it may have been that Jesus was surrounded by crowds during the day, meaning that night was the best time to approach Him to ask questions.

Nicodemus knew there was something different about Jesus and wanted to hear some of His teachings. He greeted Jesus as "Rabbi" and remarked that no one could do the things Jesus did unless God was with Him.

Jesus knew what was in the heart of Nicodemus and could discern his questions. He went right to the heart of the matter and told Nicodemus that he couldn't enter heaven without being born again. Nicodemus didn't understand what it meant to be born again and stated that it would be impossible to enter a second time into his mother's womb. Jesus replied with these words:

> Most assuredly, I say to you, unless one is born of water and the Spirit, he cannot enter into the kingdom of God. That which is born of the flesh is flesh, and that which is born of the Spirit is spirit. Do not marvel that I said to you, "You must be born again." The wind blows where it wishes, and you hear the sound of it, but cannot tell where it comes from and where it goes. So is everyone who is born of the Spirit. (John 3:5–8)

Nicodemus was still puzzled and didn't understand how these things could be. In response, Jesus went on to say:

> Are you the teacher of Israel, and do not know these things? Most assuredly, I say to you, We speak of what We know and testify of what We have seen, and you do not receive Our witness. If I have told you earthly things and you do not believe, how will you believe if I tell you heavenly things? No one has ascended to heaven but He who came down from heaven, that is, the Son of Man. And as Moses lifted up the serpent in the wilderness, even so must the Son of Man be lifted up, that whoever believes in Him should not perish but have eternal life. (John 3:10–15)

Jesus was prophesying of His upcoming death. He would soon be lifted up on a cruel Roman cross, condemned by His own people. He would be crucified, buried in a rich man's tomb, then be resurrected on the third day. Thus He provided salvation for all who believe in Him.

Jesus went on to say, *"For God so loved the world that Her gave His only begotten Son, that whoever believes in Him should not perish but have everlasting life"* (John 3:16).

The Bible doesn't complicate salvation or being born again. It is so simple that even a child can understand it. Jesus will change you if you call upon Him. Being a good citizen and upright person doesn't save you. We are all sinners. Repentance means simply talking to Jesus, telling Him that you now desire to follow Him. Jesus completed the bridge between humanity and God when He died on that cross. When you sincerely seek Him, He will not turn you away. Living life without Him is to live according to your own self-will, which ultimately leads to a Christ-less eternity in hell.

What God has prepared for us is unspeakably better than what this world has to offer.

Afterword

GOD IS STILL writing my next season of life. My wife, Lynda, is retired, and we're still travelling to Indigenous communities and internationally. This summer we'll be among the Cree people of Northern Quebec, and then we're off to East Africa for two major outreaches. I still have open invitations to Argentina, Mexico, West Africa, and the Philippines—reaching the unreached and teaching the untaught.

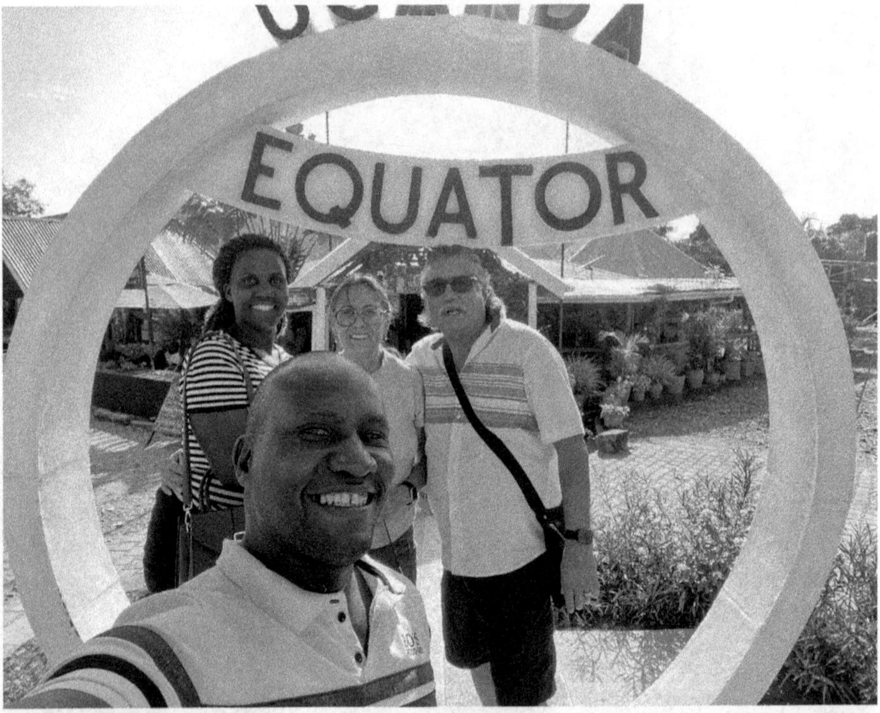
EQUATOR

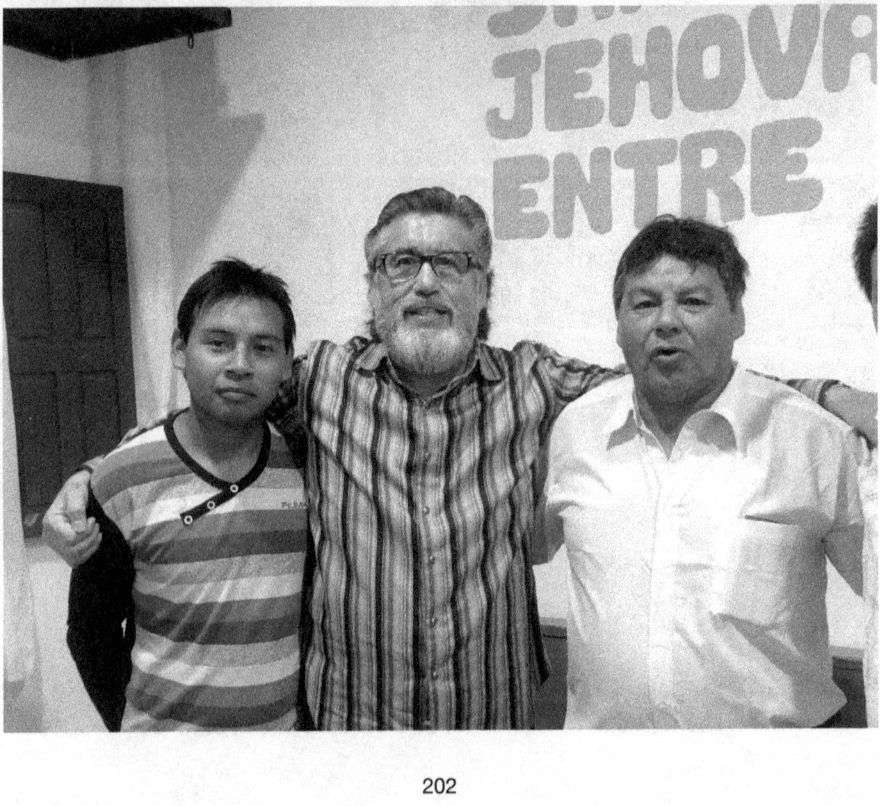
ENTRE

About the Author

Alfred M. Flett is an Indigenous person from Peguis First Nation community. He has been married to Lynda for over fifty years, and they have one married daughter, two grandchildren, and two great grandchildren. In Africa, they have three adopted families of six adults and eight grandchildren.

Alfred is an ordained minister with The Pentecostal Assemblies of Canada, a church planter, a camp and conference speaker, and now an author. He has studied with Global University and Certified Early Childhood Development. He continues travelling as an international evangelist, speaking to the next generation and winning souls for Jesus.

His next book will be a continuation of global mission work and life lessons learned through personal experience of working cross culturally.

Learn more about Alfred and his ministry at www.alfredflettministries.life.

www.ingramcontent.com/pod-product-compliance
Lightning Source LLC
LaVergne TN
LVHW041615070426
835507LV00008B/252